THE WINES OF BURGUNDY AND BORDEAUX

John Heathcote

Published by

MELROSE BOOKS

An Imprint of Melrose Press Limited
St Thomas Place, Ely
Cambridgeshire
CB7 4GG, UK
www.melrosebooks.co.uk

First published as a limited, private edition of 250 copies in 2013
First commercial edition 2016

ISBN 978-1-911280-36-1
epub   978-1-911280-37-8
mobi   978-1-911280-38-5

Printed and bound in Great Britain by:
Latimer Trend & Company Limited,
Estover Road, Plymouth PL6 7PY

For Peter

ACKNOWLEDGEMENTS

I would like to express my sincere thanks to Robert Parker for his permission to quote from the 4th edition of his book *Bordeaux* and in particular his modern classification of the principal châteaux of Bordeaux and their quality ranking. The ongoing support and encouragement in developing this improved version of the book is also greatly appreciated.

I acknowledge the very important contribution of Gill Hooper who created an orderly, attractive, and well presented manuscript from my handwritten semi-legible first drafts, which were subsequently extensively changed and corrected.

I very much appreciate the support of the Burgundy syndicate (BIVB) and Noemie Horteur who granted permission to include their superb wine maps of the five Burgundy sub-regions.

Jean-Robert Pitte published a fascinating book – 'Burgundy/Bordeaux – a Vintage Rivalry' relating to the historical conflict between the two great wine regions. I would like to thank the author for permission to quote from his book.

The wine tasting caricatures by the distinguished artist Sue Macartney-Snape adds welcome humour to the book and in particular John Steed's 'southern end of the vineyard'.

The images of Burgundy are contributed by the photographer and designer Armelle Hudelot.

The images of Bordeaux and two of the Abbey of Cîteaux are from the Cephas Picture Library.

The images of the Confrérie des Chevalier du Tastevin are contributed by photographer Jean-Louis Bernuy.

The Bordeaux wine maps and the map of the whole Burgundy wine region were commissioned from Grand Pavois by the author who retains the rights.

CONTENTS

PREFACE

One of the most exceptional and important natural phenomenon in the world is that a certain fruit as it ripens develops yeast on its skin. When that fruit is crushed the yeast on the skin converts the sugar in the juice into alcohol – a process known as fermentation. The result is a delicious, fruity, alcoholic drink. That fruit is the grape and its juice, after its sugar has been converted into alcohol, is wine.

And so the natural production of wine goes back more than 6000 years to ancient Greece and Egypt and beyond. It was important in the Roman Empire and in those parts of that vast empire, where grapes could thrive, wine was produced. The pharaohs always included amphora of wine in their burial chambers to be enjoyed in the after life.

Modern annual wine consumption worldwide now stands at around 280 million hectolitres (28,000,000,000 litres) produced in more than 60 countries.

Wine is also produced from a vast range of different grapes and there are also enormous variations in quality and price.

It also follows that wines from around the world all have their dedicated followers whether French, Italian, Spanish, New World or other excellent wine producing countries or regions. *However it is suggested that irrespective of personal choice a basic knowledge of the two great wine producing regions of France, Burgundy and Bordeaux, is important for a full understanding of the modern world of fine wine and its ancient origins.*

To the vast number of consumers, worldwide, wine appeals in a number of different ways.

For most the serving of an appropriate wine with a meal greatly enhances the enjoyment of both the food and the occasion.

For the church wine is of great symbolic importance in its religious ceremonies and in the ancient monasteries it also brought a little pleasure to the spartan way of life. This led to the great abbeys of Cîteaux and

Cluny developing the vineyards of Burgundy which still exist to the present day.

Fortunately, for a now declining number, wine represents social status. This is based on the perception that knowledge, particularly of fine and prestigious wine, has an important social kudos. This has created the 'wine snob' – limited knowledge, eloquently and boringly conveyed, to those prepared to listen and be suitably impressed.

The most attractive wine enthusiasts are those who, although highly knowledgeable and often genuine connoisseurs, have a rather irreverent and entertaining approach to wine. John Steed of the Avengers, typified this as after declaring that wine tasting 'was not my subject' he then went on to accurately identify the wine, the vintage, the vineyard and finally added 'southern end of the vineyard.'! This is superbly portrayed by the distinguished caricaturist Sue Macartney-Snape in the chapter on wine tasting which also includes several other 'wine tasters'.

A fascinating aspect of this subject is the historical and current conflict and hostility between these two great French wine regions. This is the principal subject of a superb book by a distinguished French academic, Jean-Robert Pitte, from the University of Paris Sorbonne – *'Bordeaux/ Burgundy – A Vintage Rivalry'*.

INTRODUCTION

Up to the middle of the 20th century, and for almost two decades beyond, the world-renowned wines of Burgundy and Bordeaux were enjoyed almost exclusively by great patrician families and famous institutions. The wine for those of us not so privileged was sometimes good but often little better than 'plonk'.

From the 1970's onwards the production of excellent and affordable wine started to gain momentum as global demand followed a rapid increase in worldwide affluence. This was a time when a significant part of the adult population of the developed world became enthusiastic wine drinkers.

The excellent 'modern' wines which became available were a result of improved quality in the 'Old World' vineyards of Europe, but more importantly the 'New World' wines and particularly those of Chile, South Africa, Australia, and New Zealand, which, produced through a scientific approach to winemaking in 'high tech' wineries, started to have a major impact on the world of wine and still continue to do so.

In the last fifty years mankind has experienced many dramatic changes which have fundamentally reshaped the way in which we live our lives. The most obvious is the way in which computers have become totally indispensable in just about every field of human activity.

A more important and for many a more enjoyable major development has been the availability of a whole range of excellent wines at affordable prices.

Wine also has an important place in history. It is almost certainly the world's oldest alcoholic drink. This is because wine, which is now produced in a highly sophisticated manner, can also be produced through a simple natural process as the yeast present on the skin of the grape converts the sugar in the juice of the crushed grape into alcohol. In modern winemaking, laboratory cultured yeast is often used to control and sustain this fermentation process. And so the ancient people crushed their grapes, waited for a while, and then drained off the now alcoholic fluid which gave them a delicious fruity drink which also created a rather pleasant feeling of well-being which it still does to the present day.

And so early man produced wine and the earliest recorded winemaking is around 5000BC. The Greeks certainly produced wine and the Etruscans, who originated from the Greek sphere of influence of Asia Minor, brought it to Italy and after their subjugation by the Romans it was spread throughout their great empire and many European vineyards can trace their origins back to Roman times.

In ancient Egypt the Pharaohs were buried with their amphora of wine to be enjoyed in the afterlife.

Wine also became symbolically important in many ancient religious rites and became of major significance to Christianity following the Last Supper where it represented the blood of Christ and has continued to do so in the celebration of the Eucharist and Holy Communion. Wine also continues to be of importance in a number of Jewish religious ceremonies.

Of course the world of fine wine is vast and a degree of specialisation is inevitable and so we have those whose preference is New World, France, Spanish, Italian and beyond. However, the true heritage of fine wine is that of France and in particular the two great wine regions of Burgundy and Bordeaux. Here winemaking goes back to Roman times and beyond and 'modern winemaking' can be traced back to the 12th century and possibly before. At this time the king and queen of England, Henry Plantagenet and Eleanor of Aquitaine, were both French, and Bordeaux came under the control of the English Crown and its vineyards produced 'claret' for the English market. In Burgundy the Benedictines and Cistercians founded the great abbeys of Cluny and Cîteaux and cultivated vineyards whose wine was used for their religious ceremonies and also to make their spartan way of life rather more agreeable.

It was however not until the 19th century that wine production became an organised and established commercial activity and was traded extensively across national frontiers. The first major move to classify and rank wine produced by established vineyards was in France in 1855 where the wine producers of Barsac/Sauternes and the Médoc sub-regions of Bordeaux were classified. The wines which have greatly improved since their original classification are now referred to as 'super seconds'. Also the great wines excluded in 1855 which are now considered equal in quality to first growths have been agreed and listed as such by the wine trade. Details are given in Appendix 2.

It was also France which, following the disaster of the 1860's, when the phylloxera louse infected the French vineyards and virtually wiped them out, recognised the importance of governmental regulation to ensure the quality and identity of its wines. It founded, in 1935, the *Institut National des Appellations d'Origine* (INAO)** which issued *Appellations d'Origine Contrôlées* (AOC) whose regulations for wine production are enforced by the INAO fraud squad. Every major wine region throughout the world has now followed in the implementation of governmental wine quality control regulations.

After many centuries the fine wines of France remain internationally pre-eminent and the truly great wines continue to be the most prestigious in the world. *And so irrespective of any personal wine preferences it would seem to be rather desirable to have at least a basic knowledge of both the history and modern status of France's two great wine regions, Burgundy and Bordeaux, as the cornerstone of any expertise in and knowledge of the world of fine wine.*

Fine wine is one of the most widely written about subjects in the world. The last fifty years, in particular, has produced wine critics and writers of exceptional ability and knowledge which has resulted in the publication of a plethora of great books on the subject of fine wine. Hugh Johnson, Michael Broadbent, Clive Coates, Serena Sutcliffe, Jancis Robinson, Robert Parker and others have virtually become revered household names. These publications are however rather daunting tomes full of detailed and erudite information. For instance the 4th edition of Robert Parker's book, on the Bordeaux wine region only, runs to over 1200 pages, and the sixth edition of his *Wine Buyers Guide* has over 1500 pages. Clive Coates book, not on all Burgundy, but the Côte D'Or only has almost 1000 pages. So the subject is indeed vast and detailed and these books are particularly indispensable if, for instance, precise information is required about a particular wine produced in a specific year. Let's say you intend to buy a case of 1996 Lynch Bages then you will find that Robert Parker

** now Institut National de l'Origine et de la Qualite but remains as the acronym INAO

rates its 91+ which means that it is 'outstanding'. Furthermore you will find from his tasting notes that it has, among other attributes, 'cassis fruit aromas intermixed with cedar, fruit cake and liquorice scents' etc. If you wish to contact or visit the vineyard then the telephone number and address are also given. The price you will get from your wine merchant, but make sure you are seated before you make the call.

Robert Parker was of course the first of the international wine critics and writers to introduce a numerical rating system for fine wine quality. After the initial controversy, following its inception, numerical quality rating has been accepted and adopted worldwide and other eminent critics and writers have introduced their own variations of the original system.

The problem with wine is that many of the more important aspects are complex and rather daunting and are intermingled, in the text of many books, with those parts which are interesting, entertaining, and readable. An attempt has been made here to consign important but rather detailed areas of wine 'theology' to the appendices. They therefore become optional reading but are important for reference and the acquiring of a more in-depth knowledge of the subject. An example of this is the structure and application of the legally binding quality control regulations for the production of French wine and how these evolved. This process goes to the very heart of winemaking, as if the wine trade, which is a major commercial activity, is to flourish then the end users, the consumers, must have confidence in what they are buying and that means effective quality control at source which the French government has sought to impose. Its quality control system based on AOC's is rather complex and not a particularly entertaining and exciting subject and not surprisingly many modern wine writers tend not to dwell on it. However without at least a basic understanding of the subject one is lost in a world of wine mystique.

In writing of these two great wine regions it would have been ideal to create a structure or 'template' which could apply to both. The differences however are so great that this proved to be impossible and it is necessary to describe the individual characteristics of the two regions as they are.

BURGUNDY, BORDEAUX AND THE OTHER WINE REGIONS OF FRANCE

THE SEVEN PRINCIPAL WINE REGIONS OF FRANCE

THE SEVEN PRINCIPAL WINE REGIONS OF FRANCE

BORDEAUX	LOIRE VALLEY
BURGUNDY	CHAMPAGNE
CÔTES DU RHONE	LANGUEDOC ROUSSILLON
ALSACE	

France is indisputably internationally pre-eminent in the production of fine wine. It is in fact a country that is 'truly blessed' in many ways. A magnificent Atlantic seaboard and a beautiful Mediterranean coastline, majestic Alps and great rivers. Its food and culinary achievements have impressed and influenced the world. It has a fascinating and turbulent history and has produced great scientists, artists and literary figures. Nevertheless throughout the developed world 'France' will primarily be synonymous with fine wines and the greatest of these are from the wine regions of Burgundy and Bordeaux.

The seven principal wine regions of France are:-

Bordeaux	**Loire Valley**
Burgundy	**Champagne**
Côtes de Rhône	**Languedoc-Roussillon**
Alsace	

The other wine regions of France, which produce excellent wines but are rather less well known internationally, are:-

Savoie	**Midi**
Jura	**The South West**
Provence	

The wine regions of France all have their individual history and unique characteristics. They are all different in many ways but none more so than Burgundy and Bordeaux which are the most internationally famous and acclaimed wine regions of the world. They are both, of course, French and located about 500km apart but that's where the similarity ends. It is indeed interesting to summarise their main differences.

At the outset it is important to emphasise that the differences between the two famous regions did not happen by chance but mainly through their historical conflict and hostility which exists to the present day.

A distinguished academic of the University of Paris-Sorbonne, Jean-Robert Pitte, published a book – *Bordeaux/Burgundy: A Vintage Rivalry* – which was also translated and published by the University of California. This book recognises and investigates the history and rivalry of the two regions and their long-standing hostility. The preface to the American edition opens as follows:-

> *'It is to the cause of reconciliation among the fraternal enemies of the lands of the Saône and the Yonne, on the one hand, and those of the Garonne, the Dordogne, and the Gironde, on the other, that these pages aspire to make a contribution.'*

And later:

> *'Ask the natives of these two universally renowned wine-producing regions about each other, or read what they have written, and you will not find the slightest sign of sympathy or fellow feeling. They are not from the same world – a fact they miss no occasion to proclaim loudly and clearly. Not content to ignore each other, hardly tasting each other's wines, they delight in denigrating each other more or less fiercely.'*

Going back into the mists of time the ethnic origins of the people of the two regions are quite different. The Burgundians were originally a fair skinned Germanic tribe, the Burgundii, who moved into Burgundy during the Roman period and stayed on. The Bordelais are ethnically indigenous French but historically intermixed on a multinational basis with the many different nationalities who used the important port of Bordeaux over many centuries.

The principal grape varieties of Burgundy are Pinot Noir, Chardonnay, Gamay, and Aligote and those of Bordeaux, Cabernet Sauvignon, Merlot, Cabernet Franc, Sauvignon Blanc, and Semillon. In Burgundy the wines are produced from a single grape variety which in modern terminology means that they are all 'varietals'. The wines of Bordeaux, both red and white, are all blended.

The wines of Bordeaux, starting with that of 1855, are extensively officially classified in respect of quality. St Émilion, Médoc Cru Bourgeois, and Graves have modern classifications. Burgundy has no modern classification of its wines, although the INAO, when it was formed in 1935, based the selection of the Grand Cru vineyards of Burgundy on a classification published in 1855 (the same year as the Bordeaux classification) by Dr Jules Lavalle – *Histoire et Statistique de la Vigne de Grands Vins de la Côte d'Or* with five quality groups and the vineyards in the top quality group were granted Grand Cru status by the INAO. It is important to note that the term 'classification' used here refers specifically to the formal, official listing of vineyards in a number of quality groups – a concept continued in Bordeaux but not in Burgundy after Dr Lavalle's early classification.

The vineyards of Bordeaux all have the courtesy title 'château' even when the 'house' of the vineyard is only a modest dwelling. In Burgundy when a vineyard has a great and historic château such as that of Clos Vougeot it does not feature in the name of the vineyard.

Bordeaux wine is traditionally decanted whereas Burgundy wine is normally served direct from the bottle.

The shape of the wine bottles of the two regions are quite different.

The standard Burgundy barrel is 228 litres and that of Bordeaux 225 litres.

Although wine was first produced in both Burgundy and Bordeaux by the Celts and the Romans the subsequent historic development of the vineyards of the two regions is quite different. In Burgundy the church and its monastic orders were the medieval developers of the great vineyards until the state, in waves of anti-clericalism, sequestered and sold them, particularly following the French revolution. This led to multiple ownership of the vineyards of Burgundy primarily confined to local families who were subject to the Napoleonic code of Inheritance which required them to leave their assets equally to all their children. In Bordeaux the medieval vineyards were developed by powerful families who created a thriving wine export trade initially for the English 'claret' market. The vineyards progressively came extensively under the control of foreigners through wars (Talbot, Palmer and others) and wealthy settlers (particularly the Rothschilds and Irish landed gentry). The internationalisation of Bordeaux vineyards continues to the present day. Unlike Burgundy multiple ownership of the Bordeaux vineyards hardly exists and where it does it is through a number of investors and not separate wine producers.

It would not seem unreasonable for the two great wine regions of France to adopt the same terminology (or at least a consistent one) in describing their wines at the very top of the quality spectrum. Not so:-

BURGUNDY	BORDEAUX
GRAND CRU	PREMIER GRAND CRU CLASSÉ
PREMIER CRU	GRAND CRU CLASSÉ

'CLASSÉ' means the designation is from the classification system used in Bordeaux. This is important as over two hundred other lower quality ranked châteaux are allowed, through the St Émilion AOC system, to simply display 'Grand Cru' on their bottle labels.

Furthermore the processes which led to the right to describe wines by the foregoing appellations are totally different in the two wine regions. These processes and how they are applied is quite complex but a basic understanding of their significance is important if a consumer is to rely on and be influenced by 'the display of these prestigious appellations on a wine label' and this is covered in detail in the following text.

BURGUNDY

'Burgundy for kings, champagne for duchesses,
and claret for gentlemen'

FRENCH PROVERB

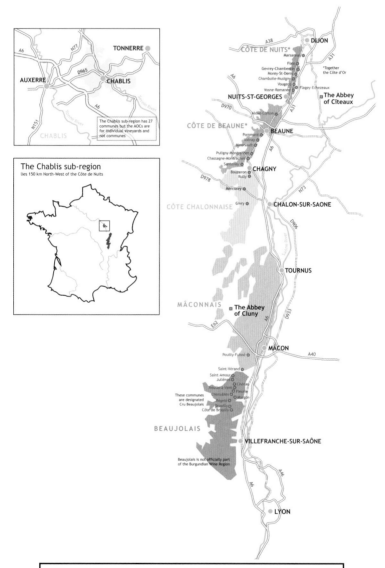

AUXERRE
TONNERRE
CHABLIS

The Chablis sub-region has 27
communes but the AOCs are
for individual vineyards and
not communes

CHABLIS

The Chablis sub-region
lies 150 km North-West of the Côte de Nuits

DIJON
CÔTE DE NUITS*
Marsannay
Fixin
Gevrey-Chambertin
Morey-St-Denis
Chambolle-Musigny
Vougeot
Vosne-Romanée
Flagey-Échezeaux
*Together
the Côte d'Or
NUITS-ST-GEORGES
The Abbey
of Cîteaux
Aloxe-Corton
CÔTE DE BEAUNE*
BEAUNE
Pommard
Volnay
Meursault
Puligny-Montrachet
Chassagne-Montrachet
Santenay
CHAGNY
Bouzeron
Rully
Mercurey
CHALON-SUR-SAONE
Givry
CÔTE CHALONNAISE

TOURNUS

MÂCONNAIS
The Abbey
of Cluny

Pouilly-Fuissé
MÂCON

Saint-Vérand
Saint-Amour
Juliénas
Chénas
Moulin-à-Vent
Fleurie
Chiroubles
Régnié
Morgon
Brouilly
Côte de Brouilly
These communes
are designated
Cru Beaujolais

BEAUJOLAIS
VILLEFRANCHE-SUR-SAÔNE

Beaujolais is not officially part
of the Burgundian Wine Region

LYON

THE BURGUNDY WINE REGION

THE BURGUNDY WINE REGION

The Burgundy wine region is geographically elongated from Beaujolais in the south to Chablis in the north a distance of around 250 kilometres. It has six wine sub-regions – Beaujolais,** Mâconnais, Côte Chalonnais, Côte de Beaune, Côte de Nuits, (together the Côte d'Or) and Chablis.

The winemaking of Burgundy has, for centuries, featured in the regions long and colourful history. The Roman Empire brought winemaking to those parts of its dominions where the climate was conducive to the cultivation of vines and that included Burgundy. There is however some evidence that the Celts may have preceded the Romans as the wine-makers of Burgundy. The Romans had acquired their wine-making capability from the Etruscans who had moved, from the Greek sphere of influence in Asia Minor, to central Italy where they were finally subjugated by the Romans. There is also evidence that the ancient Greeks also traded as far afield as the Rhône Valley as wine was a traditional part of their trade.

Later, the development of wine in Burgundy was primarily by the Church. In the year 581 Guntram, King of Burgundy, gave the vineyards of Dijon to the Abbey of Saint Benigne. This established a pattern whereby kings and nobles donated lands to the church which, experienced in viniculture, developed extensive vineyards. Charlemagne (742–814) as Holy Roman Emperor (800) was a major donor of lands to the church. In the area, now known as the Côte de Beaune, the Emperor donated 25 hectares of his family land to provide funds for the building of a church. The land was developed as the vineyards of Corton and three world famous Grand Cru wines produced from these ancient vineyards are still known as Corton, Corton-Charlemagne, and Charlemagne. In 910 and 1028 respectively the great abbeys of Cluny and Cîteaux were founded. It was to Cîteaux that Saint Bernard of Clairvaux first came. He was to go on to reform the church and actively support the crusades. The Benedictines of Cluny and the Cistercians of Cîteaux became major developers and owners of vineyards. It was the Cistercians who founded the famous Grand Cru vineyard of Clos Vougeot whose walls were completed in 1336. Its château is now the home of the Confrérie

---

** Beaujolais is *officially* not part of the Burgundy Wine Region.

des Chevaliers du Tastevin. The Cistercian nuns of Notre Dame de Tart founded the Grand Cru vineyard of Clos de Tart in the Côte de Nuits commune of Morey-Saint-Denis.

In medieval times very little of the wine of Burgundy was exported out of the region as road and water transport was limited for the movement of the large barrels in which the wine was kept. This started to change during the Avignon Papacy (1309–1378) as the opulence of the papal court generated a demand for a plentiful supply of fine wine and through the rivers Rhône and Saône and limited overland transport the Avignon demand was met from Burgundy.

In the 14th and 15th centuries Burgundy was ruled by the House of Valois, as Dukes of Burgundy. The Duchy was separated from the French crown when the French king, John II (1316–64), conferred the Dukedom on his youngest son, Philip the Bold (1362–1404), and not his eldest son Charles who succeeded him as king of France but not as the Duke of Burgundy. Philip the Bold, Duke of Burgundy, played an important role in establishing the Pinot Noir grape as the official grape for the red wines of Burgundy. The Duke issued a decree banning the Gamay grape (believed to have been brought to France as a result of the Crusades) as '*unfit for human consumption*' and '*the disloyal Gaamez (Gamay) that gives wine in abundance but full of very great and horrible harshness*' and declaring Pinot Noir as the red grape of Burgundy. From his court in Dijon the Duke's decree had a major impact on the vineyards of northern Burgundy, now known as the Côte de Nuit, which produce the great red wines of Burgundy from a single grape variety, the Pinot Noir. The south-ernmost area of the Burgundy wine region, now known as Beaujolais, was unaffected by the Duke's decree and now produces huge quantities of red wine from the Gamay grape and millions of consumers would not agree with the Duke's pronouncement on its quality.

The separated Duchy became immensely powerful and extended its control over a wide area outside Burgundy and for some time even surpassed France. Philip the Bold's grandson, Philip III (the Good), on his marriage to Isabella of Portugal created the famous chivalric order of the Golden Fleece, a highly prestigious and influential brotherhood which still exists to the present day. The present sovereigns of the Spanish and Austrian branches are Juan Carlos I of Spain and Karl von Habsburg respectively. The region was finally annexed by France following the battle of Nancy (1477) where the last Valois Duke, Charles the Bold, was killed in battle. Although the region, we now know as Burgundy, was re-integrated with France the countries which the Dukedom controlled, for instance the Low Countries, reverted to the control of the Habsburgs when Mary, daughter of Charles the Bold, married Maximilian, Archduke of Austria, who also retained the title of the Duke of Burgundy.

This renewed control of Burgundy by the French Crown was the beginning of the end for the church as owners of major vineyards which were taken over by the state and progressively sold off. Nevertheless the church still remained major vineyard owners in Burgundy but state sequestration of their lands took a dramatic turn in 1789 when a wave of anti-clericalism swept through France following the revolution. The church's vineyards were totally sequestered, divided into a number of plots, and sold to the people and the consequences of this are still felt in Burgundy to the present day. This situation was further exacerbated by the enactment of the Napoleonic Code of Inheritance which required parents to leave their estate, which could of course include ownership of part of a vineyard, equally between their children. This inevitably led to the progressive increase in multiple ownership of individual vineyards and for obvious reasons this applied more and more to the famous and prestigious vineyards as each individual 'parcel', and the wine produced from it, had considerable commercial potential. This has unfortunately led to a range of producers of different dedication and capability all labelling their wine in virtually the same manner but with a wide range of quality.

The quality ranking and rating for the wine selection process is out-lined in detail elsewhere and as the official AOC's and Classifications have proved to be too broad for this purpose most wine merchants and consumers rely on the professional reports of a number of eminent wine experts. In Bordeaux the focus is on the numerical rating and ranking of the individual châteaux whereas in Burgundy, although the same rating system exists, the emphasis is on 'best producers' due to multiple owner-ship of many of the top vineyards.

From the time (1477) when Burgundy was annexed and again became under the control of the French Crown up to the start of the French Revolution (1789) Burgundy wine had mixed fortunes. The wine was certainly greatly appreciated at the French Court, that is when it was available, as Burgundy was ravaged in this period by continual conflict and wars.

During the time of Napoleon, although the vineyards of Burgundy were sequestered they were required to continue production as casks of the wine accompanied Napoleon and his marshals throughout their campaigns.

> *'Nothing makes the future look so rosy as to contemplate it through a glass of Chambertin'* – Napoleon Bonaparte.

At that time Talleyrand, an important diplomatic and political figure throughout the revolutionary period, also expressed his approval of Burgundy wine and particularly Chambertin and is quoted as saying:-

> *'Sir, when one is served such a wine, one takes the glass respectfully, looks at it, inhales it, then having put it down one discusses it.'*

Another contemporary Alexandre Dumas is also quoted on the wine:-

> *'Nothing inspires such a rosy view of the future.'*

Burgundy has continued, since time immemorial, to produce magnificent wines (and others which are rather less memorable) despite immense upheavals and conflict. In modern times Burgundy has been embroiled in two world wars which ravaged most of Europe.

When one still enjoys a wonderful Montrachet or Meursault and a magnificent Nuit St Georges or Chambertin and others it is very clear that the spirit of Burgundy lives on.

**BURGUNDY'S BEAUTIFUL COUNTRYSIDE
AND ARCHITECTURE**

**BURGUNDY'S DISTINCTIVE AND
BEAUTIFUL ARCHITECTURE**

A WINTER SCENE IN BURGUNDY

THE WINE STRUCTURE OF BURGUNDY

The wine structure of Burgundy comprises of six sub-regions each of which has a number of principal communes. This is summarised as follows:-

REGION:-   BURGUNDY

SUB-REGIONS:-   BEAUJOLAIS
                                           MÂCONNAIS
                                           CÔTE CHALLONAIS
                                           CÔTE DE BEAUNE*
                                           CÔTE DE NUIT*
                                           CHABLIS
                                           together the Côte d'Or

THE PRINCIPAL WINE COMMUNES OF THE SUB-REGIONS OF BURGUNDY

BEAUJOLAIS	MÂCONNAIS	CÔTE CHÂLONNAISE
Saint Amour	Mâcon	Bouzeron
Juliénas	Pouilly Fuissé	Rully
Chénas	Saint Véran	Mercurey
Moulin-à-Vent		Givry
Fleurie		Montagny
Chiroubles		
Morgon		
Régnié		
Brouilly		
Côte de Brouilly		

These communes are designated Cru Beaujolais

CÔTE DE BEAUNE

Ladoix Serringny
Aloxe Corton
Pernand-Vergelesses
Savigny-lès-Beaune
Chorey-lès-Beaune
Beaune
Pommard
Volnay
Monthélie
Auxey-Duresses
Saint Romain
Meursault
Puligny-Montrachet
Chassagne-Montrachet
Saint Aubin
Santenay

CÔTE DE NUIT

Marsannay
Fixin
Geverey Chambertin
Morey St Denis
Chambolle-Musigny
Vougeot
Vosne Romanée-
    Flagey Echézeaux
Nuits St Georges

CHABLIS

In Chablis the appellations are not by commune but by vineyard which are designated as Grand Cru, Premier Cru, Villages, and Petit Chablis

THE SUB-REGIONS OF BURGUNDY AND THEIR PRINCIPAL COMMUNES

BEAUJOLAIS

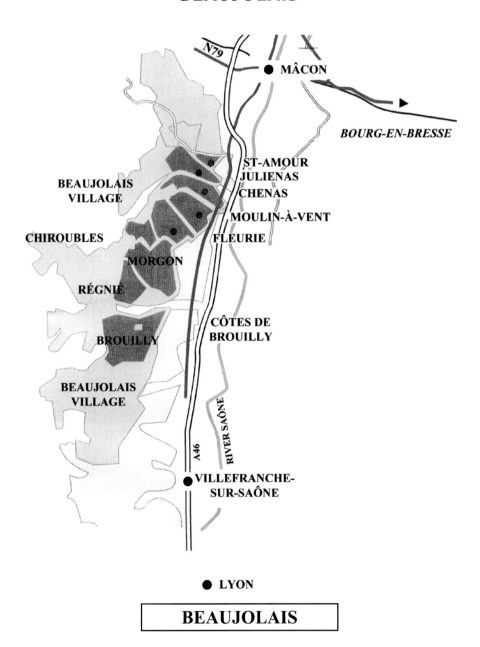

MÂCON

BOURG-EN-BRESSE

ST-AMOUR
JULIÉNAS
CHÉNAS

BEAUJOLAIS
VILLAGE

MOULIN-À-VENT

CHIROUBLES

FLEURIE

MORGON

RÉGNIÉ

CÔTES DE
BROUILLY

BROUILLY

BEAUJOLAIS
VILLAGE

RIVER SAÔNE

A46

VILLEFRANCHE-
SUR-SAÔNE

LYON

BEAUJOLAIS

Beaujolais is the most southerly part of the Burgundy wine region and is administratively in the Rhône department and immediately north of the City of Lyon. It is not officially part of the Burgundy wine region although it is generally considered to be so by the wine trade and those who write and report on Burgundy wine. Beaujolais produces more than 30% of the total wine production of Burgundy.

SUB-REGION	ANNUAL PRODUCTION (Million Bottles)	
Chablis, Côte de Nuits, Côte de Beaune, Côte Châlonnaise, Mâconnais	200	As Beaujolais is almost an entirely red wine producer, from the Gamay grape, and the other five sub-regions production is 61% white wine this means that Beaujolais produces more red wine than the rest of Burgundy.
Beaujolais	110	
TOTAL	**310**	

Beaujolais has ten principal communes which are, from south to north, Brouilly, Côtes de Brouilly, Régnié, Morgon, Chiroubles, Fleurie, Moulin-à-Vent, Chénas, Juliénas, and Saint Amour, which under the AOC system are designated Cru Beaujolais.

Despite the fact that the wine throughout Beaujolais is (with very small exceptions) produced from the Gamay grape the individual communes each produce wines of different style and character. However it is generally seen as a light fruity wine, often served chilled, and ideal for early drinking although the 'Cru' wines are moderately ageworthy.

It is probably best known internationally for what has become a wine ritual – the release of Beaujolais Nouveau on the third Thursday of November every year. Cases are deployed worldwide but only released on the first minute of the designated Thursday. In fact the celebration of the new wine of Beaujolais goes back to the 19th century when it was shipped down the Saône river to the bistros of Lyon which placed a sign outside saying '*le Beaujolais est Arrivé*'. The idea was then re-introduced in the 1960's and by the 1970's had become a major international wine phenomenon. As much as 90% of Beaujolais wine is produced by négociants and they actively promoted the 'nouveau' approach in which one of them, Georges Duboeuf, was prominent and remains so to the present day. In many years almost half of the production of Beaujolais is sold in this manner.

Although the promotion of 'Beaujolais Nouveau' as a worldwide 'brand' continues it has experienced some decline in consumer popularity and demand. This is of course against a market background of excellent and affordable wines, many from the 'New World', becoming progressively higher in quality, more competitive, and readily available internationally.

This unfortunate situation was exacerbated by scandals and law suits. The drop in sales in early 2000 was blamed on what was conceived to be a deterioration in the quality of the wine. A French wine critic, François Mauss, claimed that the consumer reaction did indeed arise from the poor quality of the wine which he referred to as '*vin de merde*'. Law suits followed and, together, with several other incidents, tended to sully the reputation of Beaujolais wine. This was a great injustice for the many producers who have over the years produced excellent, delicious wines at affordable prices and continue to do so to the present day.

Beaujolais is certainly the most beautiful area of Burgundy with picturesque vineyards, a number of which can be traced back to Roman times, on hillsides which mark the start of the Massif Centrale.

A fascinating aspect of Beaujolais wine-making, which is unique in Burgundy, is the use of a process known as carbonic maceration. A characteristic of the Gamay grape, used throughout Beaujolais, is that it has a thin skin which makes it low in tannin and easily crushed under pressure. The grapes are picked in bunches which means manual rather than machine harvesting, as it would break down the bunches, which are dumped whole into a concrete or stainless steel vat. The pressure at the lower part of the vat causes the grapes to burst and start fermenting (sugar converted to alcohol through the action of the yeast naturally present in the grape skins). This fermentation at the bottom of the vat creates heat which causes the upper grapes to ferment in their skins which retains the perfume and flavour of the grape. Through this process the wine can be made and bottled in a matter of only several weeks.

THE BEAUJOLAIS APPELLATIONS

Beaujolais has three principal appellations:-

CRU BEAUJOLAIS
BEAUJOLAIS – VILLAGES AOC
BEAUJOLAIS AOC

There are further appellations for Beaujolais Blanc and Rosé which represent less than 1% of the production of Beaujolais. As practically all the wines of Beaujolais are produced from the Gamay grape the sub-region has no Grand or Premier Cru vineyards which are confined to wines produced from the Pinot Noir and Chardonnay grapes.

Beaujolais in wine terms is divided into two distinct zones. The wine producers having the higher designations, Cru Beaujolais and Beaujolais-Villages AOC, are concentrated in the northernmost area and the vineyards having the lower classification Beaujolais AOC are in the south.

The ten communes classified as Cru Beaujolais are:-

Saint Amour	Chiroubles
Juliénas	Morgon
Chénas	Régnié
Moulin-à-Vent	Brouilly
Fleurie	Côte de Brouilly

The 'Cru' producers usually display on their labels the vineyard, village/area and producer, they do not mention 'Beaujolais'. The wines can be aged up to 5 years. The Beaujolais-Villages AOC producers usually bottle their wine in the spring of the year following the harvest when it is then ready for early drinking. Unlike the 'Cru' producers they are allowed to produce 'Nouveau' but rarely do so.

The area to the south is designated primarily Beaujolais AOC. It is used almost entirely as 'nouveau'. The wine is required to achieve a modest minimum alcohol level of 9%. If this is raised to more than 10.5% the wine may be labelled 'Beaujolais Superieur'.

THE CRU BEAUJOLAIS COMMUNES

SAINT AMOUR

The usual Roman connections exist as the village is named after a Roman soldier who converted to Christianity and was martyred for it.

The wines are light and normally consumed within a period of 3 years.

JULIÉNAS

No mistaking the Roman connection here as the village is named after none other than Caesar himself. Some of the best wines of Beaujolais are produced here. The vineyards are steep and generally cultivated by hand. These fuller bodied wines can age up to at least 5 years.

CHÉNAS

Named after the French oak trees which were common in the area. Chénas is the smallest of the Cru Beaujolais and is diminished further as the growers are allowed to label their wine Moulin-à-Vent their more famous neighbour and often choose to do so. Chénas also produces fuller bodied wines but they are usually consumed within 3 years.

MOULIN-À-VENT

Named after a 300 year old windmill which still stands and has been declared an historic monument ranking in French historical importance with the Arc de Triomphe and Notre Dame. It was at this place that Julius Caesar rested his troops after the conquest of Gaul. The wines produced are full bodied and are often aged in oak which results in wine lasting in excess of ten years. The yields are low due to the unique soil which is rich in manganese which is semi toxic to vines and reduces the yield. The rich, full, and ageworthy wine produced has resulted in Moulin-à-Vent being referred to as the 'King of Beaujolais'.

FLEURIE

We have had the 'King of Beaujolais' and now we have the 'Queen'. The wines of Fleurie are probably one of the more famous Beaujolais wines internationally. They are also produced in one of the most beautiful villages of Beaujolais. The wines are medium bodied and with their smooth fruity flavour and floral bouquet no one is concerned about longevity as they are traditionally consumed young.

CHIROUBLES

Chiroubles has the highest altitude in Beaujolais with its vineyards at around 500 metres and the village, perched on a hilltop at some 800 metres, has spectacular views. The wine produced is probably the lightest of all the Cru wines, but the best wines are delicious although they should be consumed in not more than 2 years.

MORGON

There are in fact two wine producing villages Villie-Morgon and Bas-Morgon. They are separated by a large granite hillside, the extraordinary Mont de Py. The Côte de Puy has vineyards producing some of Beaujolais's finest wines. Morgon is one of the two largest producers of the Beaujolais sub-region.

With a combination of a year of ideal climatic conditions and dedicated and competent producers the full bodied Morgon can produce great wines of international stature. This is readily demonstrated by the fact that the 2009 Morgon wine, produced by Domaine Jean Descombes (Georges Duboeuf), was rated by the Wine Spectator as 93 and the rating of Robert Parker was 90–91.

RÉGNIÉ

The view is held locally that this was the very first area in Beaujolais where the Romans cultivated vines and produced wine.

Régnié was the last village to be granted 'Cru' status when it was raised from Beaujolais-Villages AOC to Cru Beaujolais in 1989. The wines vary across the appellation with the northerly wines being more full bodied and those close to Brouilly being much lighter. Régnié is probably one of the least known appellations outside Beaujolais although the wines produced are certainly up to the top 'Cru' standard.

BROUILLY

Brouilly is dominated by an extinct volcano, the 500 metre Mont Brouilly. Another feature is the magnificent Château de la Chaize the grandest in the whole region. Brouilly is the other large 'Cru' producer and, although many light but excellent wines are produced, Brouilly does not have a great reputation for consistent quality.

CÔTE DE BROUILLY

Côte de Brouilly, whose vineyards are located on the granite slopes of Mont Brouilly, was created as a separate appellation in 1935. Although the wines are similar, in some respects, to Brouilly they benefit from vineyards with superior locations. The grapes mature more easily and have higher sugar levels. They are required to achieve an alcohol level of 10.5% compared with 10% required in Brouilly. The wines produced are generally considered excellent and more consistent than their large neighbour.

MÂCONNAIS

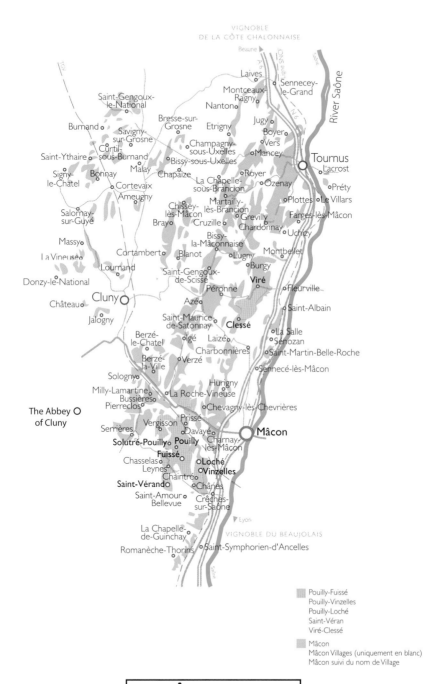

MÂCONNAIS

23

Mâconnais lies immediately north of Beaujolais but unlike its neighbour produces white wines from the Chardonnay grape. The most famous being Pouilly Fuissé. Historically Mâcon was an important Roman settlement and, as in most parts of Burgundy, they cultivated the vine and produced wine. The medieval church and a number of its religious orders were important vineyard owners and winemakers. The earliest were the Benedictines, who founded the famous Abbey of Cluny in 908, which is located in the modern Mâcon Arondissment, and were major vineyard owners. They also founded an abbey at Tournos an historic town on the northern border of Mâcon. The church of that abbey is the imposing Romanesque, St Philiberts, which dominates the town.

Mâconnais and Beaujolais are by far the largest vinicultural areas in the whole of the Burgundy wine region and Mâconnais production of pleasant and mainly undistinguished white wines, from the Chardonnay grape, is greater than the rest of the principal Burgundy sub-regions.

THE PRINCIPAL MÂCONNAIS COMMUNES AND APPELLATIONS

PRINCIPAL COMMUNES	APPELLATIONS
MÂCON	MÂCON
	MÂCON-VILLAGES
	MÂCON-CHARNAY
	MÂCON-PRISSE
	Mâcon-Vire and Mâcon-Clessé have now been awarded their own appellation – Vire-Clessé
POUILLY-FUISSÉ	POUILLY-FUISSÉ
	POUILLY-LOCHÉ
	POUILLY-VINZELLES
SAINT-VÉRAN	SAINT VÉRAN
	SAINT VÉRAND

As southern Mâconnais borders on Beaujolais (and even overlaps it) another appellation occasionally used is Beaujolais Blanc.

Production is dominated by Mâcon-Villages (around 60%), Pouilly Fuissé (around 20%) and Saint Véran (around 10%). All the other appellations each produce less than 5%.

Although Mâconnais is eligible, as a wine producer from the Chardonnay grape, for the important Burgundy appellations of 'Grand Cru' and 'Premier Cru' it qualifies for neither whereas its tiny neighbour to the north, Côte Châlonnaise, has 132 'Premier Cru' vineyards.

Although Mâconnais is predominantly a producer of white wine almost a quarter of the area is planted with the Gamay and Pinot Noir vines. Due to a problem with the ripening of these grapes in this area the wine produced from them is not always satisfactory.

Production of the wine from this area is mainly in the hands of large cooperatives a number of whom have encouraged over production resulting in thin diluted wines. This has tended to sully the reputation of the wines from the whole area despite the fact that many delicious, affordable, early drinking wines are produced. Even the reputation of the internationally famous Pouilly Fuissé, has been affected particularly as it has always commanded top prices which can only be justified if the high quality of the wine is maintained which has not always been achieved.

THE ABBEY OF CLUNY

CÔTE CHÂLONNAISE

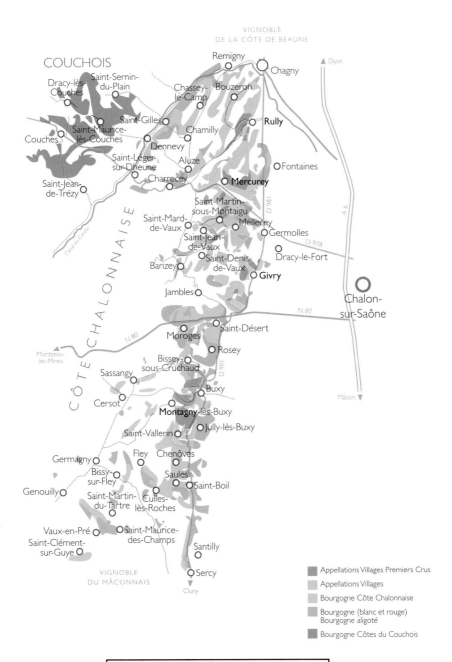

$$\boxed{\text{CÔTE CHÂLONNAISE}}$$

Côte Châlonnaise is immediately south of the Côte D'Or and north of Mâconnais. The soils and climate of the area are very similar to those of the Côte d'Or.

It has five commune AOC's which, from north to south, are Bouzeron, Rully, Mercurey, Givry, Montagny. The principal grapes are Pinot Noir, Chardonnay, Aligoté, and a limited amount of Gamay.

The sub-region is named after the town of Chalon-sur-Saône. Like other parts of southern Burgundy it was occupied by the Romans who almost certainly developed its earliest vineyards and 20,000 Roman amphorae have been found in graves in the area. It was also an important link in the central canal system developed in the 18th century to open up the markets in the north primarily for the wine trade.

THE CÔTE CHÂLONNAISE APPELATIONS

The generic appellation Bourgogne AOC can be used or that of the sub-region, Côte Châlonnaise AOC. There are also five commune appellations which are:-

BOUZERON AOC
RULLY AOC
MERCUREY AOC
GIVRY AOC
MONTAGNY AOC

THE WINE COMMUNES OF CÔTE CHÂLONNAISE

BOUZERON

Bouzeron is noted for its white wines produced from the Aligoté grape. Up to 1979 Bouzeron had no Commune or Villages AOC's and had to use the generic wine type appellation Bourgogne Aligoté AOC. In 1979 a move was made to have a Commune AOC and Bourgogne Aligoté de Bouzeron was created and in 1998 this was later changed to Bouzeron AOC the only communal appellation in Burgundy for Aligoté white wines. The move for this unique change was led by an important resident of Bouzeron – Aubert de Villaine who with his wife Pamela owns Domaine A & P Villaine in Bouzeron. More importantly Aubert de Villaine is the co-owner and director of one of the most important and internationally famous wine domaines in Burgundy – Domaine de la Romanée Conti. Bourzeron does not qualify, as a producer of wine from the Aligoté grape, for Grand or Premier Cru status.

RULLY

Côte Châlonnaise has strong Roman antecedents but Rully can actually trace its name back to a Roman settlement Rubilia Vicus. It also featured as a medieval stronghold and the 12th century Château Rully dominates the village.

The Rully AOC was created in 1939 and the appellation covers both red and white wines produced from the Pinot Noir and Chardonnay grapes respectively. Rully has 23 Premier Cru vineyards. It is also an important producer of the white sparkling wine, Cremant Bourgogne. There is also a very limited production of rosé sparkling. Some 70% of the production is white wine, the quality of which has steadily improved, and a number of producers offer excellent and affordable wine. The red wines do not enjoy the growing reputation of the whites and although positive efforts have been made to improve quality it has taken place at a much slower rate.

MERCUREY

Its name is derived from Mercury, the Roman god of eloquence, skill, trading, and thieving, who was also herald and messenger of the gods.

Mercurey is the most important and largest wine commune of the Côte Châlonnaise and dwarfs its neighbours Givry and Rully. Its appellation was created in 1936 and covers red wine from the Pinot Noir grape and white from the Chardonnay grape. Red wine dominates accounting for some 80% of total production. In the latter part of the 20th century there was a major expansion of vineyards, which tripled in area, and which has raised concerns over consistent quality. Many of the vineyards of Mercurey are owned by major wine organisations of the Côte d'Or which has increased the international profile of Mercurey wine.

Mercurey has its own wine brotherhood La Confrérie Saint-Vincent et des Disciples de la Chante Flute.

The red wines of Mercurey are full bodied and deep in colour. The

Premier Cru reds will age up to 7 years and the others 3 to 5 years. The whites are generally consumed young but will be good for up to 2 years. Mercurey has 33 Premier Cru vineyards.

GIVRY

Givry, a quaint and previously fortified village is on the outskirts of the main town of the area, Chalone-sur-Saône, and has over the years, lost vinicultural area as a result of the inevitable expansion of the town.

It is primarily a red wine producer and received its appellation in 1946. It now has 27 Premier cru vineyards. The red wines are fairly full bodied and have an ageing potential of up to 7 years. The whites are light and fragrant and are ideal for early drinking.

MONTAGNY

Once again a village with Roman antecedents as the name is derived from the Roman 'Montanum'. It is the southernmost appellation of the Côte Châlonnaise. It secured its appellation in 1936 and is confined to white wines produced from the Chardonnay grape and, uniquely, any wine which reaches an alcohol content of 11.5% may, be labelled 'Premier Cru' a condition which exists in no other appellation in France. Not surprisingly Montagny has 49 Premier Cru vineyards.

The white wines of Montagny range from ordinary to excellent and are ideal for early drinking (within 2 years)

THE CÔTE D'OR

And so we arrive at the legendary heart of the Burgundy wine region the Côte d'Or or 'golden slope'. It is certainly golden in terms of the magnificent wines which it has produced over the centuries. In modern terms it is also 'golden' for the prices we now pay for its famous wines.

The Côte d'Or comprises of the 16 communes of the Côte de Beaune in the south, famous primarily for its exquisite white wines and the 8 communes of the Côte de Nuits in the north which produce the great red wines of Burgundy. The two areas have quite distinctive characteristics and so do their individual communes and vineyards. The designation of the vineyards into Grand Cru, Premier Cru, and Villages is, by no means, distributed uniformly over the sub-region's vineyards and neither is it between those which produce red or white wine.

Before considering each of the two areas of the Côte d'Or and their individual communes it is preferable to start with a general overview or 'anatomy' of the complete area which is pre-eminent in the world of fine wine.

GENERAL OVERVIEW OF THE CÔTE D'OR

The 16 communes of the Côte de Beaune produce a total of 150,000 hectolitres (hl) of wine annually which is two and a half times that of the Côte de Nuit's 8 communes which produce 60,000 hl.

The wine production of the Côte de Beaune comprises 90,000 hl of red and 60,000 hl of white. It is particularly famous for its superb white wines of Meursault, Puligny Montrachet, and Chassagne Montrachet which together with the excellent white wines of Saint Aubin account for 50,000 hl (83%) of the white wine production of the Côte de Beaune and the two Montrachet communes have 5 out of the 8 of its Grand Cru vineyards, and Chassagne Montrachet has its highest number of Premier Cru vineyards (50).

In one small part of the northern area of the Côte de Beaune, on the Corton hill, are three Grand Cru AOC's, Corton, Corton-Charlemagne, and Charlemagne, which produce famous world class wines.

The principal communes for the production of the excellent red wines of the Côte de Beaune are Beaune, Pommard, Santenay, and Savigny-lès-Beaune which account for 50,000 hl (56%) of the Côte de Beaune's total red wine production of 90,000 hl. These four communes have 102 Premier Cru vineyards. Corton is the only red wine Grand Cru vineyard in the Côte de Beaune. The smaller commune of Volnay produces only red wines which are of outstanding quality and has 29 Premier Cru vineyards.

The 8 communes of the Côte de Nuits produce 60,000 hl of wine annually 94% of which is red. The small production of white wine is primarily from the northernmost commune, Marsannay, which also produces minute quantities of the only rosé wine of the Côte d'Or.

The Côte de Nuits has a number of world renowned communes which produce red wine of exceptional quality. Two of these Gevrey Chambertin and Nuit St George together produce over 50% of the Côte de Nuits red wine and have 67 Premier Cru vineyards and Gevrey Chambertin has the highest number of Grand Cru vineyards, 9, in the Côte de Nuit.

The two most famous and iconic wines of the world are Bordeaux's Pétrus and Romanée Conti from the Vosne Romanée commune of the Côte de Nuit. The prices of these wines, even if you can find them, are astronomical

---

The Vougeot commune of the Côte de Beaune is dominated by the huge walled vineyard, Clos Vougeot, which is historically one of the most famous vineyards of France. Founded by the Cistercian monks of Cîteaux Abbey in the early 12th century it was completed by them in 1336. The imposing Château de Clos Vougeot dates back to 1551 and is now the home of the Confrérie des Chevaliers du Tastevin which promotes the wines of Burgundy worldwide and holds regular black tie dinners in the Château. These dinners are internationally famous with 300-600 in attendance comprising of *Grand Officiers, Officiers Commandeurs, Commandeurs, and Chevaliers* and their guests. The wine, the food, the entertainment and the impeccable organisation and service make these occasions truly memorable.

THE CÔTE DE BEAUNE

The southern area of the Côte d'Or. Its 16 communes produce both red and white wine. It is however particularly renowned for its superb white wine.

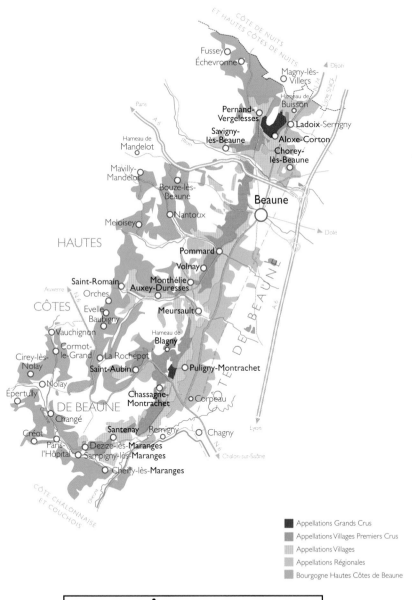

Appellations Grands Crus
Appellations Villages Premiers Crus
Appellations Villages
Appellations Régionales
Bourgogne Hautes Côtes de Beaune

THE CÔTE DE BEAUNE

The 16 principal communes of the Côte de Beaune are:-

Ladoix-Serrigny	Monthélie
Aloxe-Corton	Auxey-Duresses
Pernand-Vergelesses	Saint-Romain
Savigny-lès-Beaune	Meursault
Chorey-des-Beaune	Puligny-Montrachet
Beaune	Chassagne-Montrachet
Pommard	Saint-Aubin
Volnay	Santenay

THE PRINCIPAL COMMUNES OF THE CÔTE DE BEAUNE

LADOIX – SERRINGNY

The least known of the Côte de Beaune communes as its main claim to fame is that it shares two of the Grand Cru vineyards of the Corton Hill – Corton (red/white wine) and Corton Charlemagne (white wine) with its neighbours Aloxe-Corton and Pernand-Vergelesses. Its relatively small annual wine production, of around 4000 hectolitres, is predominately red the red/white wine ratio being 75:25. The commune has 11 Premier Cru Ladoix vineyards and 6 more, which although within the Ladoix boundaries, are designated as Aloxe-Corton Premier Crus (red only). The village, located on the side of the main route to Paris is undistinguished.

ALOXE-CORTON

The commune has three Grand Cru vineyards two of which it shares with its neighbours Ladoix-Serrigny and Pernand-Vergelesses (Corton and Corton Charlemagne) and a third, Charlemagne, which it also shares with Pernand Vergelesses. It has 14 Premier Cru vineyards eight of which are within its boundaries and six which are located in the commune of Ladoix-Serrigny but are designated as Aloxe-Corton AOC. The wine of the commune (annual production around 4500 hectolitres) is almost entirely red (white wine less than 2% of production). The village of Aloxe-Corton is one of the most attractive in Burgundy. Situated at the foot of the Corton hill it is dominated by the towers and roofs of its three impressive châteaux, Corton-Andre, Corton Grancy, and Aloxe-Corton.

hostel-Dieu.
1443.

THE HOSPICE DE BEAUNE

THE HOSPICE DE BEAUNE

THE HOSPICE DE BEAUNE

PERNAND-VERGELESSES

The commune has 3 Grand Cru vineyards two of which, Corton, and Corton-Charlemagne, are shared with both its neighbours Aloxe-Corton and Ladoix-Serrigny and a third, Charlemagne, is also shared with Aloxe-Corton. The commune has 8 Premier Cru vineyards. Its annual wine production at around 6000 hectolitres is higher than its neighbours to the north and it also produces a greater quantity of white, the red/white wine ratio being 50:50. Like Aloxe-Corton the village of Pernand Vergelesses is attractive and located close to the Corton hill.

SAVIGNY-LÈS-BEAUNE

The commune is a large producer of mainly red wine (annual production of almost 14,000 hectolitres 85% of which is red wine). The village lies in a valley and the hillsides on either side have different soils and exposure and the wines produced on each differ considerably. The southern hillside produces lighter bodied less alcoholic, early drinking wines while those produced on the northern hillside are much more full bodied which can age up to 10 years. The commune has no Grand Cru vineyards but has 22 Premier Cru vineyards. The village of Savigny-lès-Beaune is attractive and fairly large with around 1500 inhabitants.

CHOREY-LÈS-BEAUNE

The commune is one of only two in the Côte de Beaune which has neither Grand Cru or Premier Cru vineyards. Its relatively small annual production of around 5000 hectolitres is almost entirely red wine (around 95%). The soil of the commune is far from ideal for viniculture but despite this a number of competent and dedicated winemakers are now producing excellent wine at reasonable prices. Being only a few kilometres away from the historical medieval city of Beaune, the village is rather overshadowed by it and visitors use Beaune hotels and restaurants as a base when visiting the nearby area and certainly the commune of Chorey-lès-Beaune.

BEAUNE

The acknowledged capital of the wine region of Burgundy. This famous, medieval, walled city, from which the commune takes its name, is both historically renowned and commercially important. It has excellent facilities – hotels, restaurants and shops, and is an ideal base when visiting the Côte de Beaune. The commune is one of the larger wine producers which is around 16,000 hectolitres annually. It is predominantly a red wine commune with a red/white wine ratio of 85:15. The commune has no Grand Cru vineyards but has the second highest number of Premier Cru vineyards in the Côte d'Or – 42 (the highest being Chassagne Montrachet with 50). Beaune is also a major base for Burgundy négociants and most of the commune's wine is produced by them. The red wines of Beaune are traditionally lighter than those of its northerly neighbours in the Côte de Nuits and do not have the same international renown.. The small quantities of white wines produced are excellent but are overshadowed by the great, internationally famous white wines of the southern Côte de Beaune.

The Hospice de Beaune is famous as an important historical institution and also for the annual auction of its wines. The Hospice was founded in 1443 by Nicolas Rolin, Chancellor of Burgundy, as a hospital for the poor and needy. The original building, the Hotel Dieu, an architectural masterpiece, is now a museum. A major international event, which started in 1851, is the charity auction of the Hospice's wines on the third Sunday of November each year. It is part of a three day festival 'Les Trois Glorieuses' which opens with a black tie dinner at the château of Clos Vougeot. The Hospice, over the centuries, was endowed with lands and currently has over 60 hectares of vineyards the wines of which are auctioned to support the Hospice as a charitable organisation. The auction is now conducted by Christies and in the order of 500 bidders participate on a worldwide basis using the telephone and internet. The prestigious nature of the Hospice wines means that the prices achieved are generally higher than commercial market values but they are used as a benchmark for each vintage.

POMMARD

This entirely red wine commune has no Grand Cru vineyards and 27 Premier Cru vineyards. It is one of the largest communes, producing annually around 13,000 hectolitres of wine. The wines are powerful, full-bodied, and long lasting but for many experts lack finesse and elegance, and the Villages appellations even less so. The contrast between the light, delicate, red wines of its immediate neighbours, Beaune, to its north and Volnay to its south is quite remarkable. The village of Pommard is pleasant but unremarkable and visitors tend to be based in nearby Beaune. The village does however have the impressive Château Pommard which has extensive cellars.

VOLNAY

Volnay is also an entirely red wine commune with a medium level of production annually of around 8000 hectolitres. The commune has no Grand Cru vineyards and 29 Premier Cru vineyards. It is known for its attractive, light, elegant, and fragrant wines although in certain parts its soil and topography result in wines which are more robust and closer to those of Pommard. The commune wine producers have an excellent reputation for their wine-making skills and dedication. The village of Volnay is tiny and lies above its vineyards. It was a favourite holiday place for the Dukes of Burgundy but sadly their château was destroyed in the 18th century.

MONTHÉLIE

A smaller (production less than 5000 hectolitres annually) and a less well-known commune than many of its illustrious neighbours. It is also a predominantly red wine commune with a red/white wine ratio of 87:13. The commune has no Grand Cru vineyards and 15 Premier Cru vineyards. Before the commune received its AOC in 1937 its tradition was to produce rustic wines for local consumption although some wines were bottled as Pommard and Volnay. There are now a number of winemakers who are producing excellent reasonably priced wines but elsewhere the tradition of producing wines with limited finesse continues. The small hilltop village of Monthélie is very attractive and seems to have changed little over the centuries. It has of course its ancient Romanesque church and also a château which dominates the village.

AUXEY-DURESSES

Auxey Duresses is also one of the smaller and lesser known communes of the Côte de Beaune and many producers, until recently, labelled their wine Côte de Beaune Villages which was better known than the commune appellation. Its red/white wine ratio is 67:33. The commune has no Grand Cru vineyards and 9 Premier Cru vineyards. The quality and reputation of the wines varies considerably. The quality of the wine of the best producers is excellent and moderately priced whereas the rest can be disappointing and certainly undistinguished. The village of Auxey-Duresses is attractive with important archaeological remains and a 14th century church. An important resident of the village is Madame Lalou Bize-Leroy whose family are influential and important vineyard owners of Burgundy.

SAINT ROMAIN

The commune is the smallest wine producer of the Côte de Beaune with production less than 4000 hectolitres annually. White wine production slightly exceeds that of red with a red/white wine ratio of 46:54 with the whites being generally superior to the reds. The commune has no Grand Cru or Premier Cru vineyards. The wines produced are pleasant and of modest quality. The village is however famous for an important barrel maker (tonneleries), François Freres, who sells his barrels to important winemakers throughout the international market. The village of Saint Romain is best known for its magnificent panoramic views, its grottos and of course its ancient church.

MEURSAULT

The commune of Meursault is the largest wine producer of the Côte de Beaune with over 18,000 hectolitres of mainly white wine (98%). The commune has no Grand Cru vineyards and 19 Premier Cru vineyards. The great white wines of Meursault are quite magnificent and internationally acclaimed. There is however the almost inevitable wide range of quality with the estate bottled wines superior to those of the négociants and many Villages appellation wines fail to live up to the great name of the commune. In the year 1920 Meursault decided to follow the wine auction and 'trois glorieuses' celebrations of Beaune with their own festival. The idea is that the producers bring along bottles of their best wine and enjoy it with their friends who together can number as many as 600. The village of Meursault is interesting and pleasant but less picturesque than those of its neighbours.

PULIGNY MONTRACHET

The commune is a fairly large producer of around 11,000 hectolitres annually of almost entirely white wine (99%). It has 4 Grand Cru vineyards, two of which it shares with its neighbour Chassagne Montrachet, and 17 Premier Cru vineyards. The white wines which they produce are amongst the most famous and prestigious in the world of fine wine. They are also of course amongst the most expensive. Of the Grand Cru vineyards two, Montrachet and Batard-Montrachet, extend across the border into the commune of Chassagne Montrachet and these Grand Cru vineyards are shared by both communes. The other two Grand Cru vineyards Bienvenue-Batard-Montrachet and Chevalier Montrachet are entirely within the commune of Puligny Montrachet. The commune, like many others in the Côte d'Or, has a wide range of quality from sublime to very ordinary. Producing from a commune, with an internationally celebrated name, there is always the temptation for the lesser appellations to resort to the highest allowable yields which impacts on quality. The village is pleasant but one of the most ordinary in the Côte d'Or but clearly a very interesting place to visit and particularly the important domaines which together with their owners are full of character. The name 'Montrachet' is derived from the name of the rather bare rocky hillside Mont Rachet but, as I have been frequently reminded, when you put the two words together to form Montrachet the 't' in the middle is silent.

CHASSAGNE MONTRACHET

The commune of Chassagne Montrachet is one of the largest wine producers of the Côte de Beaune (around 16,000 hectolitres annually). Unlike its northerly neighbours the commune produces substantial quantities of red wine (red/white wine ratio 33:67). The commune has 3 Grand Cru vineyards two of which it shares on a cross border basis with Puligny Montrachet (Montrachet and Batard-Montrachet) and the other Grand Cru vineyard, Criots-Batard-Montrachet, is entirely within the communes borders. The commune of Chassagne Montrachet has the highest number of Premier cru vineyards, 50, in the entire Côte d'Or. The commune is to some extent eclipsed by the prestige and international status of its two northerly neighbours, Meursault, and Puligny Montrachet despite the fact that it produces some of the most exquisite white wines which are often incomparable. The commune also has the reputation for consistently producing excellent wines throughout its appellation structure. The village is small and rather basic with no hotels and restaurants and remarkably for a French village it does not even have a bar.

SAINT AUBIN

If there can be a rising star in the Côte de Beaune then many wine experts believe it would be the commune of Saint Aubin as it has attracted a number of young, competent, and dedicated wine-makers. It has no Grand Cru vineyards but has 20 Premier Cru vineyards, more than Meursault and Puligny Montrachet to its near north. The commune produces both red and white wine in the red/white wine ratio of 25:75 with a moderate total annual production of slightly over 8000 hectolitres. The red wines produced are fairly full bodied and generally of good or excellent quality and will age up to 7 to 10 years. The delicious white wines, although not as elegant and refined as those of its northerly neighbours, are similar in style and character. Saint Aubin is so small (population less than 300) it is often referred to as a hamlet. It does however have the impressive Château Gamay and has the hamlet of Gamay after which the grapes of Beaujolais are named.

SANTENAY

The most southerly commune of the Côte de Beaune. It has a large mainly red wine production of around 14,000 hectolitres annually with a red/white wine ratio of 84:16. The commune has no Grand Cru vineyards and 11 Premier Cru vineyards. Santenay, over the years, has not managed to improve its image and, despite marked improvements in style and quality, this does not appear to have been recognised and Santenay remains a rather undistinguished wine producer. It is in fact probably more famous for its casino and springs 'Source Carnot' which are reputed to have therapeutic properties particularly for gout which is apparently not uncommon in Burgundy. The commune has three villages Saint Jean, Santenay Le Bas, and Santenay Le Haut where the casino and springs are.

THE CÔTE DE NUITS

The northern area of the Côte d'Or. The 8 principal communes of the Côte de Nuits are world famous for their great red wines produced from a single grape variety, the Pinot Noir. Only a few percent of the total production is devoted to white wine.

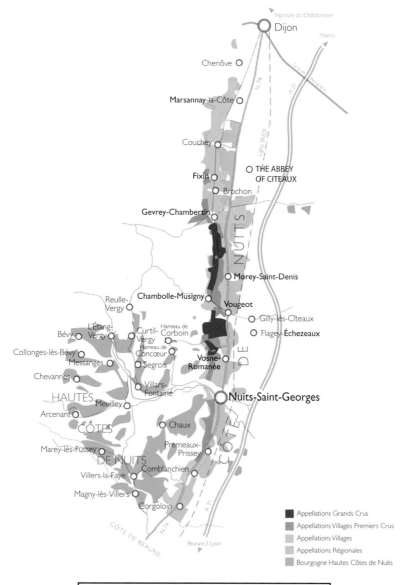

Appellations Grands Crus
Appellations Villages Premiers Crus
Appellations Villages
Appellations Régionales
Bourgogne Hautes Côtes de Nuits

THE CÔTE DE NUITS

The 8 principal communes of the Côte de Nuits are:-

<table>
<tr><td>Marsannay</td><td>Chambolle-Musigny</td></tr>
<tr><td>Fixin</td><td>Vougeot</td></tr>
<tr><td>Gevrey-Chambertin</td><td>Vosne-Romanée and Flagey-Echézeaux</td></tr>
<tr><td>Morey-St-Denis</td><td>Nuit-St-Georges</td></tr>
</table>

THE PRINCIPAL COMMUNES OF THE CÔTE DE NUIT

MARSANNAY

The most northerly commune of the Côte de Nuit, Marsannay produces red, white, and rosé wines with a total annual production of almost 10,000 hectolitres. Its red/white/rosé wine ratio is 67:18:15. The commune has no Grand Cru and Premier Cru vineyards. The wines produced are pleasant and usually ideal for early drinking but in comparison to those of its neighbours are not distinguished. The communes rosé wines are however considered to be some of the best in France and rival those produced in Provence a traditional region for this type of wine. Marsannay is a small town with a population of about 6000 located on the outskirts of the city of Dijon. It has a modern hotel, restaurants, and shops and with Dijon is often a base for those visiting the Côte de Nuit.

FIXIN

The commune of Fixin is a small producer of mainly red wine, (only minute quantities of white wine are produced). Its annual wine production is around 4000 hectolitres. The commune has no Grand Cru vineyards and 5 Premier Cru vineyards 4 of which, Arvelets, Hervelets, Clos de Chapitre and Clos Napoleon are within the Fixin boundaries and a fifth, Clos de Perriere is located partly in the commune of Brochon. Over the last 25 years or so a number of dedicated, and highly competent winemakers, have raised the standard of Fixin wine to an extent where it is now favourably compared with those of its illustrious neighbours. A far cry from the time when Fixin wines were blended with those of Gevrey Chambertin or simply labelled 'Côte de Nuit-Villages'. The Fixin wines are traditionally robust, full bodied, more tannic and ageworthy than most of the wines of the Côte de Nuits but when they open the wine experts credit them with fragrance and finesse.

THE ABBEY OF CÎTEAUX

THE ABBEY OF CÎTEAUX

THE ABBEY OF CÎTEAUX

The village of Fixin is also a tourist attraction because of its association with Napoleon. Captain Noisot, who served with Napoleon's Imperial Guard, was overcome by the departure of Napoleon from Fontainebleau in 1815 after the 100 days when he bade farewell to the Imperial Guard, known as the 'Cour des Adieux'. Noisot purchased land in Fixin in 1846 and created a park, in honour of Napoleon. He commissioned a sculpture by François Rude 'The Awakening of Napoleon' and the sculptures of members of the Imperial Guard are buried upright, ready to move, when the Emperor awakens. The depiction of Napoleon is controversial as it is not particularly complimentary to the great man. There is also a small museum with Napoleon memorabilia. Despite the growth of the nearby city of Dijon, and the tendency for neighbouring villages to grow as 'dormitories', Fixin has retained its rural charm and the population is still less than 1000. Part of the commune of Fixin, Fixey, has a fine church, the Oratory of St Anthony, with a square tower and tiled roof, which dates back to 902. The eastern and western parts of the nave were rebuilt in the 12th and 13th centuries. The apse was enlarged in 1720. The other church, St Martin, which is 12th century, is located in the centre of the village.

GEVREY-CHAMBERTIN

The commune of Gevrey-Chambertin is, by far, the largest wine producer of the Côte de Nuits and the second largest in the whole of the Côte d'Or. It produces only red wine with an annual production of over 17,000 hectolitres. The commune has 9 Grand Cru vineyards, the highest number in the Côte d'Or, and 26 Premier Cru vineyards. As one Grand Cru vineyard can officially use different names and two have names which are interchangeable this sometimes gives rise to a little confusion. A famous Grand Cru vineyard is named simply 'Chambertin'. However an equally famous Grand Cru vineyard, Chambertin-Clos de Bèze, may officially shorten its name to 'Chambertin'. Charmes-Chambertin and Mazoyeres-Chambertin have the official right to interchange their names. The famous name 'Chambertin' comes from Burgundian folk-lore. In the 12th century a farmer named Bertin had fields next to the vineyards of the Abbey of Bèze and was so impressed by the Abbey's wine that he decided to cultivate vines and produce his own wine. Bertin was so successful that he actually surpassed the quality of the wine of his great neighbour and called his wine 'Chambertin' which literally means Bertin's fields. The Abbey's vineyard evolved into Chambertin-Clos de Bèze but because of its neighbourly vineyard's prestige and importance it secured the right to drop the 'Clos de Bèze' and also calls its wine 'Chambertin'.

Gevrey-Chambertin is of course a famous name in the world of wine and indeed produces exceptional wine mainly from its Grand Cru and Premier Cru vineyards. The great name is of course also used for the Villages and Commune appellations which are the largest in the Côte de Nuit. Unfortunately there is a wide variation in the quality of these 'Gevrey Chambertin' wines as they frequently fail to live up to the illustrious name of the commune. The top quality wines are full bodied with strong aromas and flavours. They are also age worthy with the Grand Cru's lasting up to at least 20 years. The best Villages wines can also last up to 10 years. Gevrey Chambertin with a population of around 3000 is a small town with excellent hotels and restaurants.

MOREY-ST-DENIS

A small, predominantly red wine commune, with an annual total production of less than 4000 hectolitres. Its red/white wine ratio is 96:4. Morey-St-Denis's 5* Grand Cru vineyards and 20 Premier Cru vineyards produce many excellent and outstanding wines which due to a quirk of perception or fashion, are often, unjustifiably, underrated.

The commune is also to a great extent overshadowed by its acclaimed neighbours. However for many the cloud has passed and there is now a much greater recognition and appreciation in the wine trade and by consumers of the excellent wines of Morey-St-Denis. The wines are rich, fragrant, and ageworthy with relatively low levels of tannin. The Grand Cru wines will last up to 20 years and the Premier Crus 10–15 years. The general standard of the Villages appellation wines is good to excellent as the commune has the reputation for maintaining a high standard of wine-making. Morey-St-Denis village is small with around 650 inhabitants. It was originally within the domain of the great Cistercian Abbey of Cîteaux. The village has a history of misfortune as it was burnt down in the 17th century, decimated by the plague, and strangely, in the past, known as a haven for social misfits. Fortunately the village has fully recovered and now with a hotel, renowned for its comfort and service, it is often attractive as a base for visitors to the area.

one of which, Bonnes-Mares, is shared with Chambolle Musigny

CHAMBOLLE-MUSIGNY

The commune of Chambolle-Musigny is almost entirely a red wine producer with only minute quantities of white wine produced. It has an annual production of around 6000 hectolitres. The red wines have almost unique characteristics as they are particularly light and fragrant with an exquisite bouquet. Not surprisingly they are known as the 'queen' or 'feminine' wines of the Côte de Nuit. The commune has 2* Grand Cru vineyards and 25 Premier Cru vineyards. The characteristics of the wine require a delicate touch in the wine-making if the full potential is to be realised. Unfortunately this does not always extend to the Villages appellation producers and the results can often be disappointing. The delicate wines of Chambolle-Musigny have, over the years, attracted ardent supporters. The famous French poet Gaston Roupnel described the wine as '*a wine of silk and lace; supremely delicate with no hint of violence yet much hidden strength.*' The tiny village of Chambolle-Musigny has no hotels or restaurants. It does of course have a church and the rather bizarre painting of Christ on its door features in Burgundian folklore.

one of which, Bonnes-Mares, is shared with Morey-St-Denis

VOUGEOT

The commune of Vougeot has a number of unique characteristics. It is first of all dominated by a single vineyard, Clos Vougeot, which is the largest Grand Cru vineyard of the Côte de Nuit. The commune also has the smallest wine production of all the communes of the Côte d'Or with a total annual production of slightly more than 2000 hectolitres of red wine only. Clos Vougeot, which was founded by the monks of the Cistercian Abbey of Cîteaux in the 11th century, with its walls completed by them in 1336, also has a magnificent château which is now the home of the Confrérie des Chevaliers du Tastevin. In addition to the Grand Cru

CLOS DE VOUGEOT WITH THE BANNERS OF THE CONFRERIE DU TASTEVIN

vineyard of Clos Vougeot the commune has 4 Premier Cru vineyards. Clos Vougeot is one of the most historically famous vineyards of France. One story of the vineyard which has passed into folklore relates to an incident when a French colonel, Bisson, returning with his troops from the eastern front, passed Clos Vougeot where Bisson ordered his men to halt and present arms, a salute afforded only to a commander-in-chief.

In the introductory section 'The Burgundy Wine Region' the historical process which led to the selling of the church's vineyards which was followed by the enactment of the Napoleonic Code of Inheritance are described. This led to the multiple ownership of vineyards particularly in Burgundy and the resulting wide range of quality of wines, from individual owner/producers, which all bear the same label except for the name of producer or negociant. Because of its Grand Cru status, and its fame, Clos Vougeot has tended to become the focal point for a certain disenchantment of Burgundy wine arising from multiple ownership of vineyards and the resulting wide range in quality which ostensibly have the same 'pedigree'. There are many owners who are producing superb Clos Vougeot wines who are understandably aggrieved by their great vineyard being singled out, as the 'whipping boy' for this Burgundy phenomenon. Nevertheless Cos Vougeot is a very large vineyard and its 'terroir' varies considerably from the excellent, soil, exposure, and topography of its slope to the flat area and alluvial soil near the road. It also has more than 80 individual owners who either produce their own wine or do so collectively or through négociants who all display 'Clos Vougeot – Grand Cru' on their labels. The village (or hamlet) of Vougeot with less than 200 inhabitants is one of the smallest and most insignificant of the Côte d'Or.

VOSNE-ROMANÉE AND FLAGEY-ECHÉZEAUX
Vosne Romanée has an annual production of around 6000 hectolitres of entirely red wine. The communes 8 Grand Cru vineyards and 15 Premier Cru vineyards produce the most sumptuous and expensive wines of the Côte de Nuit. The pinnacle is the vineyard of Romanée Conti which together with Pétrus of Bordeaux shares the 'accolade' of the worlds most expensive and iconic wines. In contrast the Village appellation wines, as in many of the Côte de Nuits communes, appear to rely on the fame and prestige of the great wines, rather than the quality of their own offerings,

ROMANEE CONTI

which results in wines that are often disappointing. A feature of the top wines of Vosne Romanée is that they are mainly produced from small or even tiny vineyards (Romanée Conti is only 1.8 hectares) which unlike many others in the Côte d'Or have a single owner (called a monopole) or are operated by a single entity. The Grand Cru vineyards of Romanée Conti and La Tache are monopole's of Domaine Romanée Conti, La Grand Rue is a monopole of Domaine Larmarche and La Romanée is a monopole of Comte Liger-Belair. Domaine Romanée-Conti also has substantial holdings in the Grand Cru vineyards of Richebourg, Romanée-St Vivant, Echézeaux, and Grand Echézeaux. The village of Vosne-Romanée and the hamlet of Flagey-Echéveaux are relatively simple working places with very limited facilities for visitors which the nearby town of Nuit-St-Georges, only a few kilometres away, provides with excellent hotels and restaurants.

NUITS-SAINT-GEORGES

The second largest wine producer (around 12,000 hectolitres annually of almost entirely red wine) of the Côte de Nuit, the largest producer being Gevrey Chambertin. The commune of Nuits-Saint-Georges has no Grand Cru vineyard but one of the highest number of Premier Cru vineyards, 41, of the Côte d'Or and the highest of the Côte de Nuit. Due to the wide ranging difference in soil and topography throughout this large commune there is a considerable diversity of both quality and characteristics in the wines produced. The Burgundians believe that the greater the production of the commune the greater the attention required in selecting the wine. This is certainly true in Nuit-Saint-Georges where the wines produced vary from exceptional and sublime to those which are certainly not so, and the Villages appellations are particularly variable in quality. The great wines of Nuit-Saint-George are powerful, robust, and ageworthy with the 'Premier Cru' lasting for up to 15 years. The small town of Nuits-Saint-Georges with some 6000 inhabitants ranks in terms of commercial importance and services only after Beaune and Dijon. The town also has a hospice which like the renowned Hospice-de-Beaune owns vineyards and also auctions its wine production annually but on a more modest basis compared with that of Beaune.

CHABLIS

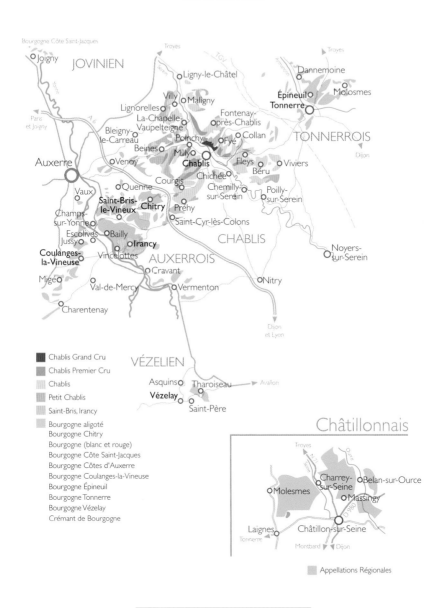

Chablis Grand Cru
Chablis Premier Cru
Chablis
Petit Chablis
Saint-Bris, Irancy
Bourgogne aligoté
Bourgogne Chitry
Bourgogne (blanc et rouge)
Bourgogne Côte Saint-Jacques
Bourgogne Côtes d'Auxerre
Bourgogne Coulanges-la-Vineuse
Bourgogne Épineuil
Bourgogne Tonnerre
Bourgogne Vézelay
Crémant de Bourgogne

Appellations Régionales

CHABLIS

The most northerly sub-region of Burgundy which produces only white wine from the Chardonnay grape. Its venerable name was for decades defiled around the world as it was used to describe any white wine produced from various grape varieties. A largely successful campaign was launched to eradicate the mis-use of the name 'Chablis'.

Its wines, although produced from the same grape variety, Chardonnay, as the wines of the Côte-de-Beaune, are quite different in character. The Chablis wines are traditionally sharp and 'flinty' or 'gout de Pierre a fusil' – tasting of gun flint. This arises from the climate, soil and type of barrel used. In the Côte de Beaune the oak of the new barrels with different levels of 'charring' have an important affect on the wine whereas the older barrels used in Chablis have very little. This is however progressively changing and some Chablis wines are now more 'oaked'. The Chablis sub-region has 27 communes throughout which the vineyards are spread and the Chablis AOC created in 1938 applies not to communes but to vineyards which were classified as Grand Cru, Premier Cru, and Chablis AOC. In 1944 a lower classification 'Petit Chablis' was added. The vineyard areas of the two lower classifications have increased considerably over the last 50 years or so, and continue to do so. The current approximate vineyard areas are:-

APPELLATION	VINEYARD AREA (HECTARES)
Grand Cru	110
Premier Cru	800
Chablis AOC	3000
Petit Chablis	750
TOTAL	**4660**

The sub-region has 7 Grand Cru vineyards and 40 Premier Cru vineyards which account for less than 20% of total production. Chablis, over recent years, has come under quite severe criticism by wine critics and experts for the poor quality of some of its wines particularly those of the lower appellations, Chablis AOC and Petit Chablis which they, at least, partly blame on the extensive use of mechanical harvesting, high yields, and the predominance of young vines as a result of vineyard expansion. It is clear that Chablis is capable of producing good, excellent and outstanding wines but unfortunately this is not always so. The village of Chablis is pleasant but ordinary and provides minimal facilities for visitors. The nearby city of Auxerre, with its historical churches and the Cathedral of St Étienne combined with modern facilities including excellent hotels is usually the base for visitors to Chablis.

THE SELECTION OF BURGUNDY WINES

TERMINOLOGY

Firstly it is important to address and understand three important terms, relating to wine selection, which feature prominently in Burgundy wine terminology. These are:- TERROIR, CLIMAT and LIEU-DIT.

The location where vines are planted is subjected to the prevailing microclimatic conditions of the area and has ground, which invariably has several soil types (gravel, clay, minerals, etc, both surface and subsoil). Also altitudes, aspects, and terrains vary considerably in different locations.

The foregoing have an important affect on the characteristics of the grapes of these vines and the wine which is produced from them in respect of sugar, alcohol, acidity, taste, colour and quality. The other very important influence on the style and quality of the wine produced is of course the expertise and dedication of the winemaker. Together in Burgundy they produce some of the world's greatest wines.

The distinctive features of vinicultural locations as outlined above are collectively known as 'terroir' which is a term extensively used in many places where wine is produced and certainly throughout France. It is particularly important in Burgundy where widely differing terroirs can exist often in close proximity.

In Burgundy wine goes back to the Roman Empire and possibly beyond. Later the great abbeys of Cluny and Cîteaux were founded (in 910 and 1028 respectively) and the Benedictine and Cistercian monks established vineyards which still exist to the present day. These were required to provide the wine for the celebration of the Eucharist, where it represents the blood of Christ, and also to add a little cheer to the spartan way of life of the monks.

The monks became skilled viniculturists and winemakers and they soon realised that the wine produced from different areas or 'plots' often in close proximity or even adjacent produced wines of different style and quality. The monks delineated those areas which produced a distinctive and consistent style and quality of wine, which meant in modern terminology that the delineated plots had identifiable and unique terroirs, and each of these was called by the monks a *climat*, a concept which still exists to the present day and is extensively used throughout Burgundy.

In 1935 when the INAO (the French wine governing body) was established the climats were officially recognised and apply to the Burgundy appellations. There are more than 1000 Burgundy climats of which 669 are Premier Cru. There are also 39 Grand Cru Burgundy vineyards.

In July 2015 a Burgundian team led by Aubert de Villaine (co-owner and co-director of Romanée Conti) secured UNESCO World Heritage recognition for the climats of Burgundy for '*Outstanding Universal Value*' which is the highest level that it is possible to achieve, and:-

> '*joint works of man and nature, together with the areas including the archaeological sites which have an exceptional universal value from the historic, aesthetic, ethnological or anthropological perseptive.*'

Another term used extensively in Burgundy for a delineated area of land is '*lieu-dit*' (plural lieux-dits). These have formal legal status as they are listed in the French Land Registry which was first established in 1807 – the Napoleonic period.

It is frequently stated that climats and lieux-dits are 'interchangeable'. It is not clear what purpose this serves. Of course certain climats are located within the boundaries of lieux-dits (and vice versa) and the wines produced do, in certain instances, state the name of the lieu-dit on the label. However one is *a delineated area of land with a particular and consistent terroir which is now part of the INAO appellation system* (**climat**) and the other *is a legally delineated area of land listed in the official French Land Registry dating back to the Napoleonic period* (**lieu-dit**).

266/600   Oxidised

WINE SELECTION

With Burgundy wine there is, remarkably, a widespread misconception that the great communes, and particularly those of the Côte d'Or are individual, undivided entities and that for instance the wines of Nuits-St-Georges, Gevrey-Chambertin or Chambolle-Musigny etc. each have a singular unique characteristic. How many times have you heard '*my favourite wine is Nuit-St-Georges or, although both are excellent I prefer Gevrey-Chambertin to Chambolle-Musigny.*'

The reality is quite different as these great communes produce a very extensive range of wines of widely differing quality and price many of which do indeed prominently display the name of the commune on their labels.

The Burgundy quality hierarchy is as follows:-

> Grand Cru AOC
> Premier Cru AOC *
> Villages AOC *
> Commune AOC *
> Sub-Region AOC
> Bourgogne AOC

* The wines of these appellations boldly display the name of the commune on their bottle labels.

GRAND CRU AOC

The Grand Cru appellations are restricted to the Pinot Noir and Charonnay grapes and are granted to single vineyards. They account for around 2% of Burgundy wine production. The allowable yield is 35 hl/ha.

The INAO, when it was formed in 1935, based the selection of the Grand Cru vineyards on a classification published in 1855 (the same year as the Bordeaux classification) by Dr Jules Lavalle – *Histoire et Statistique de la Vigne de Grands Vins de la Côte d'Or* with five quality groups and the vineyards in the top quality group were granted Grand Cru status by the INAO.

The Grand Cru producers display the names of the vineyard and their names on the labels:-

JOHN HEATHCOTE

CLOS VOUGEOT
GRAND CRU
ALAIN HUDELOT-NOELLAT

Of the six sub-regions of Burgundy only Chablis, Côte-de-Nuits, and Côte-de-Beaune have Grand Cru vineyards. Mâconnaise, Côte Châlonnaise, and Beaujolais do not as they did not have their vineyards historically included in Dr Jules Lavelle's top quality group of his 1855 classification and some also produce their wine from 'non qualifying' grapes (Gamay and Aligote).

The distribution of the Grand Cru vineyards over the three sub-regions is as follows:-

Côte-de-Beaune	-	8
Côte-de-Nuits	-	24
Chablis	-	7
		39

The Grand Cru vineyards have multiple ownership (and are known as *'morsellated vineyards'*) which resulted from the State sequestering and selling off the Church vineyards, mainly to local families, combined with the enactment of the Napoleonic Code of Inheritance which required any Inheritance to be left equally to all of the children. Clos Vougeot is often used as an example of this as it is divided between 80 owners who produce wine individually, through small groups collectively, or through négociants. This means that there are more than 50 producers of Clos Vougeot Grand Cru wine from different terroirs from within this large vineyard and with widely varying winemaking expertise and dedication. All the producers label their wine almost identically as Clos Vougeot, Grand Cru, prominently displayed, and the name of the producer.

The foregoing results in a wide range of quality and price for wines produced from a single Grand Cru vineyard which are all labelled in a similar manner.

Many of the international wine experts publish a 'best producers' list and also numerically quality rate the different wines.

International wine merchants also post their prices on the internet wine searcher system.

The foregoing results in the following for four of the 'best producers' of Clos Vougeot.

PRODUCER	YEAR	PRICE - EUROS PER BOTTLE	AVERAGE NUMERICAL QUALITY RATING
JEAN GRIVOT	2007 2009	100–125 150–170	91 93
JOSEPH DROUHIN	2007 2009	90–110 120–200	92 91
LOUIS JADOT	2007 2009	80–120 80–110	91 92
DOMAINE LEROY *	2007 2009	1000–1100 900–1400	96 97

SOURCE: Internet Wine Searcher System

**CLOS VOUGEOT GRAND CRU VINEYARD –
A SELECTION OF PRODUCERS, THEIR WINE PRICES
AND AVERAGE, NUMERICAL, QUALITY RATING
MID 2016 WINE PRICES**

The foregoing demonstrates that there are significant price differences between producers even though their numerical quality ratings are virtually the same for three of the four producers with Domaine Leroy being significantly higher. There are also wide variations in the offer prices for each producer in the international wine market posted on the internet wine searcher system.

All this makes wine selection quite a challenge.

> ** Lalou Bize-Leroy was formerly co-owner and co-director of Romanée Conti (a role now taken over by a member of her family). The Domaine Leroy has been successfully developed into one of Burgumdy's top wine producers and the Domaine's wine prices are often significantly higher than those of other distinguished producers.*

PREMIER CRU AOC

The Premier Cru appellations of Burgundy are granted to a number of climats located in the delineated Premier Cru areas of the principal wine communes. For instance Vosne Romanée, Volnay, Morey Saint-Denis, and Pomard have 15, 29, 20, 27, Premier Cru climats respectively (see table at end). They account for approximately 12% of Burgundy wine production. The allowable yield is 45 hl/ha.

Under the INAO regulations wine can be produced from a single Premier Cru climat in which case the name of the commune and the climat together with the name of the producer are displayed on the label.

GEVREY CHAMBERTIN	–	*COMMUNE*
PREMIER CRU (or 1er CRU)	–	*APPELLATION*
CLOS-ST-JACQUES	–	*CLIMAT*
BRUNO CLAIR	–	*PRODUCER*

The regulations however allow wines to be blended from several Premier Cru climats from within a commune in which case the label would display only the name of the commune, the producer, and Premier Cru (or 1er Cru).

The Premier Cru climats have, like the Grand Cru vineyards, multiple ownership. Details of the following two climats are given by way of example:-

COMMUNE: GEVREY-CHAMBERTIN		**COMMUNE:** NUITS-ST-GEORGES	
CLIMAT:	CLOS-SAINT-JACQUES	**CLIMAT:**	AUX BAUDOTS
SIZE:	6.7 hectares	**SIZE:**	6.3 hectares

OWNER/PRODUCER	**OWNER/PRODUCER**
ARMAND ROUSSEAU	LALOU BIZE-LEROY
SYLVIE ESMONIN	JEAN GRIVOT
BRUNO CLAIR	MEO CAMUZET
LOUIS JADOT	NICOLAS POTEL
JEAN-MARIE FOURRIER	JEAN TARDY

GEVREY-CHAMBERTIN HAS 35 PREMIER CRU CLIMATS	NUIT-SAINT-GEORGES HAS 41 PREMIER CRU CLIMATS

Again as in the case of the Grand Cru vineyards the Premier Cru climats with their multiple ownership have considerable differences in prices between producers even though their numerical quality ratings are more or less the same.

There are also again wide variations in the offer prices for each producer in the international wine market posted on the internet wine searcher system.

The foregoing is clearly shown by the following table:-

PRODUCER	YEAR	PRICE - EUROS PER BOTTLE	AVERAGE NUMERICAL QUALITY RATING
ARMAND ROUSSEAU	2007	320–500	94
	2009	450–650	94
SYLVIE ESMONIN	2007	80–125	93
	2009	100–130	92
BRUNO CLAIR	2007	120–135	91
	2009	140–150	94
JEAN-MARIE FOURRIER	2007	250–450	94
	2009	350–500	95
LOUIS JADOT	2007	100–120	93
	2009	100–150	92

SOURCE: Internet Wine Searcher System

**THE CLOS-SAINT-JACQUES PREMIER CRU
CLIMAT OF GEVREY-CHAMBERTIN –
A SELECTION OF PRODUCERS,
THEIR WINE PRICES AND AVERAGE
NUMERICAL QUALITY RATINGS
MID 2016 WINE PRICES**

The foregoing again demonstrates the challenge to be faced in selecting a Burgundy Premier Cru wine although, as in the case of the Grand Crus, a great deal of market information and expert opinion is available.

THE DISTRIBUTION OF THE BURGUNDY PREMIER CRU CLIMATS OVER THE SUB-REGIONS AND COMMUNES

SUB REGION	COMMUNE	NUMBER OF PREMIER CRU CLIMATS	SUB REGION	COMMUNE	NUMBER OF PREMIER CRU CLIMATS
CÔTE DE CHÂLONNAISE	RULLY	23	CÔTE DE NUIT	FIXIN	5
	MERCUREY	33		GEVREY CHAMBERTIN	35
	GIVRY	27		MOREY SAINT-DENIS	20
	MONTAGNY	49		VOSNE-Romanée	15
	TOTAL	132		NUITS-SAINT-GEORGES	41
CÔTE DE BEAUNE	LADOIX SERRIGNY	17		TOTAL	145
	ALOXE CORTON	8	CHABLIS	-	89
	PERNAND	8		TOTAL	89
	SAUIGNY-LÈS-BEAUNE	22	GRAND TOTAL		669
	BEAUNE	42	MARSANNAY IN THE CÔTE-DE-NUIT AND CHOREY-LÈS-BEAUNE AND SAINT ROMAN IN CÔTE-DE-BEAUNE DO NOT HAVE ANY PREMIER CRU CLIMATS		
	POMMARD	27			
	VOLNAY	29			
	MONTELIE	15			
	AUXEY-DURESSES	9			
	MEURSAULT	24			
	PULIGNY MONTRACHET	20			
	CHASSAGNE MONTRACHET	50			
	SAINT-AUBIN	21			
	SANTENAY	11			
	TOTAL	303			

VILLAGES AOC

This appellation, in the quality hierarchy, is the third level after Grand Cru and Premier Cru. The other appellations – Commune AOC, Sub-Region AOC and the generic Bourgogne AOC are mainly for local and national consumption and do not feature to any great extent in the international wine market. These 'lesser' appellations account for approximately 50% of Burgundy wine production.

The Villages wines account for approximately 36% of Burgundy wine production. They have an allowable yield of 50 hl/ha. The Villages AOC climats are delineated areas around the wine producing communes. They vary considerably in size for instance Gevry-Chambertin's Villages climat is 360 hectares whereas Morey-St-Denis is only 64 hectares.

The Villages AOC climats are divided into a number of vineyards. Wine can be produced from a single vineyard in which case the label displays the appellation (Villages AOC) the name of the commune and also the name of the vineyard. If the wine is blended from a number of vineyards from within the climat then no vineyard name is displayed.

Many Village AOC wines are of excellent quality and are modestly priced. Selection however is particularly difficult as the 'best producer' lists and numerical quality ratings are not readily available. Nevertheless the standards maintained for Burgundy Villages wines are of the highest order and it would be rare and a great disappointment to find a less than satisfactory Villages wine.

SUMMARY OF YIELDS

The Burgundy Grand Cru, Premier Cru, and Villages appellations have allowable yields 35hl/ha, 45hl/ha, and 50hl/ha, respectively. These are the basic INAO yields (rendement de base). These yields can be increased by 20% (plafond limite de classement or PLC) depending on a tasting evaluation.

CONFRÉRIE DES CHEVALIERS DU TASTEVIN – TASTEVINAGE

In relation to the very large wine production of the Burgundy wine region there exists a relatively small but highly effective wine quality evaluation system known as Tastevinage. Burgundy has a major, prestigious inter-national organisation – the brotherhood of the Confrérie des Chevaliers du Tastevin with headquarters at Château Vougeot where each year two wine tasting and quality evaluation sessions are held for wines submitted from throughout the Burgundy wine region (including the Cru vineyards of Beaujolais).

The number of wines tested has steadily risen since the inception of the wine tasting and quality evaluation in 1950 and now exceeds annually the wines of more than 1500 producers.

The wines which pass the exacting evaluation are awarded the right to display the prominent and colourful Tastevinage emblem on their wine bottles.

A detailed description of the Confrérie des Chevaliers du Tastevin and the Tastevinage are included n Appendix l(D).

Robert Parker considers that the Tastevinage has a role to play in the selection of the wines of Burgundy:-

> *'virtually every wine I have ever tasted with the Tastevin label has been at least good. In most cases the wines are good to excellent.'*

CONCLUSION

In conclusion there is a vast range of Burgundy wines which vary in quality from good to excellent and exceptional with prices to match.

Of course Burgundy is one of the most famous and acclaimed wine regions of the world but what makes Burgundy exceptional in the world of fine wine is its unique pattern of terroirs which can differ considerably even when they are in close proximity or even adjacent. As the terroirs differ so does the characteristics of the wine produced in respect of quality and style.

This phenomenon was discovered by the skilled viticulturalists and winemaking monks of the great abbeys of Cluny and Cîteaux a thousand years ago. They called a plot of land which had a unique and identifiable terroir a climat which is a term still used in the same way to the present day.

Burgundy also has, of course, many winemakers of exceptional skill and dedication and of international renown which combined with the principal grape varieties, Pinot Noir and Chardonnay, which are ideally suited to Burgundy's remarkable terroirs, results in the production of many of the world's greatest wines.

BORDEAUX

"A great claret is the queen of all natural wines and…the highest perfection of all wines that have ever been made. It is delicate and harmonious beyond all others."

H. WARNER ALLEN
British wine writer

"One never tires of summer sunsets; they are always beautiful and yet they never are quite the same…That is also the secret of the appeal which Claret has for all wine lovers; it is the most perfectly balanced wine and in ever a new garb; harmony without monotony."

ANDRÉ SIMON
A Wine Primer

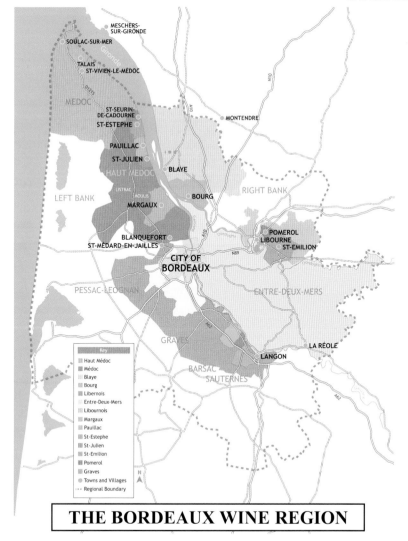

Key
- Haut Médoc
- Médoc
- Blaye
- Bourg
- Libernois
- Entre-Deux-Mers
- Libournois
- Margaux
- Pauillac
- St-Estephe
- St-Julien
- St-Emilion
- Pomerol
- Graves
- Towns and Villages
- Regional Boundary

THE BORDEAUX WINE REGION

THE BORDEAUX WINE REGION

The Romans also found Bordeaux an ideal place to cultivate their vines and produce wine and, as in Burgundy, they were almost certainly preceded as winemakers by the Celts. The early and medieval history of the wine of Bordeaux was however quite different to that of Burgundy. From the 12th century onwards the development of Bordeaux wine from the Gascon territory of south west France was driven by a new phenomenon, an export market, that of England, where the wines of Bordeaux were called 'claret' and still are to the present day. This all started with a famous lady, Eleanor, Duchess of Aquitaine, whose lands extended from the Loire to the Pyrenees. Eleanor became Queen of France in 1137 when she married King Louis VI. This marriage was annulled in 1152 and 8 weeks later Eleanor married Henry Plantagenet whose mother Mathilda, the daughter of the Norman king, Henry I 'Beauclerc', and granddaughter of William the Conqueror, had married Geoffrey of Anjou. It was from his Angevin father that the name of the English royal line, Plantagenet, came. Geoffrey wore a sprig of broom (Planta Genista) in his hat and adopted the name 'Plantagenet' which he passed to his son, the first Plantagenet king of England. Two years after his marriage Henry became King of England, with Eleanor as his queen, the lands of Aquitaine and the vineyards of Bordeaux were then under the control of the English Crown and some time later, during the early reign of King John, the son and second successor (Richard Cœur de Lion was the first) of Henry and Eleanor, the export of wine to England was actively encouraged by abolishing the export tax of Aquitaine (Grande Coutune). This led to the rapid development and expansion of the vineyards of Bordeaux and after the fall of La Rochelle in 1224, to the French, Bordeaux was established as the principal port for the wine trade.

This early control of Bordeaux was not to last indefinitely as the French Kings from the House of Valois were determined to drive the Plantagenet English kings out of France and repudiate their claim to the French throne. And so a war lasting more than 100 years started in 1337. It ended in 1453 when the English were finally defeated at the Battle of Castillon near Bordeaux and expelled from France except for Calais. The English commander, John Talbot, who had been made 1st Earl of

Shrewsbury by King Henry VI (founder of Eton College for 'twenty five poor and needy scholars to learn grammar') was killed, together with his son, at the battle, and after 300 years of English control, Gascony and Bordeaux were restored to the French Crown. Talbot had earlier acquired a Bordeaux vineyard which still bears his name.

The Duke of Burgundy, Philip the Good, (1419–1467) had, during the '100 year war', allied Burgundy, which at that time was independent of the French Crown, with King Henry V of England under the Treaty of Troyes (1423) and it was the Burgundians who captured and handed over Joan of Arc to the English. She was tried at an ecclesiastical court and condemned to be burnt at the stake (1431 – aged 19 years).

Another foreign presence in France and certainly Bordeaux was that of the Irish. This started with King Henry VIII establishing England as a protestant nation in 1534. His daughter Queen Mary attempted to return it to Roman Catholicism followed by her half sister Queen Elizabeth who was equally determined to follow her father as a protestant Monarch. This led through the succession of James I, Charles I (who although abstemious drank a glass of claret before his execution in 1649) and Charles II, to James II who was committed to re-establishing Catholicism in England and was deposed and exiled for it. Throughout all this the Irish, although under the control of the English Crown, remained staunchly catholic. When James II was removed from the throne of England and fled to France in 1688 he sought help from the French and Irish Catholics. Their joint force was defeated at the Battle of the Boyne (1690) by the Northern Ireland protestants who had been brought in by James I. Many of the Irish landed gentry moved to France to avoid English reprisals and many settled in Bordeaux. The Lynch family came from Galaway and the O'Briens claim to have founded Haut Brion, the French version of their name (nice story but not true), and were many others. The most famous were the MacMahons who produced a French Marshal and President and the family still hold the French hereditary title of Duke of Magenta. It is not clear whether the Scottish Dukes of Montrose were the early owners of Château Montrose, but it certainly makes the wine especially popular in Scotland.

An important feature of Bordeaux wine is that the vineyards have the right to use the title of 'Château'. This has got nothing to do with a grand house or mansion (which a number of the vineyards have) but it is a courtesy title which may be used even if the 'chateau' is a modest house. The opposite of course is true of Burgundy and even when a vineyard has an imposing château, such as for instance Clos Vougeot, it does not feature in the name of the vineyard.

There also tends to be a modern perception that the great chateaux of Bordeaux go far back to antiquity particularly when it is well known that 'claret' was being exported to England in the early 13th century when Bordeaux was a domain of the English Crown.

This is not so as at that time the vineyards were small and generally operated by tenant farmers on the basis that the crops were shared with the owners.

Most of the large estates, which evolved into major vineyards, to be eventually known as 'châteaux' throughout Bordeaux, can only be traced back to the 17th century. This process first started in the sub-region of Graves and the area of Pessac from where the early 'claret' was exported to England.

Probably the first vinicultural area to be established as an 'estate' exists to the present day as Château Pape Clement. First planted in the late 13th century it was presented to Bertrand de Goth, upon his appointment as Archbishop of Bordeaux, by his brother, Berald. Bertrand went on to be elected Pope Clement V in 1305 and in 1309 he moved the papal court from Rome to Avignon where it remained until 1376. The estate in Bordeaux which he had received as a gift from his brother was endowed by Pope Clement to the archbishops of Bordeaux but it was named after him – Château Pape Clement.

Another famous early estate, Chateau Haut Brion, also from Pessac in Graves, was founded in the 16th century and later featured in the early history of 'claret' in London. The first records of its presence in the city were the cellar records of King Charles II (reigned 1660–85), where it was called Hobriono, and the diary of Samuel Pepys which recorded his tasting of the wine at the Royal Oak Tavern on the 10th of April 1663 *'drank a sort of French wine called Ho Bryen that hath a good and most particular taste I ever met with'*.

The vineyards of the Médoc did not however play a significant part in this early activity as up to the end of the 16th century a large part of the peninsular was waterlogged and marshy and only a limited area, which is now part of the Haut Médoc, was suitable for viniculture.

This all changed in 1599 when a Dutchman, Conrad Gaussen, arranged for a famous Dutch engineer, Humphrey Bradley, to drain the Médoc peninsular.

The resulting 'terroir' proved to be exceptional and the great wine producing communes and estates developed rapidly and to such an extent that the 1855 classification of red wine was totally dominated by the Medoc châteaux.

This was followed by concern, in the early 18th century, over excessive planting of vines at the expense of other important produce. From 1725 strict government laws were passed forbidding the planting of new vineyards which if contravened resulted in stiff penalties and the ploughing up of new vineyards. By the late 18th century the situation had stabilised and the pattern of châteaux established at that time was much the same as it is at the present day.

The Bordeaux wine region is dominated by its three rivers. The *Garonne*, the most southerly, passes through the city of Bordeaux and meets the *Dordogne*, with a confluence to the north of the city, to form the *Gironde* estuary which flows north westwards into the Bay of Biscay.

Over a vast period of time the rivers carried downstream pebbles, gravel, minerals, and fertile silt which, when deposited on the river banks, created the perfect geology for viniculture. In the present day the rivers also have a moderating influence on the Bordeaux microclimate which combined with the geology creates the perfect 'terroir' for the world famous wine region.

The Bordeaux wine region, in the international wine trade, has also been traditionally divided by the rivers with the areas on the left bank of the Gironde estuary and the Garonne river and those on the right bank of the Gironde estuary and the right bank of the Dordogne river being referred to as the *'Left Bank'* and the *'Right Bank'* respectively.

THE LEFT BANK

On the left bank of the Gironde estuary is the Médoc peninsular most of which is a vinicultural area. The southern part – the Haut Médoc with its world famous communes of St Estèphe, Pauillac, St Julien, and Margaux, is an area of special importance. In the 1855 classification of Bordeaux the red wines of these communes contributed 60 out of the 61 châteaux classified.

To the south of the city of Bordeaux and the left bank of Garonne river is a large viticultural area – the Graves. The northern part, almost adjacent to the city, is Pessac-Leognan. At the southern end of the Graves are the famous sweet wine communes of Sauternes and Barsac.

THE RIGHT BANK

On the right bank of the Gironde estuary immediately north of the confluence of the Garonne and Dordogne rivers are the communes of Bourg and Blaye.

On the right bank of the Dordogne river and in the immediate vicinity of the town of Libourne are the famous sub-regions of Pomerol and St Émilion together with a number of communes designated as 'satellite appellations'.

Between the Garonne and Dordogne river is the large sub-region of Entre-Deux-Mers also with a number of 'satellite appellations' located within its boundaries – a major producer of white wine.

THE SUB-REGIONS AND PRINCIPAL COMMUNES OF BORDEAUX – AN OVERVIEW

SUB-REGION/ COMMUNE	SIZE - HECTARES UNDER VINE	BOTTLES ANNUALLY (MILLION)	RED / WHITE	GRAPE VARIETIES	
ST ÉMILION	5500	36.0	RED	MERLOT CABERNET FRANC CABERNET SAUVIGNON	
POMEROL	800	5.3	RED	MERLOT CABERNET FRANC CABERNET SAUVIGNON MALBEC	
PAULLIAC**	1200	8.5	RED*	MERLOT CABERNET FRANC CABERNET SAUVIGNON PETIT VERDOT	L O C A T E D I N H A U T M E D O C
ST ESTÈPHE**	1250	9.0	RED	MERLOT CABERNET FRANC CABERNET SAUVIGNON PETIT VERDOT CARMENERE MALBEC	
ST JULIEN**	900	6.5	RED	MERLOT CABERNET SAUVIGNON CABERNET FRANC	
MARGAUX**	1400	9.5	RED	MERLOT CABERNET SAUVIGNON CABERNET FRANC PETIT VERDOT	
GRAVES (GRAVES AOC AND GRAVES SUPERIEURES AOC)	3500	24.4	RED and WHITE (DRY AND SWEET)	**RED** MERLOT CABERNET SAUVIGNON CABERNET FRANC PETIT VERDOT MALBEC **WHITE** SAUVIGNON BLANC SEMILLON MUSCADELLE	G R A V E S S U B R E G I O N
PESSAC-LÉOGNAN	1350	9	RED and WHITE	**RED** MERLOT CABERNET SAUVIGNON **WHITE** SAUVIGNON BLANC SEMILLON	
SAUTERNES	1800	4.5	WHITE (SWEET)	SAUVIGNON BLANC SEMILLON MUSCADELLE	
CERONS	95	0.35			
BARSAC	830	1.8			

* Château Mouton Rothchild is now producing a fine white wine – Sauvignon Blanc/Semillon Blanc blend

** The four great communes of the Haut Médoc

THE LEFT BANK

MÉDOC AND GRAVES

MÉDOC

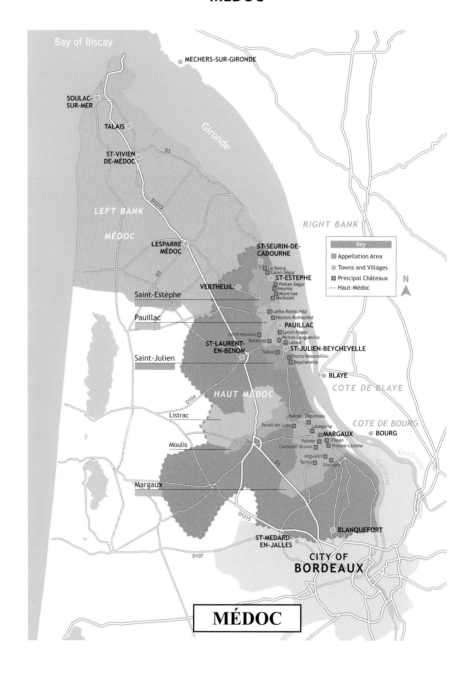

The peninsular that is north of the city of Bordeaux and on the left bank of the Gironde is geographically known as the Médoc Peninsular.

In respect of wine production an area running close to the left bank of the Gironde from Blanquefort, on the outskirts of the city of Bordeaux, to St Vivien-de-Médoc, close to the northern tip of the peninsular, is a vinicultural area which received its appellation from the INAO in 1936 as Médoc AOC.

The southern part of this area from Blanquefort to the northern boundary of the commune of St Estèphe immediately south of Saint-Seurin-de-Cadbourne was also granted an appellation by the INAO in 1936 as Haut Médoc AOC. Furthermore the four great wine producing communes within the Haut Médoc – St Estèphe, Paulliac, St Julien, and Margaux together with two further but lesser important communes, Listrac and Moulis, were also granted their own appellations in 1936.

The Haut Médoc established its extraordinary fine wine status in 1855 when the red wines of Bordeaux were classified and 60 Haut Médoc châteaux were classified out of a total of 61. Although challenged in modern times, particularly by the great right bank wines of Pomerol and St Émilion, the exceptional wines of Haut Médoc have retained their pre-eminent position in the world of fine wines, particularly its four first growths of 1855 (châteaux Lafite, Latour, Margaux and Mouton).

THE FOUR GREAT COMMUNES OF THE HAUT MÉDOC

ST ESTÈPHE

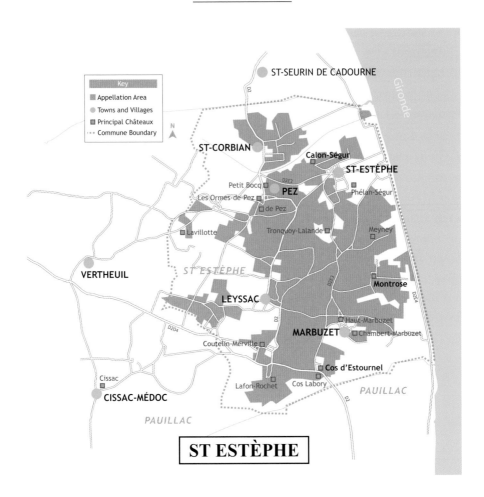

ST ESTÈPHE

The characteristics of St Estèphe wines has always been that they are high in tannin and slow to mature. In the modern world of fine wine low tannin and early maturity are 'fashionable' and many St Estèphe châteaux have increased the Merlot in their blends. Cos d'Estournel now has 38% Merlot and Montrose 25%. The highest are La Haye, Houissant, and Marbuzet with 59%, 60% and 62% respectively. Of course terroir influences the characteristics of the wine and St Estèphe, the most northerly of the four great communes of the Haut Médoc, has less gravel and more clay than its neighbours to the south.

Almost forty years ago Alexis Lichine described the commonly held perception of St Estèphe wine at that time which to a great extent has continued to the present day, but to a lesser extent:

> *"With the possible exceptions of Cos d'Estournel, Montrose, and Calon-Ségur, one doesn't look for any great mystery and subtlety in Saint-Estèphe wines, which usually lack the breeding or finesse that are hallmarks of Pauillac, Saint-Julien, and Margaux, and sometimes incline to be rustic. However, they can be beautifully generous, full wines, appealing to the consumer who is fond of a big mouthful that lingers on the palate long after the wine is swallowed."*

In the classification of Bordeaux châteaux St Estèphe has not fared well compared with its 'illustrious' neighbours.

In the Bordeaux classification of red wines in 1855 St Estèphe had the lowest score of the Médoc communes with only 5 châteaux included compared with 21, 18, and 11 for Margaux, Paulliac and St Julien respectively.

In Robert Parker's modern classification of 181 châteaux of Bordeaux St Estèphe fared little better with only 8 châteaux included compared with 19, 16, and 12 for Margaux, Paulliac and St Julien respectively, except that St Estèphe had two of the first growths – Cos d'Estournel, and Montrose.

As well as producing one of the most distinguished wines of the Haut Médoc Cos d'Estournel has almost certainly the most 'bizarre' château in Bordeaux. It was built by Louis Gaspard d'Estournel at the beginning of the 19th century and reflected his love for Chinese culture and architecture. The 'pagodas' originally had gold temple bells but sadly these were lost during the last war. The ornate door is quite remarkable and came from the palace of the Sultan of Zanzibar.

The Haut Médoc now has many chateaux which are officially classified as Cru Bourgeois which are producing wine of outstanding quality. The first official classification of Cru Bourgeois was in 1932 when 444 châteaux were classified. It was replaced in 1978 by a new official classification of 127 châteaux which remains in effect. St Estephe châteaux are prominent in this classification with eight of the eighteen châteaux classified Crus Grands Bourgeois Exceptionnels.

CHÂTEAU COS D'ESTOURNEL

THE ST ESTÈPHE APPELLATION

APPELLATION AREA – covers part of the commune of St Estèphe only

SIZE OF COMMUNE – 3757 hectares

AOC AREA UNDER VINE – 1250 hectares

AREA OF CLASSIFIED GROWTHS – 230 hectares

OTHER AOC – approximately 5 hectares of vineyards within the
commune of St Estèphe are Pauillac AOC

ST ESTÈPHE – CLASSIFIED CHÂTEAUX

	1st	2nd	3rd	4th	5th
1855	-	COS d'ESTOURNEL MONTROSE	CALON SÉGUR	LAFON ROCHET	COS LABORY
ROBERT PARKER	COS d'ESTOURNEL ———— MONTROSE	CALON SÉGUR	-	LAFON-ROCHET	CHAMBON MARBUZET HAUT-MARBUZET ———— MEYNEY ———— LES ORMES DE PEZ

PAUILLAC

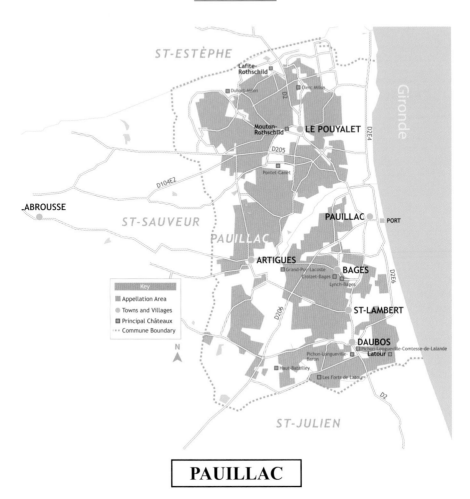

PAUILLAC

Of the four great communes of Haut Médoc, St Estèphe, Pauillac, St Julien, and Margaux, it is Pauillac which is generally considered the pre-eminent commune with its three famous first growth châteaux – Lafite, Latour, and Mouton.

Furthermore the river port town of Pauillac is often seen as the capital of Haut Médoc and the important wine syndicate '*la Commonderie du Bontemps de Médoc des Graves de Sauternes et de Barsac*' has its head-quarters in the town. The ceremonial dress of the Commanderie includes a hat or toque which is called a Bontemps – the dish in which eggs are mixed to make the 'fining' for wine.

The port of Pauillac is also where the French aristocrat, Lafayette, departed from to add his support to George Washington and the American War of Independence. He returned to be an important participant in the French Revolution of 1787 which led to the execution of a number of Bordelais aristocrats.

The 1855 classification, now 160 years old, has remained unchanged with the exception of the elevation of Château Mouton Rothschild from second to first growth in 1973 (Château Cantermerle was left out in error and added in 1856). Robert Parker has provided a modern classification and the comparison of the two classifications in respect of Pauillac is certainly interesting. The three Pauillac first growths remain so and two 1855 second growths Châteaux, Pichon-Longueville-Baron and Pichon Lalande both retain their positions as second growths. However three outstanding Pauillac châteaux, Clerc-Milon, Grand-Puy-Lacoste and Lynch-Bages, were elevated by Robert Parker from 1855 fifth growths to second growths.

The three great first growth châteaux of Pauillac in many ways epitomise the grandeur and fame of the Bordeaux châteaux and the magnificent wines which they produce. Their history is briefly outlined:-

CHÂTEAU LAFITE

The estate goes back to 1234 when it was owned by Gombaud de Lafite. In the 17th century the estate was purchased by the Ségur family who were responsible for planting the vineyard.

The Ségur family ownership ended in 1794 when Nicolas Pierre de Pichard Ségur was executed, following the French Revolution of 1787, and the estate passed into public ownership.

The estate was later acquired by the Dutch Vanlerberghe family followed by an English banker Sir Samuel Scott.

In 1868 the estate was bought by Baron James Mayer Rothschild and ownership has remained with Rothschild family to the present day.

Lafite which is derived from La Hite a Gascon word for small hill as the estate is the highest land in Pauillac. The name through the ages has been spelt with two 't's' or two 'f's'.

There is friendly rivalry between Lafite and Mouton as both are owned by the extended Rothschild family and the two estates touch at one point. The two vineyards are planted with the same four grape varieties but the

CHÂTEAU LAFITE ROTHSCHILD

balance between them is quite different with for instance 25% Merlot at Lafite and only 8% at Mouton. As only 30%–50% of total vineyard production is accepted for the first growth wines there is ample scope, in both vineyards, for deciding the make up of the final blend from the four grape varieties depending on the seasonal conditions in a particular year and how it affects the different grape varieties. For instance the great 1961 Lafite vintage was produced from 100% Cabernet Sauvignon grapes.

VINEYARD PLANTING

	CABERNET SAUVIGNON	MERLOT	CABERNET FRANC	PETIT VERDOT
LAFITE	70%	25%	3%	2%
MOUTON	80%	8%	10%	2%

The château is 18th century and appears on the Lafite wine labels. An interesting feature is the weather vane on the 'pepperpot' tower which is made up of five arrows. These represent the five Rothschild brothers who, in the ghetto of Frankfurt, established the family fortune in the late 18th century.

Besides possessing the oldest bottle of its own wine (1797) of any château in the Médoc, the château also has the famous 'Bismarck' desk, brought from Château Ferrière, the Rothschild residence outside Paris. It was at Ferrière that the Iron Chancellor learned of the Rothschild agreement to advance the funds for payment of the huge indemnities he had demanded as a condition to end the Prussian occupation of France in 1870. Apparently, the chancellor had fully expected his demands to be impossibly high, but the combined financial muscle of the Rothschild banks provided the money. On hearing the news, the enraged Bismarck slammed his fist on the desk with such force that the inkwell jumped from its stand, spilling ink all over the top. The desk, complete with ink stain, is now in one of the private rooms of the château.

CHÂTEAU MOUTON ROTHSCHILD

Although the estate which is now Château Mouton Rothschild was established much earlier it only started to achieve prominence when it became an important vineyard in the early 19th century. Until 1833 the owner was Baron de Brane and Seigneur de Mouton who changed the name from Château Pouyallet to Château Brane-Mouton. After brief ownership by a Paris banker named Thuret the estate was acquired by Nathaniel de Rothschild, from the English branch of the family, in 1853. He changed the name to Château Mouton Rothschild and it has remained in the family to the present day. Nathaniel's uncle, James, from the French branch of the family bought the neighbouring vineyard, Château Lafite, in 1868.

In the official classification of 1855 Mouton was included as a second growth although at that time it was considered equal to the four first growths. The belief was that it was not given the top classification because the owner was of Anglo-Jewish heritage. Nathaniel responded with the following:-

"First I cannot be, second I do not choose to be, Mouton I am".

This was finally changed in 1973 when Jacques Chirac, then the French Minister of Agriculture, through a Presidential Decree, elevated Mouton to a first growth.

Nathaniel's children and grandchildren showed little interest in wine but his great grandson Philippe (1902–1988) became a dedicated wine enthusiast and was committed to developing Mouton into one of the world's finest and most prestigious wines.

Baron Philippe de Rothschild took over the management of Château Mouton, the family vineyard, in 1922 aged 20. He was highly progressive, innovative, and dedicated to achieving the highest standards of quality.

In 1924 Philippe took the decision to château bottle the wine of Mouton. At that time all the wine was shipped in bulk and bottled by the merchants with possible adulteration and dubious provenance. Many of the important châteaux soon followed his lead. Surprisingly this did not include Château Margaux which shipped in bulk up to the 1948 vintage.

He also had an interest in art and its relation to wine and subsequently opened a museum at the château which displayed wine related historical artefacts, many of great value and rarity.

This interest in art also led to Philippe deciding to embellish the wine labels of his top growth with the work of famous contemporary artists.

The first being in 1924 by Jean Carlu and was followed by many of the most famous names in 20th century art – Miro, Chagall, Braque, Picasso, Francis Bacon, Henry Moore, Lucian Freud… In 2004 Charles, Prince of Wales, was the artist as it was the 100 year anniversary of the Entente Cordiale signed by France and Britain in 1904. The artist's 'reward' for their artistic contribution is ten cases of Château Mouton Rothschild, 5 cases of the vintage of the year of the artist's contribution and 5 cases of other vintages.

| Marc Chagall 1970 | The original 1924 label designed by Jean Carlu | Pablo Picasso 1973 |

On two occasions two labels were used for the same vintage. In 1978 the Canadian artist, Jean-Paul Riopelly, submitted two designs. Baron Philippe considered them both outstanding and split the production and used both. In 1993 artist Balthus submitted a pencil drawing of a reclining nymphet which was banned in the United States by the Bureau of Alcohol, Tobacco and Firearms. The bottles exported to America had blank labels. All are now collectors items.

The original art was established as a travelling exhibition and was displayed in over 40 locations worldwide. In 2013 a permanent art gallery was established at the château to display the original art of the labels.

In the 1930's, Philippe, after a run of poor vintages (1930, 1931, 1932) discontinued the second label Carruades de Mouton and introduced a generic Bordeaux wine, Mouton Cadet. This proved to be an outstanding success and is now one of the best selling wines in the world (in 2002 fifteen million bottles were sold). From the original wine the 'brand'

CHÂTEAU MOUTON ROTHSCHILD

was expanded to white and rosé wines and a range of 'Mouton Cadet Reserve' – red Médoc, red Saint Émilion, red Graves, white Graves, white Sauternes.

In 1993 a second label was introduced – Le Petit Mouton de Mouton produced from grapes from the younger vines of the first growth vineyard and with the highest standards of vinification. Its outstanding success can be judged by Robert Parker's ratings of 92 and 91 for the 2009 and 2010 vintages respectively.

A further outstanding success was the introduction of a white wine, Aile d'Argent in the early 1980's when a small part of the main Mouton vineyard was planted with 57% Semillon, 42% Sauvignon Blanc, and 1% Muscadelle. It is now one of the finest white wines of Bordeaux with the 2009 vintage rated 93 by Robert Parker and 90 by the Wine Spectator.

The fascinating story, of how the wine got its name, is provided by Baron Philippe de Rothschild's daughter Baroness Philippine:-

> 'Aile d'Argent....Two unusual words that floated up from the depths of time, a link between the past and present, between my father Baron Philippe de Rothschild and myself. When I was a little girl, my father made up a fairy tale for me, the hero of which was a magic teapot. Its incredible adventures enchanted me and beguiled my childhood. The teapot was called Aile d'Argent, Silver Wing.'
>
> War broke out and my father was arrested. In prison, from memory, he wrote down the story, which he called Aile d'Argent la Magique (Magical Silver Wing), the title under which it was published by Gallimard in 1947.
>
> Aile d'Argent...I am glad that the words which once inspired my dreams are taking on form and colour again."

Baron Philippe de Rothschild also expanded the initial wine business to an international wine 'empire' with the following principal vineyards added to his top growth, Château Mouton Rothschild:

Château d'Armailhac	-	Bordeaux
Château Clerc Milon	-	Bordeaux
Domaine de Lambert	-	Languedoc
Baron'Arques	-	Languedoc
Opus One	-	Napa Valley
Almaviva	-	Chile

The 'brand' Baron Philippe de Rothschild now also covers a wide range of wines from different grape varieties (including Pinot Noir and Chardonnay).

Despite all the outstanding achievements there was an event which took place in Paris in 1976, in which Château Mouton Rothschild participated, which was to prove rather embarrassing for the world famous wines of Burgundy and Bordeaux. An American journalist, George Taber, also increased its impact by eventually calling it 'The Judgement of Paris', a famous event in ancient mythology. This event was set up to taste and compare four white and four red wines of Burgundy and Bordeaux respectively with six white and six red wines of the Napa Valley, America. This process was repeated in 1978 and again in 1986 and 2006 for the red wines only where the Napa Valley wines progressively increased their superiority. Full details are provided in Appendix 7.

The end of an era came in 2014 when Baroness Philippine de Rothschild died. She had taken over the management of what had become an extensive wine 'empire' from her father Baron Philippe de Rothschild in 1988. She maintained the standards and momentum which he had established in over sixty years of control. In 2013 the achievements of Baroness Philippine were recognised with the prestigious Lifetime Achievement Award by the Institute of Masters of Wine.

CHÂTEAU LATOUR

The site, which is now Château Latour, has been occupied since the 14th century when the original tower, Tor à Saint Lambert, was built 300 metres from the banks of the Gironde as a military fortification and was occupied by the English during the One Hundred Years War and lost and destroyed when they were defeated by the French army at the Battle of

Castillon (1453). The present circular tower was built in the 17th century – La Tour of Saint Lambert, from which the name of the estate came.

Notable early owners of the estate were Humphrey, first Duke of Gloucester (1391–1447), who served at Agincourt under his brother King Henry V of England, Gaston de Foix, Duke of Nemours (1489–1512) brilliant French military commander, and Jean de Dunois, illegitimate son of the Duke of Orleans (1402–1468).

The estate has a very long line of family ownership starting in the 17th century when it was acquired in 1695 through marriage by Alexandre Ségur who already had extensive holdings to which he added Château Lafite in 1716 before his death in 1718. His son Nicolas Alexandre Ségur subsequently added Château Latour and Château Calon-Ségur. He was named the 'Prince of Vines' by King Louis XV as his wine was greatly appreciated at the royal court.

Upon the death of Alexandre Ségur in 1755 the ownership became extremely complex. Alexandre had four daughters. The eldest Marie-Therese married a cousin, Alexandre de Ségur-Calon who through his wife controlled both Lafite and Latour. He decided to pass ownership of Latour to the families of two of his sisters-in-law the youngest sister Charlotte – Emily was unmarried. And so the ownership of Latour passed to:-

1. Comte de Ségur-Cabanac (the son of Alexandre's second daughter Angelique-Louise)
2. Comte de la Pallu succeeded by the Courtrivon family
                              and
    Marquis Andre de Beaumont (who was married to the daughter of Alexandre's third daughter Marie-Antoinette-Victoire)

During the early part of the French Revolution (which started in 1787) Comte de Ségur-Cabanac fled the country. Although advised to do so his two co-owners failed to buy his share of Latour (20%). It was auctioned in 1794 and passed through a number of owners.

PIGEONNIER OF CHÂTEAU LATOUR

In 1841 the family put the complete Latour estate up for sale and bought it back including the 20% which was outside the family control. In 1842 the Société Civile de Château Latour was established which owned the estate with shareholding exclusive to the family.

The estate of Château Latour finally passed out of family control in 1963 when 75% was sold to Lord Cowdray's Pearson Group. In 1989 ownership of Château Latour was acquired by Allied Lyons but in 1993 was returned to French ownership when it was bought by Francois Pinault's Artemis Group.

The vineyard planting is 80% Cabernet Sauvignon, 15% Merlot and 5% Cabernet Franc and Petit Verdot. This results in very slow maturing wines but superb when they finally open up.

THE PAUILLAC APPELLATION

APPELLATION AREA – Part of the commune of Pauillac and part of the following communes:-

ST SAVEUR – 34 hectares
ST JULIEN – 16 hectares
ST ESTÈPHE – 5 hectares
CISSAC – 1 hectare

SIZE OF COMMUNE – 2540 hectares
AOC AREA UNDER VINE – 1200 hectares
AREA OF CLASSIFIED GROWTHS – 840 hectares

PAUILLAC – CLASSIFIED CHÂTEAUX

	1st	2nd	3rd	4th	5th
1855	LAFITE LATOUR MOUTON	PICHON LONGUEVILLE BARON PICHON LALANDE	–	DUHART MILON	PONTET-CANET BATAILLEY GRAND-PUY-LACOSTE GRAND-PUY-DUCASSE HAUT-BATAILLEY LYNCH-BAGES LYNCH MOUSSAS MOUTON-BARONNE-PHILIPPE (now d'Armhailac) HAUT-BAGES-LIBERAL PÉDESCLAUX CLERC-MILON- ROTHSCHILD CROIZET-BAGES
ROBERT PARKER	LAFITE LATOUR MOUTON	CLERC MILON GRAND-PUY-LACOSTE LYNCH BAGES PICHON LONGUEVILLE BARON PICHON LONGUEVILLE CONTESSE LALANDE	DUHART-MILON PONTET-CANET	D'ARMAILHAC LES FORT DE LATOUR	BATAILLEY GRAND-PUY DUCASSE HAUT BAGES LIBERAL HAUT BATAILLEY

ST JULIEN

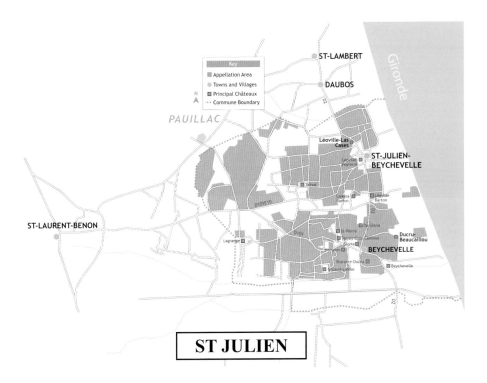

St Julien is the smallest of the four great communes of the Haut Médoc with 26 vineyards covering a planted area of 900 hectares.

The commune has a distinguished reputation for producing wines which are consistently of the highest quality. This goes back to the 1855 classification when eleven of its châteaux were included and in the modern era 12 are included in Robert Parker's classification including two first growths (Ducru Beaucaillou and Léoville-las-Cases).

Throughout Haut Médoc the vineyards are located (or clustered together) on 'hills' of gravel and this is certainly the case in St Julien.

A distinctive characteristic of the commune is that the estates are large (for instance around 40% larger than those of Margaux). Another feature is that of the 900 hectares planted in the commune a small area of around 16 hectares is in Pauillac AOC which complicates the concept of communal boundaries and appellations. St Estèphe the most northerly commune of the Haut Médoc produces full bodied slow maturing wines whereas the most southerly commune, Margaux, produces lighter early maturing

THE WINES OF BURGUNDY AND BORDEAUX

'delicate' wines and St Julien is often seen as the wine halfway between the wine of these communes in respect of wine type.

Château Beychevelle is a beautiful estate overlooking the Gironde which in 1587 was acquired by the Duc d'Epernon – the Grand Admiral of France. All vessels passing the estate were required to strike their sales, 'baisser les voiles', as a mark of respect and this is still depicted on the bottle label.

Two Bordeaux families, the Rothschilds in Pauillac (Mouton) and the Bartons in St Julien, are current owners of châteaux which they owned at the time of the 1855 classification. Thomas Barton arrived in Bordeaux from Ireland in 1725, and became an important wine merchant. His grandson, Hugh, bought Château Langoa in St Julien in 1821 and later acquired part of the Léoville estate which later became Léoville-Barton and which was classified as a second growth in 1855 with Langoa-Barton a third growth. The Barton family still own the estates and recently acquired a further estate, Château Mauvesin, in the commune of Moulis to which they have now added the family name.

One modern success story of St Julien is the founding and development of Château Gloria. It started with the purchase of six hectares in 1942 which has steadily increased through acquisition of land from neighbouring classed vineyards and is now 48 hectares. Although not classed it is considered an outstanding wine and in Robert Parker's modern classification it is classed as a third growth.

Finally St Julien is recognised for a 'famous' monstrosity. At the entry to the town is a huge hideous wine bottle, 5 metres high and resting on a pedestal. Despite endless pleas over the years for its removal it remains steadfastly in place.

ST JULIEN APPELLATION

APPELLATION AREA – covers part of commune of St Julien only
SIZE OF COMMUNE – 1550 hectares
AOC AREA UNDER VINE – 900 hectares
AREA OF CLASSIFIED GROWTHS – 630 hectares
OTHER AOC – Approximately 16 hectares of vineyards within the commune of St Julien are Pauillac AOC

ST JULIEN – THE CLASSIFIED CHÂTEAUX

	1st	2nd	3rd	4th	5th
1855	———	LÉOVILLE-LAS CASES LÉOVILLE-POYFERRE LÉOVILLE-BARTON GRUAUD-LAROSE DUCRU-BEAUCAILLOU	LA GRANGE LANGOA-BARTON	ST PIERRE BRANAIRE TALBOT BEYCHEVELLE	
ROBERT PARKER	DUCRU-* BEAUCAILLOU LÉOVILLE-* LAS CASES	GRUARD-LAROSE LÉOVILLE* BARTON LÉOVILLE-POYFERRE	BRANAIRE-DUCRU LA GRANGE	GLORIA ST PIERRE TALBOT LANGUA-BARTON	BEYCHEVELLE

* THESE CHÂTEAUX TOGETHER WITH PICHON-LONGUEVILLE AND COS D'ESTOURNEL ARE KNOWN IN THE WINE TRADE AS 'SUPER SECONDS' – SEE APPENDIX 2B

MARGAUX

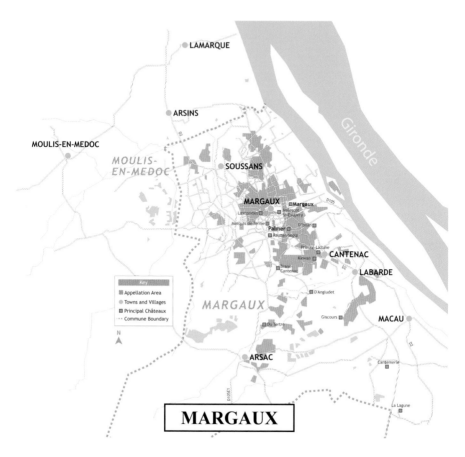

Of the four great communes of the Haut Médoc, Margaux is the largest with approximately 1400 hectares planted and on an annual production of 9.5 million bottles.

The Margaux commune appellation covers not only the commune of Margaux but the vineyards of four other nearby communes which, if they comply with INAO regulations are entitled to describe their wine as 'Margaux AOC'. These other four communes are Cantenac, Arsac, Labarde, and Soussans.

THE COMMUNES OF THE MARGAUX APPELLATION

COMMUNE	SIZE OF COMMUNE	APPROX. AOC AREA UNDER VINE
ARSAC	3220 ha	100 ha
CANTENAC	1430 ha	420 ha
LABARDE	475 ha	130 ha
MARGAUX	843 ha	400 ha
SOUSSANS	1560 ha	165 ha
TOTAL	**7508 ha**	**1215 ha**

The foregoing results in a number of the châteaux of Margaux AOC producing their wine from grapes from two or more vineyards located in the five communes covered by the Margaux appellation. For instance:-

CHÂTEAU	LOCATION OF VINEYARDS	
GISCOURS	LABARDE	ARSAC
LASCOMBES	MARGAUX	SOUSSANS
PALMER	MARGAUX	LABARDE
PRIEURÉ-LICHINE	ALL FIVE COMMUNES	

In the 1855 Classification Margaux had the highest number of classified châteaux (19), including a first growth, château Margaux, out of a total of the 61 châteaux classified.

The foregoing clearly demonstrates the potential which Margaux has for producing great wines. However in the modern era there has been criticism by international wine experts of the consistency and quality of a number of the Margaux châteaux. This is certainly reflected in the comparison of the 1855 and Robert Parker's modern classification, although the two truly great châteaux, Margaux and Palmer, have clearly retained their status as great international wines.

CHÂTEAU MARGAUX

Château Margaux, probably the most magnificent château of Bordeaux, was built by the Marquis de la Colonilla, Bertrand Douat, at the beginning of the 19th century. He commissioned the leading architect of Bordeaux, Louis Combes, to create the château in the First Empire Style. It was completed in 1812.

The estate however has a long history going back to the 12th century when it had a fortified castle known as La Mothe. Limited wine production started in the 15th century. In the early 18th century the wine progressed to a reasonable standard and in 1771 the wine from the estate was the first claret sold by Christies and Thomas Jefferson declared it as one of the *'four top wines of quality'*.

Following the French Revolution of 1787 the owner of the estate, Elie du Barry, was executed and the estate was badly neglected before it was acquired by Bertrand Douat who built the present château and put the estate back into good order.

In modern times the estate was bought by a Bordeaux wine merchant, Fernand Ginester, in 1925 and the estate remained in the family until 1973 when it was acquired by Andre Mertzelopoulos and remains in the family to the present time.

The other great estate of Margaux, Château Palmer, a third growth in the 1855 Classification but now considered a first growth by Robert Parker, also has an interesting history.

The estate was originally part of the ancient estate of Château d'Issan. It was divided by the Foix Candale family in 1748 and part was inherited by the Gascq family and became Château Gascq.

In 1814 Château Gascq was sold to an English general, Charles Palmer, who had served in the Peninsular War and as the ADC to the Prince Regent.

Charles Palmer was very active in developing and extending the estate and achieved a standing, as Château Palmer, equal to that of Château Margaux. Palmer ran into financial difficulties in the early 1840's and was forced to sell the estate to Madame Francoise-Marie Bergerac in 1843. In modern times a syndicate of local families acquired the estate in 1938 and remain owners to the present day.

THE MARGAUX APPELLATION

TOTAL AREA OF ALL FIVE COMMUNES – 7508 ha
TOTAL AOC AREA UNDER VINE – 1215 ha
AREA OF CLASSIFIED GROWTHS – 900 ha

		1st	2nd	3rd	4th	5th
1855		MARGAUX	RAUZAN-SELLA RAUZAN-GASSIES DUFORT-VIVENS LASCOMBES BRANS-CANTENAC	GISCOURS KIRWAN D'ISSAN MALESCOT-ST EXUPÉRY CANTENAC-BROWN PALMER DESMIRAIL FERRIERE MARQUIS-D'ALESME-BECKER BOYD-CANTENAC	POULET PRIEURÉ-LICHINE MARQUIS-DE-TERME	DU-TETRE DAUZAC
ROBERT PARKER		MARGAUX PALMER	MALESCOT-ST EXPUREY MAROJALLIA RAUZEN-SELLA	CANTENAC D'ISSAN KIRWAN	GISCOURS	D'ANGLUDET CANTENAC BROWN DUFORT VIVENS LABÉGORCE-ZÉDÉ LASCOMBES MARQUIS-DE-TERME PAVILLON ROUGE DU Château MARGAUX PRIEURÉ-LICHINE SIRAN DUTERTE

THE FOUR GREAT COMMUNES OF THE HAUT MÉDOC AN OVERVIEW

COMMUNE	APPROX. HECTARES PLANTED	APPROX. NUMBER OF BOTTLES PRODUCED	NUMBER OF CLASSIFIED CHÂTEAUX					
			1st	2nd	3rd	4th	5th	
ST ESTÈPHE	1250	7.0m	–	2	1	1	1	1855
			2	1	–	1	4	ROBERT PARKER
PAUILLAC	1200	6.5m	3	2	–	1	12	1855
			3	5	2	2	4	ROBERT PARKER
ST JULIEN	900	4.7m	–	5	2	4	–	1855
			2	3	2	4	1	ROBERT PARKER
MARGAUX	1400	7.0m	1	5	10	3	2	1855
			2	3	3	1	10	ROBERT PARKER

THE LESSER KNOWN APPELLATIONS OF THE MÉDOC

The Médoc is dominated by the four great communes of the Haut Medoc – St Estèphe, Pauillac, St Julien and Margaux.

However, the sub-region has other important but lesser known vinicultural areas.

The appellation system of the Médoc is rather complex. The complete vinicultural area of the peninsular is covered by the Médoc appellation, but the southern area has its own appellation – Haut Médoc; furthermore six communes, located within the Haut Médoc, have their own individual appellations – the four great communes of St Estèphe, Pauillac, St Julien and Margaux, and the two lesser communes – Listrac and Moulis.

Those vineyards within the six communes use the commune appellation, providing they can meet the applicable INAO regulations. Those vineyards outside the communes but within the Haut Médoc would use the Haut Médoc appellation, again providing they meet the relevant INAO regulations and those vineyards that could not use the Médoc appellation but that situation rarely occurs.

The area of the Médoc vinicultural area to the north of the Haut Médoc is covered the Médoc appellation.

MÉDOC, HAUT MEDOC, AND THE COMMUNES OF MOULIS AND LISTRAC

AN OVERVIEW

SUB-REGION / COMMUNE	SIZE HECTARES UNDER VINE	BOTTLES ANNUALLY (MILLION)	RED / WHITE	GRAPE VARIETIES
MÉDOC	4700	30-6		CABERNET SAUVIGNON
HAUT MÉDOC	4200	24-0	RED	CABERNET FRANC
MOULIS	550	4-2		MERLOT
LISTRAC	700	5-0		PETIT VERDOT

GRAVES

POMEROL

ST-EMILION

CITY OF **BORDEAUX**

MÉRIGNAC

BÈGLES

PESSAC   TALENCE

ENTRE-DEUX-MERS

GRADIGNAN

CESTAS   CAMBES

LÉOGNAN

PESSAC-LÉOGNAN   LA PRADE

LA BRÈDE   VIRELADE

GRAVES   SAUCATS   PODENSAC

ST-MICHEL-   CÉRONS
DE-RIEUFRET

Key   BARSAC

Pessac-Léognan Area   CABAGNAC-ET-   CÉRONS   BARSAC
Graves Area   VILLAGRAINS

Cérons Area   PREIGNAC

Barsac Area   ST-MACAIRE

Sauternes Area   LANGON

Towns and Villages

SAUTERNES

SAUTERNES   ROAILLON

GRAVES

The Graves sub-region of Bordeaux, which lies on the left bank of the Garonne and immediately south of the city of Bordeaux is one of Bordeaux's most ancient and famous vinicultural areas.

Although the Romans and the church were early producers of wine in Bordeaux the events, which led to the development of the export trade in Bordeaux wine, started in the 12th century and over the centuries progressed to what is now a major global trade in wine with Bordeaux a leading participant.

The 'English' period in Bordeaux started with the area coming under the control of the English Crown through the marriage of Eleanor of Acquitaine to Henry Plantagenet in 1152, who in 1154 was crowned Henry II, King of England. It ended in 1453 when the English Army was defeated by the French at the Battle of Castillon. It was during this period that the export trade of Bordeaux wine, initially with England, started. The early wine exported was known as claret to the English (and still is) and was produced in Graves. The most famous being Haut Brion which was mentioned by Samuel Pepys in 1663.

The estate was owned by the Pontac family from the 16th century until 1935. Francois Auguste de Pontac opened a tavern in London called *Pontac's Head* in 1666.

Probably the first 'estate', (planted around 1300) which is now Château Pape Clement, was presented to Bertrand de Goth, upon his appointment as Archbishop of Bordeaux, by his brother Berald. Bertrand went on to be elected Pope Clement V in 1305 and later moved the Papal Court from Rome to Avignon.

Thomas Jefferson (1743–1826) who was the principal author of the American Declaration of Independence and was the third American President (1801–1809) spent from 1785 to 1789 (the period immediately prior to the French Revolution) as the United States Minister to France and became a noted wine connoisseur.

While in Bordeaux Jefferson sent a relative in America six dozen of *'what is the very best Bordeaux wine. It is of the vineyard of Obrion, one of the four established as the very best, and it is of the vintage of 1784, the only very fine one since the year 1779'*.

Jefferson's own purchases also provide an interesting insight into the predominance of the other first growths of the 1855 classification even before the French Revolution which started in 1789. He bought Château Margaux wine 1784 and wrote, *'it is the best vintage that has happened in nine years, and is one of the four vineyards which are admitted to possess exclusively the first reputation. I may safely assure you therefore that, according to the taste of this country and of England, there cannot be a bottle of better Bordeaux produced in France. It cost me at Bordeaux three livres a bottle, ready bottled and packed. This is very dear'*.

In February 1788 he wrote to President Pichard asking to buy 250 bottles of 'La Fite' 1784, asking him to put it in bottle and *'emballer chez vous'*, as this would be a guarantee that the wine was natural and the racking, etc. had been well done. He also requested that while in France and after his return to America he might apply to him for his wines.

The letter was sent on to Pichard at Libourne, as the Parlement was then situated there, but in April the President replied that he had no '*vin de Lafitte*' 1784 left, and though he would like to serve Jefferson in future he only had the 1786 which was not yet drinkable.

With regard to Jefferson's request for 250 bottles of '*La Fite*' and Pichard's reply that he had no '*Vin de Lafitte*' 1784 left. The record auction price for a bottle of wine ($156,000) was for a 1787 Château Lafite which, it was claimed, was owned by Thomas Jefferson.

At the time of the Exposition Universelle de Paris, Emperor Napoleon III called for the classification of Bordeaux's finest wines. In this 1855 classification of red wines all came from the Médoc sub-region with a single exception – a Graves, Haut Brion, which was classified as one of the original four first growths. At the same time the sweet white wines of Bordeaux were also classified and all were wines from the Graves communes of Sauternes Barsac, Bommes, Fargues, and Preignac.

In the modern era the wines of Graves are of course produced under the INAO (Institut National des Appellations d'Origine) regulations.

The Graves sub-region has six AOC'S:-

GRAVES AOC GRAVES SUPERIEURES	–	Which cover most of the Graves sub-region
PESSAC-LÉOGNAN	–	The northern part of the Graves sub-region and on the outskirts of the city of Bordeaux
SAUTERNES BARSAC CERON	–	The southern part of the Graves sub-region

GRAVES AOC

This AOC applies to most of the Graves sub-region for both red and dry white wine produced from 3000 hectares of vineyards.

GRAVES SUPERIEURES AOC

This AOC also applies to most of the Graves sub-region and is an appellation for sweet white wines produced from 500 hectares of vineyard.

The PESSAC-LÉOGNAN, SAUTERNES/BARSAC and CERON appellations are dealt with separately in following sections.

Graves also has a modern classification for dry red and white wines. As all the classified châteaux are located in Pessac-Léognan details are provided in that section.

THE GRAVES SUB-REGION

AN OVERVIEW

GRAVES AOC'S	AREA UNDER VINE (HECTARES)	BOTTLES ANNUALLY (MILLION)	RED/ WHITE/ SWEET	GRAPE VARIETIES
GRAVES	3000	22	RED/ DRY WHITE	**RED** CABERNET SAUVIGNON MERLOT CABERNET FRANC PETIT VERDOT MALBEC **WHITE** SAUVIGNON BLANC SEMILLON
GRAVES SUPERIEURES	500	2.4	SWEET WHITE	SAUVIGNON BLANC SEMILLON MUSCADELLE
PESSAC-LÉOGNAN	1350	9	RED/ DRY WHITE	**RED** CABERNET SAUVIGNON MERLOT PETIT VERDOT MALBEC **WHITE** SAUVIGNON BLANC SEMILLON
CERONS *	95	0.35	SWEET WHITE	SAUVIGNON BLANC SEMILLON MUSCADELLE
BARSAC	830	1.8		
SAUTERNES	1800	4.5		

* Also produces Graves AOC red and dry white wines and Graves Superieures AOC sweet wines.

PESSAC LÉOGNAN

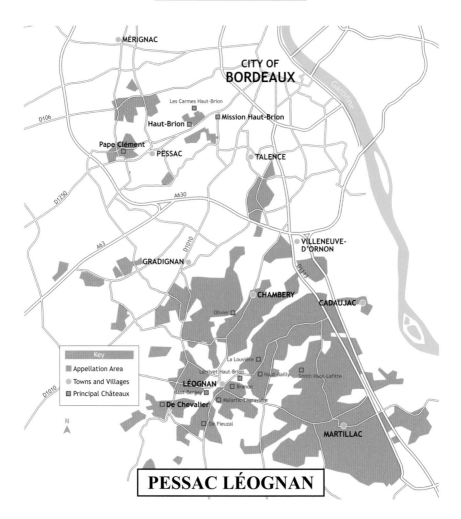

PESSAC LÉOGNAN

This appellation, for red and dry white wines, covers the northern part of the Graves sub-region and is on the outskirts of the city of Bordeaux.

The wines of Pessac-Léognan are noted for their exceptional quality with the most famous being Château Haut Brion which was the only non-Médoc red wine classified as one of the original four first growths in the 1855 classification.

In recent times the red and dry white wines of Graves were officially classified in 1953 and updated in 1959. Seven châteaux were classified for both red and dry white wines, six for red only, and three for dry white only. Details are provided in Appendix 2A.

All the wines in the classification are from the six communes of Pessac-Léognan AOC:-

> Pessac
>
> Léognan
>
> Talence
>
> Martillac
>
> Villenave-d'Ornon
>
> Cadaujac

The combined vineyard area of the six communes is 1350 hectares with an annual production of nine million bottles.

The only change to the classification was the discontinuing of the Château La Tour Haut-Brion label after the 2005 vintage. The production of the vineyard is now integrated with that of the adjoining Château La Mission Haut-Brion.

ROBERT PARKER CLASSIFICATION OF PESSAC LÉOGNAN

GROWTH	CHÂTEAUX
1st	HAUT BRION MISSION HAUT BRION
2nd	PAPE CLEMENT SMITH-HAUT-LAFITE
3rd	LES CARMES HAUT BRION DOMAINE DE CHEVALIER HAUT-BATAILLY HAUT- BERGEY LARRIVE HAUT BRION
4th	DE FIEZAL LA LOUVIERE
5th	BAHANS HAUT BRION

CHÂTEAU HAUT BRION

SAUTERNES AND BARSAC

SAUTERNES AND BARSAC

Both Barsac and Sauternes have AOC'S except that Barsac can label its wine Sauternes AOC but not vice versa. There are five communes covered by the Sauternes AOC:-

Sauternes
Barsac (which also has its own AOC)
Bommes
Fargues
Preignac

The communes are located at the southern end of the Graves sub-region and produce sweet white wines of exceptional quality which are internationally famous.

Like many of the vinicultural areas of Bordeaux the wines of the Graves sub-region go back in history as far as Roman times.

The wines were certainly well established by the late 18th century as Thomas Jefferson, a dedicated wine connoisseur, certainly sampled the sweet wines of Sauternes and Barsac during his time in France (1785–1789) and on his return to America, where in 1801 he was elected as the third President, and imported thirty cases of Château d'Yquem for his private cellar.

In 1855 the red wines of Bordeaux (from the Médoc with one exception) were classified together with the sweet white wine of Graves which all came from the communes now covered by Sauternes AOC as follows:-

1855 CLASSIFICATION – SWEET WHITE WINES

COMMUNE	PREMIER CRU SUPERIEUR	PREMIER CRU FIRST GROWTHS	DEUXIEME CRU SECOND GROWTHS
SAUTERNES	1 (CHÂTEAU d'YQUEM)	1	4
BARSAC		2	8
BOMMES		6	-
FARGUES		1	1
PREIGNAC		1	1
TOTAL	1	11	14

In the 1855 classification of 61 red wines and 26 sweet white wines of Bordeaux only one was considered so exceptional that it was rated on its own above all others as a first great growth – Château d'Yquem.

CHÂTEAU D'YQUEM

Ramon Felipe Eyquem bought the estate in 1477. It subsequently passed through a number of owners until it was acquired by the de Lur-Saluces family in 1785 and remained in the family until 1996.

Thomas Jefferson the United States Minister to France (1785–89) was a particular Château d'Yquem enthusiast and shipped the wine home for his own cellar and that of President Geoge Washington.

In modern times the estate was managed by Comte Alexandre de Lur-Saluces from 1968 with dedication and competence and with annual production rising in a good vintage to 100,000 bottles.

In 1996 the Comte's brother Alexandre sold his share of the estate to the French luxury goods company LVMH (Louis Vuitton, Moet, Hennessey) who acquired a controlling interest in the estate.

The vineyard is 126 hectares although only 100 hectares are producing at any one time. The average annual production is 65,000 bottles. In very poor vintages the wine is sold and not bottled as Château d'Yquem. (this happened nine times in the 20th century.)

The northern part of Graves, Pessac Léognan, is known for its covering of deep gravel. This is considered highly beneficial as it provides drainage and also forces the roots of the vine to penetrate to great depths to reach the range of minerals which are essential if the grapes are to produce wine of character and finesse. Château d'Yquem at the southern end of Graves is totally different. It is on a hillside on a dome of clay and marl covered with a thin layer of sand and gravel. In its natural form the land would be totally unsuitable for viniculture. And so the property was extensively drained using earthenware pipes.

The buried drainage pipes are estimated to be 100 kilometres long that is approximately one kilometre per hectare.

CERONS

Finally we have in terms of size but not quality the 'minnow' of the sweet wine communes of the southern part of the Graves sub-region, which lies to the north of Barsac.

The commune has its own AOC which allows higher yields of 40 hl/ha compared with 25hl/ha for the Sauternes and Barsac AOC'S.

The AOC area under vine and annual production are minimal compared with its distinguished sweet wine neighbours and is certainly less well known.

As well as producing excellent sweet white wine under its AOC, Cerons also produces red and dry white Graves AOC wine and sweet white Graves Superieures AOC wine from vineyards of approximately 100 hectares.

CHÂTEAU D'YQUEM

THE RIGHT BANK

ST ÉMILION, POMEROL
AND THE SATELLITE APPELLATIONS

ST ÉMILION

ST ÉMILION

AREA OF ST ÉMILION SUB-REGION	–	8000 hectares
AOC AREA UNDER VINE	–	5500 hectares
AREA OF CLASSIFIED GROWTHS	–	3850 hectares

St Émilion has an official modern classification of its châteaux which was first introduced in 1955 and updated in 1969, 1985, 1996 and 2006 which was controversially suspended after four demoted châteaux mounted a legal challenge. The last update was in 2012 which remains in effect. It comprises of 4 Premiere Grand Cru Classé (A) and 14 (B) and 64 Grand Cru Classé a total of 82 châteaux. Details are given in Appendix 2.

ST ÉMILION

CHÂTEAU CHEVAL BLANC

In addition to the official classification over 200 other St Émilion châteaux can, under the basic appellation rules, use 'Grand Cru' on their labels but are deemed to be of a lesser quality than the Grand Cru <u>Classé</u> châteaux of the official classification.

GRAND CRU   **GRAND CRU CLASSÉ**

St Émilion is considered to be the oldest wine sub-region of Bordeaux and it is by far the largest.

Viniculture in St Émilion goes back to Roman times and the 4th century Latin poet Ausonius, fourth consul of Rome, had a villa here and it is claimed that Château Ausone was built on its foundations. The Knights of St John of Jerusalem had a commanderie in the area probably at the time following the crusades.

To the immediate east of St Émilion near the town of Castillon a battle took place which changed the course of history for Bordeaux. The region had been under the control of the English Crown following the marriage in 1192 of Eleanor of Aquitaine and Henry Plantagenet who two years later became King Henry II of England. The English control lasted until 1453 when the English army under the command of John Talbot, Earl of Shrewsbury, was defeated by the French army at Castillon and control of Bordeaux reverted to the French Crown after 300 years.

The remarkable success of the Confrérie du Tastevin, in Burgundy, following its founding in 1934 led to the revival of a medieval assembly in St Émilion – The Jurade. It was first established by John Lackland when he was crowned King John of England in 1199 and dissolved at the time of the French Revolution.

The sub-region is also scenically attractive with the historical and beautiful walled town of St Émilion being a major tourist attraction.

In December 1999 St Émilion was declared a World Heritage Site by UNESCO recognising the extraordinary nature of this lively landscape. '*St Émilion vineyards have been shaped by successive generations of wine-makers. They have managed to develop and modernise while preserving the remarkable testimonies of its history. With its Medieval and Roman churches, St Émilion has a spectacular architectural heritage. This legacy equally comprises of picturesque cellars, mills and dovecotes. Besides the centuries of interaction between the people and the landscape,*' UNESCO has also rewarded the particular attention of the professionals in St Émilion. Since 1993, any changes to the structure of a soil or other plantations on the land would have to be approved by a commission. It is composed of members of the INAO, winemakers, representatives of the concerned town hall, and the Chamber of Agriculture. This is what **guarantees the sustainability of the exceptional 'cultural landscape'** of St Émilion!

St Émilion wines are dominated by two grape varieties – Merlot and Cabernet Franc with only a very limited planting of Cabernet Sauvignon.

This results in lighter wines with lower tannin and earlier maturity compared with those of Médoc and Graves.

An interesting and controversial development in St Émilion has been the emergence in the 1980's of the 'vin de garage' or 'garage wines' and in Bordeaux the winemakers are known as 'garagistes'. Le Pin in neigh-bouring Pomerol is usually considered the first garage wine which started as a one hectare vineyard in 1979.

The concept then spread to St Émilion and in 1989 Jean-Luc Thunevin and his wife Murielle Andraud bought a 0.6 hectare plot in St Émilion near Château Pavie-Macquin, and using a former garage as a winery, pro-duced their first vintage of 1500 bottles in 1991. More land was acquired and Château Valandraud is now 4.5 hectares and for the 1995 vintage Robert Parker rated it higher than Pètrus and in his modern classifica-tion of the Château of Bordeaux includes it as a second growth. In the 2012 official classification of the Châteaux of Bordeaux Valandraud is a Premier Grand Cru (B) and can now be considered the 'flagship' of the garage wine movement. Although Robert Parker has enthusiastically sup-ported the garage wine development, a number of which he rates highly, his views are not shared by a number of international wine experts who,

THE WINES OF BURGUNDY AND BORDEAUX

as traditionalists, are derogatory and hostile to the garage wine phenomenon. Nevertheless the 'genie is out of the bottle' and is spreading to the other sub-regions of Bordeaux.

ST ÉMILION IN ROBERT PARKER'S MODERN CLASSIFICATION OF THE CHÂTEAUX OF BORDEAUX

Growths	Overall	St Émilion
1st	20	4
2nd	41	18
3rd	25	8
4th	22	7
5th	73	20
TOTAL	**181**	**57**

JURADE ST ÉMILION

POMEROL

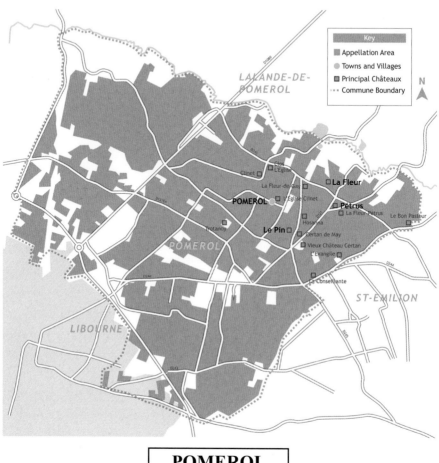

POMEROL

AREA OF POMEROL SUB-REGION – 1200 hectares
AOC AREA UNDER VINE   – 800 hectares

The wines of Pomerol have similar characteristics to those of St Émilion, its immediate neighbour, as Merlot and Cabernet Franc are also Pomerol's principal grape varieties which result in lighter wines with lower tannin compared with those of Médoc and Graves.

CHÂTEAU PÉTRUS

For Pomerol there has been a dramatic improvement in quality compared to many years ago and beyond and its great wines, led by Pètrus, are prestigious, expensive, and internationally renowned.

It is interesting to look back almost a generation and to a distinguished writer on wine, and particularly those of Bordeaux, who wrote almost fifty years ago:-

> *"The finer wines of Pomerol are the most immediately attractive red wines of Bordeaux; even more than those of the neighbouring St Émilion. They are soft, lacking much of the tannin that marks the Médocs and the Graves when immature and they may be drunk fairly young, a consideration these days when the accent is on quick turnover. Consequently it is no surprise that the Pomerols have won many adherents in the last twenty years; and with demand prices have risen sharply too."*
>
> Edmund Penning-Rowsell

Pomerol was an area where the Romans also planted their vines and later the Knights of St John of Jerusalem had a strong presence following the crusades with hostels and hospitals as Pomerol was on the pilgrimage route to Santiago Compostila in Spain. The Knights also replanted vines following the devastation of the 100 year war which ended in nearby Castillon in 1453.

The Dutch who were important wine traders in Bordeaux in the 16th and 17th centuries had an important influence in Pomerol where white wines were produced to supply the Dutch, Baltic, and Hanseatic markets.

This continued until the late 19th century when the prices for red wine were much higher and the steady transition to red wine took place. In 1936 the INAO granted Pomerol its AOC which specifically precluded the production of white wine.

As Pomerol steadily gained international status to reach what is now considered a pre-eminent status in the world of fine wine it is important to recognise the contribution made by certain Bordelais families.

Before the second world war the Moueix family had a negociant business in Libourne. After the war they progressed from first securing the exclusive rights for Château Pètrus to majority shareholders in 1964 with full control over the winemaking. The family also acquired the Châteaux of Trotanoy, La Fleur-Pètrus, Lagrange, La Grave, Latour à Pomerol and Hosanna. Control over winemaking and the introduction of creative techniques resulted in a rapidly developing recognition of Pomerol wines in the world markct.

Another major contributor to the evolution and international recognition of Pomerol wines was a Pomerol born and internationally distinguished oenologist – Michel Rolland. He grew up on the family estate in Pomerol, Le Bon Pasteur, and graduated from the Bordeaux Oenology Institute together with his future wife Dany.

In addition to the profound and beneficial influence on Pomerol winemaking Michel Rolland has clients throughout the fine wine producing countries of the world.

POMEROL IN ROBERT PARKER'S MODERN CLASSIFICATION OF THE CHÂTEAUX OF BORDEAUX

Growths	Overall	Pomerol
1st	20	5
2nd	41	9
3rd	25	4
4th	22	2
5th	73	10
TOTAL	**181**	**30**

The above demonstrates Pomerol's remarkable status in the 'Bordeaux quality league' according to Robert Parker. His modern classification of 181 Bordeaux châteaux has the highest number in St Émilion (57) and second highest number in Pomerol (30). However St Émilion at 5500 hectares is almost seven times larger than Pomerol which has a mere 800 hectares.

CHÂTEAU LE PIN

THE SATELLITE APPELATIONS OF BORDEAUX

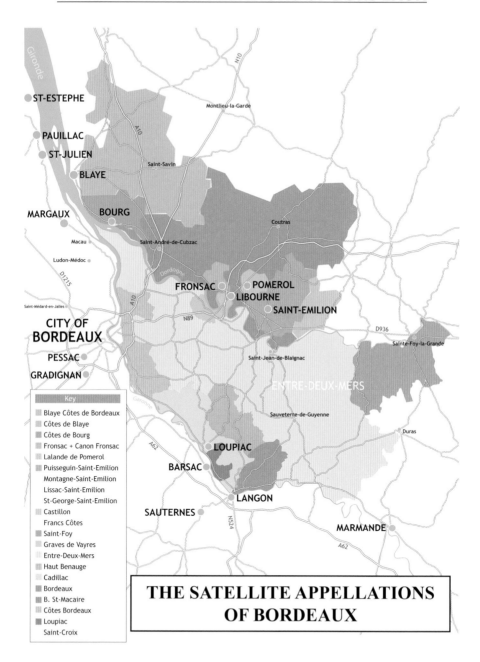

Key

- Blaye Côtes de Bordeaux
- Côtes de Blaye
- Côtes de Bourg
- Fronsac + Canon Fronsac
- Lalande de Pomerol
- Puisseguin-Saint-Emilion
- Montagne-Saint-Emilion
- Lissac-Saint-Emilion
- St-George-Saint-Emilion
- Castillon
- Francs Côtes
- Saint-Foy
- Graves de Vayres
- Entre-Deux-Mers
- Haut Benauge
- Cadillac
- Bordeaux
- B. St-Macaire
- Côtes Bordeaux
- Loupiac
- Saint-Croix

THE SATELLITE APPELLATIONS OF BORDEAUX

What has preceded this part has been all about the prestigious and expensive wines of Bordeaux which have achieved international acclaim.

That is, by no means, the full story of Bordeaux wine.

On the Right Bank are the 'satellite appellations of Bordeaux' producing huge quantities of excellent wine at affordable prices. Robert Parker undertakes wine tasting in these areas and considers that the wines represent 'outstanding bargains'.

Details of the satellite appellations are given in the 'overview' and are located as follows:-

> On the right bank of the Dordogne estuary and immediately north of the confluence of the Garonne and Dordogne rivers are two satellite appellations – the communes of **BOURG** and **BLAYE.**
>
> On the right bank of the Dordogne river are nine satellite appellations located around the sub-regions of Pomerol and St Émilion. (*CANON FRONSAC, FRONSAC, LALANDE DE POMEROL, PUISSEGUIN ST ÉMILION, MONTAGUE ST ÉMILION, LUSSAC ST ÉMILION, ST GEORGE ST ÉMILION, CASTILLON CÔTE DE BORDEAUX, FRANCS CÔTE DE BORDEAUX*).
>
> Between the Garonne and Dordogne rivers is the large sub-region of Entre-Deux-Mers which has eight satellite appellations within its boundaries. (*GRAVES DE VAYRES, ENTRE DEUX MERS, ENTRE-DE-MERS HAUT BENUGE, BORDEAUX HAUT BENAUGE, CADILLAC CÔTES DE BORDEAUX, PREMIERES CÔTE DE BORDEAUX, CÔTE DE BORDEAUX SAINT-MACAIRE, LOUPIAC, ST CROIX DU MONT*.)
>
> To the east of Entre-Deux-Mers and adjoining Bergerac is the satellite appellation of *SAINT-FOY-BORDEAUX.*

Many of these areas are attracting highly competent winemakers which is significantly lifting the quality of the wine to new levels of excellence.

The vinicultural area of the satellite appellations ia approximately the same as that of the famous sub-regions (Pomerol, St Émilion, and Graves) and the four great communes of the Haut Médoc (St Estèphe, Pauillac, St Julien, and Margaux) – 22,000 hectares. This demonstrates the importance of the satellite appellations as part of the Bordeaux wine region.

THE SATELLITE APPELLATIONS OF BORDEAUX
AN OVERVIEW

APPELLATION	SIZE HECTARES UNDER VINE	BOTTLES ANNUALLY (MILLION)	RED/ WHITE	
BLAYE CÔTE DE BORDEAUX CÔTE DE BLAYE	7500	27.0	RED/ WHITE	RIGHT BANK OF THE GIRONDE ESTUARY
CÔTES DE BOURG	3900	31.2	RED/ WHITE	
FRONSAC	850	6.6	RED	LOCATED AROUND THE SUB-REGIONS OF POMEROL AND ST ÉMILION
CANON FRONSAC	30	0.25	RED	
LALANDE DE POMEROL	560	6.0	RED	
PUISSEGUIN ST ÉMILION	1000	6.9	RED	
MONTAGNE ST ÉMILION	1600	11.4	RED	
LUSSAC ST ÉMILION	1400	9.3	RED	
ST GEORGE ST ÉMILION	180	1.1	RED	
CASTILLON CÔTES DE BORDEAUX	3000	19.0	RED	
FRANCS CÔTES DE BORDEAUX	900	2.9	RED/ WHITE	
SAINT-FOY BORDEAUX	120	0.75	RED/ SWEET WHITE	BETWEEN EN-TRE-DEUX-MERS AND BERGERAC
GRAVE DE VAYRES	645	6.5	RED/ WHITE	ALL LOCATED IN THE SUB-REGION OF ENTRE-DEUX-MERS
ENTRE-DEUX-MERS ENTRE-DEUX-MERS HAUT BENAUGE	2400	15	WHITE	
BORDEAUX HAUT BENAUGE	100	0.5	WHITE	
CADILLAC CÔTES DE BORDEAUX	1100	6.5	RED	
PREMIERES CÔTE DE BORDEAUX	3300	24	RED/ WHITE	
CÔTE DE BORDEAUX SAINT-MACAIRE	40	0.2	SWEET WHITE	
LOUPIAC	350	1.4	SWEET WHITE	
ST CROIX DU MONT	430	2.1	SWEET WHITE	

GRAPE VARIETIES

RED	WHITE
CABERNET SAUVIGNON	SAUVIGNON BLANC
MERLOT	SEMILLON
CABERNET FRANC	MUSCADELLE
MALBEC	COLOMBARD
PETIT VERDOT	UGNI BLANC
CARMENERE	

THE SELECTION OF BORDEAUX WINES

Up to the late 1970's the fine wines of Bordeaux were almost entirely confined to exclusive clubs, famous colleges, and distinguished families. Their wine selection was based on expertise, built up over many years, often recorded and passed down from generation to generation, together with their long term knowledge of their chosen great châteaux, which they knew intimately, and in which they had great trust.

By around 1970 the world of fine wine started to change dramatically as global prosperity and the international availability of excellent afford-able wine produced scientifically in high tech wineries in America and the so called 'New World' countries of Chile, South Africa, Australia and New Zealand started to have a major impact.

Nevertheless the greatest and most prestigious wines of the world remained French and in particular those produced in the wine region of Bordeaux and the new wave of affluent 'connoisseurs' were determined to join the old 'claret' elite but without their experience in the selection of great wine built up over decades.

Bordeaux does provide a basic official guide to wine quality ranking through a classification system first introduced in 1855 when 59 châteaux of Médoc were classified and one (Haut Brion) from Graves. They were divided into five quality groups called 'growths'. The only changes to this classification since its inception was the addition of Château Cantermerle (omitted in error) a year after its publication and the elevation of Château Mouton Rothschild from a second to a first growth by Presidential Decree in 1973. The châteaux classified in 1855 have, remarkably, retained the right to describe their wines as 'Premier Grand Cru Classé' (first growths) and 'Grand Cru Classé' (the other four growths) to the present day. This right is still exercised by a number of Médoc châteaux as the sub-region does not have a modern official classification. For instance Château Latour has on its label 'Premier Grand Cru Classé' and Lynch Bages 'Grand Cru Classé' both based on the 1855 Classification and other châteaux of Médoc do likewise. There are however a number of châteaux which acknowledge the origin of their 'accolade' by displaying 'Grand Cru Classé en 1855' for example Château Branaire, Château Giscours and others but the majority do not assert their right to display the top quality designations based on 1855.

THE WINES OF BURGUNDY AND BORDEAUX

This 'ancient' classification is more than 150 years old, is limited in scope as it excluded the châteaux of Pomerol, St Émilion, and Graves (except Haut Brion) and has never been updated (with only a single exception). In view of this the retention and display of a top quality designation based on what existed in 1855 would seem to be rather meaningless in the 21st Century. Nevetheless the 1855 classification has somehow managed to hold on to its prestigious status even in the modern world of fine wine.

The sweet white wines of Sauternes/Barsac were also classified in 1855. Château d'Yquem was the only 'First Great Growth' followed by 11 'First Growths' and 14 'Second Growths'. As in Médoc the sub-region does not have a modern official classification. Here also the right to display the top quality appellations on their wine labels, based on the 1855 Classification, has been retained. Château d'Yquem however does not deign to describe its great wines, based on its supreme 1855 rating. Its labels simply display '*Château d'Yquem, Lur Saluces*' and the year in which it was produced and most other châteaux do likewise.

The official classification of Bordeaux wines moved into the present era as the sub-regions of St Émilion and Graves and also the Cru Bourgeois of the Médoc have modern classifications.

THE ST ÉMILION CLASSIFICATION

The St Émilion classification for red wines was first introduced in 1955 and amended by decree in 1958 it listed 12 Premier Grand Cru Classé and 63 Premier Cru Classé. The classification was updated 1969, 1985, 1996 and 2006 (which was disputed by a number of châteaux). The current classification is that of 2012 which has 18 Premier Grand Cru Classé: 4 – (A) and 14 – (B) and 64 Grand Cru Classé. It s important to note that there are more than 200 châteaux, excluded from the classification which, through the St Émilion appellation, are allowed to label their wine 'Grand Cru' which is a quality ranking significantly lower than Grand Cru Classé.

THE GRAVES CLASSIFICATION

The Graves classification for both red and white wine was established in 1959 and includes 14 red wine and 8 white wine châteaux. As 6 châteaux are classified for both red and white wine the total number of châteaux included in the Graves classification is 15.

136

THE CRU BOURGEOIS CLASSIFICATION

The first classification was in 1932 when 444 châteaux were included. This was revised in 1978 with 127 châteaux classified as follows:-

Cru Grand Bourgeois Exceptionnel	–	18
Cru Grand Bourgeois	–	41
Cru Bourgeois	–	68
TOTAL		**127**

Full details of all the Bordeaux classifications are included in Appendix 2A.

The modern classification system of Bordeaux châteaux is clearly of some limited help in wine selection insofar as they are deemed to be superior to those châteaux excluded. But their value is further limited for wine selection due to the fact that the modern classifications are made up of a number of quality groups (or growths) and the châteaux in each group are listed in alphabetical order not quality. That means for instance that the 64 Grand Cru Classé châteaux in the St Émilion classifcation are effectively deemed to be equal in quality.

And so it can be concluded that the Bordeaux classifcation system provides only a limited quality hierarchy (the great wines of Haut Médoc, Pomerol, and Sauternes/Barsac do not have modern classifications) but is not particularly useful for wine selection. By the 1970's the world of fine wine started to change dramatically. As stated at the outset:-

> 'The new wave of affluent 'connoisseurs' were determined to join the old "claret" elite but without their experience in the selection of great wine built up over decades.'

The void on wine selection was first filled in the late 1970's by an American, Robert Parker, and he was soon joined by a number of international wine experts who provided detailed information on wine selection.

To provide an unbiased quality rating of the individual châteaux of Bordeaux, (and as quality varies from year to year the quality rating has to be repeated annually) was an immense undertaking and it was initiated by Robert Parker, who has now become a legendary figure throughout the world of fine wine. He gave up his career as a lawyer in 1978 and moved into the tasting and reporting of fine wine with the publication of the two-monthly 'Wine Advocate' which followed an earlier newsletter. Robert Parker revolutionised the quality evaluation and rating of fine wines through the introduction of a numerical quality rating system combined with detailed tasting notes, structured as follows:-

THE NUMERICAL QUALITY RATING SYSTEM

96–100	Extraordinary
90–95	Outstanding
80–89	Above average to very good
70–79	Average
50–69	Below average to poor

This proved to be highly controversial initially but it was eventually universally accepted and a number of other eminent wine critics and writers adopted similar numerical rating systems (Jancis Robinson and Clive Coates both rate out of 20).

In addition to the foregoing, in which the principal châteaux are numerically rated annually for quality, a regional overview, covering the main sub-regions and their principal châteaux is important in showing the quality pattern of the present time throughout the entire Bordeaux wine region.

The 1855 Classification was intended to do this but at that time the perception was that top wine quality was confined to Médoc, a single Graves (Haut Brion) and Sauternes/Barsac.

Since 1855 the quality pattern throughout the Bordeaux wine region has of course changed fundamentally. To demonstrate this Robert Parker has published a classification similar in basic structure to that of 1855 but reflecting modern reality. The following shows the perceived increase in the number of châteaux which now merit classification compared with 1855.

190/600   Dry & Unexciting

CHÂTEAUX LISTED

	1855	ROBERT PARKER
FIRST GROWTHS	5	21
SECOND GROWTHS	14	41
THIRD GROWTHS	14	25
FOURTH GROWTHS	10	22
FIFTH GROWTHS	18	73
	61	**181**

The following highlights the fact that the châteaux of the sub-regions, omitted from the 1855 Classification, and in particular the châteaux of St Émilion and Pomerol, would now dominate a modern classification for the entire Bordeaux wine region:-

SUB-REGION OR COMMUNE	NUMBER OF CHÂTEAUX IN CLASSIFICATIONS	
	1855 CLASSIFICATION	ROBERT PARKER CLASSIFICATION
Margaux	21	19
Pauillac	18	16
St Estèphe	5	8
St Julien	11	12
Graves	1	10
Haut Médoc	5	2
St Émilion	–	57
Pomerol	–	30
Others	–	27
Totals	**61**	**181**

Details of the above classifications are included in Appendix 2.

To complete the wine quality overview of Bordeaux Robert Parker also ranks the principal château of each sub-region and those of the major communes in five quality groups:-

OUTSTANDING

EXCELLENT

VERY GOOD

GOOD

OTHER NOTABLE PROPERTIES

This is shown by way of example for the great Médoc commune of Pauillac:-

OUTSTANDING
Lafite-Rothschild, Latour, Lynch Bages, Latour, Mouton-Rothschild, Pichon-Longueville, Pichon-Longueville-Comtesse de Lalande

EXCELLENT
Clerc-Milon, Grand-Puy-Lacoste, Pontet-Canet (since 1994)

VERY GOOD
Duhart-Milon, Les Forts de Latour, Haut-Batailley

GOOD
d'Armaihac, (known as Mouton-Baronne-Philippe between 1956 and 1989) Batailley, Carruades de Lafite, Grand-Puy-Ducasse

The rankings, on the foregoing basis, of the châteaux of the sub-regions of St Émilion, Pomerol, Graves, Sauternes/Barsac, and the Médoc communes of St Estèphe, Pauillac, St Julien, and Margeaux are included in Appendix 2 except that the last quality category 'Other Notable Properties' has been omitted throughout.

An attempt has been made in the foregoing to recognise the important role played by the governmental (INAO) regulations in maintaining basic control over wine quality but that these regulations are not particularly helpful in the wine selection process which is the very cornerstone of the trade in fine wine.

The foregoing resulted in the emergence and progressive impact of the international wine experts whose published quality ranking of fine wine, now usually based on a numerical rating system, virtually dominate the selection of fine wine, and of course its price, worldwide.

Although there is a certain amount of resentment of the influence which the wine experts have in the quality rating of fine wine, and the consequences of their judgement on the price we pay for it, nevertheless the reality is that there is no credible alternative available for the selection of fine wine.

APPENDIX 1

BURGUNDY

A – THE GRAND CRU AND PREMIER CRU VINEYARDS OF BURGUNDY

The Burgundy sub-regions of Beaujolais and Mâconnais have no Grand Cru or Premier Cru vineyards. These top appellations are confined to vineyards which produce their wine from the Pinot Noir and Chardonnay grapes, Beaujolais wine is produced almost entirely from the Gamay grape and Mâconnais, although producing huge amounts of wine from the Chardonnay grape, has no vineyards which qualify for these top appellations.

CÔTE DE CHÂLONNAISE

The vineyards of Bouzeron produce practically all their wine from the Aligoté grape and therefore have no Grand Cru or Premier Cru vineyards

RULLY

Premier Cru vineyards:-

◆ Le Meix Caillet	◆ Rabource	◆ Le Meix Cadot
◆ Marissou	◆ Chapitre	◆ Les Montpalais
◆ La Fosse	◆ Les Preaux	◆ Gresigny
◆ Les Pierres	◆ Molesme	◆ Les Margotes
◆ Pillot	◆ Agneux	◆ La Renarde
◆ Raclot	◆ La Bressande	◆ Vauvry
◆ Les Cloux	◆ Les Champs Cloux	◆ La Pucelle

The following Premier Cru vineyards are located in the commune of Chagny:
• Clos due Chaigne   • Clos Saint-Jacques

MERCUREY

Premier Cru vineyards:-

- Clos Marcilly
- Les Puillets
- Les Saumonts
- Les Croichots
- La Cailloute
- Les Combins
- Les Champs Martin
- Clos des Barraults

- Clos des Myglands

- Le Clos l'Eveque
- Clos Voyens
- Grand Clos Fortoul
- Clos des Grands Voyens
- Les Naugues
- Les Crets
- Clos Tonnerre
- Les Vasees

- Les Byots

- Sazenay
- La Bondue
- La Levriere
- La Mission
- Le Clos du Roy
- Grifferes
- Les Velley
- Clos Château de Montaigu

- Les vignes de Maillonges

The following Premier Cru vineyards are located in the commune of Saint-Martin-sous-Montaigu:

- Les Montaigus
- Clos des Montaigus

- Les Fourneaux
- La Chassiere

- Les Ruelles
- Clos de Paradis

GIVRY

Premier Cru vineyards:

- Clos due Cras Long
- Clos du Vernoy
- Les Grandes Vignes
- Clos Marceaux
- Les Grands Pretans
- Clos de la Baraude
- Petit Marole
- Cellier aux Moines
- Clos Charle

- En Cras Long
- La Baraude
- En Choue
- La Grande Berge
- La Plante
- Le Paradis
- Le Petit Pretan
- Le Vigron
- Les Bois Gautiers

- Clos Jus
- Servoisine
- Les Bois Chevaux
- Clos Saint-Pierre
- Clos Saint-Paul
- Clos Salomon
- Clos Marole
- A Vigne Rouge
- Crauzot

MONTAGNY
Premier Cru vineyards:-

- Vignes Saint-Pierre
- Les Combes
- Saint-Ytages
- Les Charmelottes
- Champ Toizeau
- Vignes dur le Cloux
- Les Garcheres
- Vignes Couland
- Les Bouchots
- Les Burnins
- Les Perrieres

- Les Treufferes
- Montcuchot
- Vigne due Soleil
- Les Maroques
- Les Beaux Champs
- Les Macles
- Creux de Beaux Champ
- L'Epaule
- Les Platieres
- Les Jardins

- Saint-Morille
- Les Vignes Derriere
- Les Bordes
- Les Las
- Les Gouresses
- Les Paquiers
- Montorge
- Les Resses
- Le Cloux
- Sous les Feilles

The following Premier Cru vineyards are located in the commune of Buxy:

- La Grande Piece
- Le Clos Chaudron
- Les Vignes des Pres
- Le Vieux Château
- La Condemine du Vieux Château

- Le Clouzot
- Les Pidances
- Les Coudrettes
- Les Vignes Longues

- Cornevent
- Mont Laurent
- Les Bonneveaux
- Les Bassets

- Le Craboulettes
- Les Chaniots

- Le Coères
- Chazelle (commune of Jully-lès-Buxy)

- La Moulliere
  (commune of Saint-Vallerin)

CÔTE DE BEAUNE

LADOIX-SERRIGNY
Premier Cru vineyards:-

Red and White wines	Red wines only	White wines only
La Corvee	Les Buis	Les Grechons
Le Clou d'Orge	Les Joyeuses	En Naget
La Micaude	Bois Roussot	Le Rognet et Corton
Basses Mourottes		
Hautes Mourottes		

Ladoix-Serrigny vineyards designated as Aloxe-Corton Premier Cru:-
- Clos des Marechaudes
- Les Moutottes
- La Marechaude
- Les Petites Lolieres
- La Coutiere
- La Toppe au Vert

ALOXE-CORTON
Premier Cru vineyards:-
- Les Valozieres
- Les Chaillots
- Les Guerets
- Les Paulands
- Les Fournieres
- Les Vercots
- Les Marechaudes
- Clos du Chapitre

The six vineyards designated as Aloxe-Corton Grand Cru but which are located in Ladoix Serrigny are listed under that commune.

PERNAND-VERGELESSES
Premier Cru vineyards:-
- Sous Fretille (*white wine only*)
- Creux de la Net
- Les Fichots
- Clos Berhet (*white wine only*)
- En Caradeux
- Les Vergelesses
- Clos du Village (*white wine only*)
- Ile des Vergelesses

THE THREE GRAND CRU VINEYARD OF CORTON HILL
The three Grand Cru vineyards of Corton hill overlap and are shared by the communes of Ladoix-Serrigny (LS), Aloxe-Corton (AC), and Pernand-Vergelesses (PV) as follows:-
- Corton (red and white wine) LS, AC, PV
- Corton-Chalemagne (white wine) LS, AC, PV
- Charlemagne (white wine) AC, PV.

SAVIGNY-LÈS-BEAUNE
Premier Cru vineyards:-
- Les Charnieres
- Aux Gravains
- Les Peuillets
- Les Talmettes
- Petits Godeaux
- Les Marconnets
- Les Vergelesses
- Aux Serpentieres
- La Dominode
- Batailliere
- Aux Clous
- Les Jarrons
- Basses Vergelesses
- Aux Guettes
- Les Hauts Jarrons
- Aux Fourneaux
- Les Rouvrettes
- Redrescul
- Champ Chevrey
- Les Narbantons
- Les Hauts Marconnets
- Les Lavieres

CHOREY-LES-BEAUNE

Chorey-les-Beaune has no Grand Cru or Premier Cru vineyards:-

BEAUNE

Premier Cru vineyards:-

- Les Boucherottes
- Les Vignes Franches
- Clos des Ursules
- Les Couacheux
- Les Epenotes
- Le Clos des Mouches

- Les Seurey
- Clos de la Mousse
- Les Reversees
- Les Sceaux
- Les Teurons
- Clos du Roi

- Les Perrieres
- Les Bressandes
- Les Toussaints
- Les Greves
- Sujr les Greves
- Sur les Greves-Clos Sainte-Anne

- Les Montrevenots
- Les Aigrots
- Les Sizies
- Pertuisots
- Clos Saint-Landry
- Les Avaux
- Les Tuvilains
- Belissand

- Blanches Fleurs
- A l'Ecu
- Clos de l'Ecu
- Les Feves
- Les Cent Vignes
- Les Marconnets
- En Genet
- En l'Orme

- Aux Cras
- Le Bas des Teurons
- Aux Coucherias
- Clos de la Feguine
- Montee Rouge
- La Mignotte
- Clos des Avaux
- Champs Pimont

POMMARD

Premier Cru vineyards:-

- Les Rugiens-Bas
- Les Rugiens-Haut
- Les Grands-Epenots
- Les Petits-Epenots
- Clos des Epeneaux
- Les Charmots
- Les Arvelets
- La Platiere
- La Chaniere

- Les Pezerolles
- Les Saucilles
- Les Boucherottes
- En Largilliere
- Clos de Verger
- Clos de la Comaraine
- La Refene
- Clos Blanc
- Derriere Saint-Jean

- Les Chaponnieres
- Les Croix Noires
- Les Poutures
- Le Clos Micault
- Les Combes-Dessus
- Les Bertins
- Les Fremiers
- Les Jarolieres
- Les Chanlins-Bas

VOLNAY

Premier Cru vineyards:-

- Pitures-Dessus
- Lassolle
- Clos des Ducs
- Le Village
- Clos de la Cave des Ducs
- Clos de l'Audignac
- Clos de la Chapelle
- Clos du Château des Ducs
- Clos de la Rougeotte
- Fremiets-Clos de la Rougeotte

- Clos de la Barre
- Clos de la Bousse d'Or
- Les Brouillards
- Mitans
- Les Angles
- Fremiets
- La Gigotte
- Les Lurets
- Robardelle

- Carelle sous la Chapelle
- Le Ronceret
- Champans
- Les Caillerets
- Les Caillerets-Clos des 60 Ouvrees
- En Chevret
- Taille Pieds
- Clos du Verseuil
- Clos des Chenes
- Pointes d'Angles

Five Premier Cru red wine vineyards located in the commune of Meursault are designated Volnay-Santenots (see Meursault)

MONTHÉLIE

Premier Cru vineyards:-

- Les Riottes
- Sur la Velle
- Le Meix Bataille
- Le Clos Gauthey
- Les Vignes Rondes

- Le Cas Rougeot
- La Taupine
- Les Champs Fulliot
- Le Village
- Le Château Gaillard

- Les Duresses
- La Barbiere
- Le Clou-des Chenes
- Les Clous
- Le Clos des Toisieres

AUXEY-DURESSES

Premier Cru vineyards:-

- Climat du Val
- Clos du Val
- Les Breterins

- La Chapelle
- Reugne
- Les Duresses

- Bas des Duresses
- Les Grands Champs
- Les Ecusseaux

SAINT-ROMAN

Saint-Roman has no grand Cru or Premier Cru vineyards.

MEURSAULT

Premier Cru vineyards:-

- Les Cras
- Les Caillerets
- Les Santenots Blancs (*Santenots*)
- Les Plures (*Santenots*)
- Le Santenots du Milieu (*Santenots*)
- Les Santenots du Dessous (*Santenots*) – red only
- Les Vignes Blanches (*Santenots*) – red only

- Charmes
- La Jeaunelotte (*Blagny*)
- La Piece sous le Bois (*Blagny*)
- Sous le dos d'Ane (*Blagny*)
- Sous Blagny (*Blagny*)
- Perriers
- Clos des Perriers

- Genevrieres
- Le Porusot
- Les Boucheres
- Les Gouttes d'Or
- Les Ravelles

Meursault has nine Premier Cru vineyards within its boundaries which are designated Premier Cru in the communes of Volnay-Santenotes (5) and Blagny (4).

PULIGNY-MONTRACHET

Puligny-Montrachet has two Grand Cru vineyards entirely within its boundaries:-

- Bienvenues-Batard-Montrachet
- Chevalier-Montrachet

Two Grand Cru vineyards cross communal borders with Chassagne-Montrachet.

- Montrachet
- Batard-Montrachet

Premier Cru vineyards:-

- Sous le Puits (Blagny)
- La Garenne (Blagny)
- Hameau de Blagny (Blagny)
- La Truffière
- Champ Gain
- Les Chalumaux

- Champ Canet
- Clos de la Garenne
- Les Folatieres
- Le Cailleret
- Les Demoiselles
- Les Pucelles

- Clavaillon
- Les Perrieres
- Clos de la Mouchere
- Les Combettes
- Les Referts

Puligny Montrachet also has three vineyards within its boundaries which are designated Blagny Premier Crus.

CHASSAGNE-MONTRACHET

Chassagne-Montrachet has one Grand Cru vineyard entirely within its boundaries:-
♦ Criots-Batard-Montrachet

It also shares on a cross boundary basis:-
♦ Montrachet   ♦ Batard-Montrachet

Premier Cru vineyards:-
♦ Les Baudines
♦ Les Embazees
♦ Clos Pitois
♦ Francemont
♦ Tete du Clos
♦ Les Grands Clos
♦ Les Petits Clos
♦ Bois de Chassagne
♦ La Romanée
♦ Les Grandes Ruchotte
♦ La Grande Montagne
♦ En Virondot
♦ Les Fairendes

♦ La Grande Borne
♦ Clos Chareau
♦ Les Boirettes
♦ La Chapelle
♦ Ez Crottes
♦ Guercheres
♦ Les Chaumes
♦ Champs Jendreau
♦ La Boudriotte
♦ Les Champs-Gains
♦ En Cailleret
♦ Vigne Derriere
♦ La Maltroie

♦ Les Macherelles
♦ Les Vergers
♦ Clos Saint Jean
♦ Les Combards
♦ Les Chenevottes
♦ Les Pasquelles
♦ Petingerets
♦ Les Chaumets
♦ Les Combes
♦ En Remilly
♦ Blanchot Dessus
♦ Les Bondues
♦ Chassagne du Clos Saint-Jean

♦ Vigne Blanche
♦ Morgeot
♦ Les Brussonnes
♦ La Cardeuse

♦ Ez Cretz
♦ Les Places
♦ Les Rebichets
♦ Chassagne

♦ Les Murees
♦ La Roquemaure
♦ Les Petites Fairendes

SAINT-AUBIN
Premier Cru vineyards:-

- Derriere la Tour
- En Creot
- Les Champlots
- Sur Gamay
- La Chateniere
- En Remilly
- Les Murgers des
- Dents de Chien

- Les Combes
- Le Charmois
- Village
- Les Castets
- Derriere chez Edouard
- Le Puits

- Les Frionnes
- Sous Roche Dumay
- Vignes Moingeon
- Pitangeret
- Les Perrieres
- Les Cortons
- Sur le Sentier du Clou

SANTENAY
Premier Cru vineyards:-

- La Comme
- Les Gravieres
- Clos de Tavannes
- Beauregard

- Clos Faubard
- Clos des Mouches
- Beaurepaire
- Passetemps

- La Maladiere
- Grand Clos Rousseau
- Clos Rousseau

CÔTE DE NUIT

MARSANNAY
Marsannay has no Grand Cru or Premier Cru vineyards

FIXIN
Premier Cru vineyards:-

- Arvelets
- Hervelets
- Clos Napoleon

- Clos du Chapitre
- Clos de la Perriere (located partly within the commune of Brochon)

GEVREY-CHAMBERTIN
Grand Cru vineyards:-

- Chambertin
- Chambertin-Clos de Bèze
- Charmes-Chambertin
- Mazoyeres-Chambertin
- Chapelle-Chambertin

- Griotte-Chambertin
- Latricieres-Chambertin
- Mazis-Chambertin
- Ruchottes-Chambertin

Premier Cru vineyards:-
- La Bossiere
- La Romanée
- Poissenot
- Estournelles-Saint-Jacques
- Clos des Varoilles
- Lavaut Saint-Jacques
- Les Cazetiers
- Clos du Chapitre
- Clos Saint-Jacques
- Champeaux
- Petits Cazetiers
- Combe au Moine
- Les Goulots
- Aux Combottes
- Bel Air
- Cherbaudes
- Petite Chapelle
- En Ergo
- Clos Prieur
- La Perriere
- Au Closeau
- Issarts
- Les Corbeaux
- Craipillot
- Fonteny
- Champonnet

MOREY-SAINT-DENIS
Grand Cru vineyards:-
- Clos de Tart
- Clos des Lambrays
- Clos Saint-Denis
- Clos de La Roche
- Bonnes-Mares (shared)

Premier Cru vineyards:-
- Les Genavrieres
- Monts Luisants
- Les Chaffots
- Clos Baulet
- Les Blanchards
- Les Gruenchers
- La Riotte
- Les Millandes
- Les Faconnieres
- Les Charrieres
- Clos des Ormes
- Aux Charmes
- Aux Chesaux
- Les Chenevery
- Le Village
- Les Sorbes
- Clos Sorbe
- La Bussiere
- Les Ruchots
- Côte Rotie

CHAMBOLLE-MUSIGNY
Grand Cru vineyards:-
- Bonnes-Mares (shared)
- Musigny

Premier Cru vineyards:-
- Les Veroilles
- Les Sentiers
- Les Baudes
- Les Noirots
- Les Lavrottes
- Les Charmes
- Les Plantes
- Aux Combottes
- Derriere la Grange
- Les Gruenchers
- Les Chatelots
- Les Cras
- Les Carrieres
- Les Chabiots
- Les Amoureuses

- Les Fuees
- Les Grands Murs
- Aux Beaux Bruns
- Aux Echanges

- Les Groseilles
- Les Combottes
- Les Feusselottes

- Les Borniques
- Les Hauts Doix
- La Conmbe d'Orveau

VOUGEOT
Grand Cru vineyard:-
- Clos de Vougeot

Premier Cru vineyards:-
- Les Cras
- La Vigne Blanche

- Les Petits Vougeots
- Clos de la Perriere

VOSNE-ROMANÉE
Grand Cru vineyuards:-
- La Tache
- La Grande Rue
- La Romanée

- Romanée-Conti
- Romanée-Saint-Vivant
- Richebourg

And in Flagey-Echézeaux:
- Echézeaux

- Grands Echézeaux

Premier Cru vineyards:-
- Les Beaux Monts
- Les Suchots
- Aux Brulees
- La Croix Rameau
- Clos des Reas
- Les Gaudichots

- Les Chaumes
- Aux Malconsorts
- Au-dessus des Malconsorts
- Cros Parentoux
- Aux Reignots
- Les Petits Monts

In the commune of Flagey-Echézeaux:
- Les Beaux Monts
- Les Rouges
- En Orveaux

NUITS-SAINT-GEORGES

Premier Cru vineyards:-

- Aux Champs Perdrix
- En la Perrier Noblot
- Les Damodes
- Aux Boudots
- Aux Cras
- La Richemone
- Aux Murgers
- Aux Vignerondes
- Aux Chaignots
- Aux Thorey
- Aux Argillas
- Aux Bousselots

- Les Perriers
- Les Hauts Pruliers

- Les Porrets Saint-Georges
- Clos des Porrets Saint-Georges
- Les Vallerots
- Les Poulettes
- Les Chaboeufs
- Les Vaucrains
- Château Gris
- Les Crots
- Rue de Chaux
- Les Proces
- Les Pruliers
- Ronciere

- Les Saint-Georges
- Les Cailles

- Clos des Corvees
- Clos des Corvees Pagets
- Clos Saint-Marc
- Les Argillieres
- Clos des Argillieres
- Chaines Carteaux
- Clos des Grandes Vignes
- Clos de la Marechale
- Clos Arlot
- Les Terres Blanches
- Les Didiers
- Clos des Forets Saint-Georges

- Aux Perdrix

CHABLIS

Grand Cru vineyards:-

- Bourgros
- Les Preuses
- Vaudesir
- Grenouilles

- Valmur
- Les Clos
- Blanchot
- La Moutonne*

* *Claims Grand Cru status and labels its bottles thus but is not officially recognised*

Premier Cru vineyards:-

- **Mont de Milieu**
- **Montee de Tonnerre**
- Chapelot
- Pied d'Aloue
- Côte de Brechain
- **Fourchaume**

- Les Lys
- Melinots
- Roncieres
- Les Epinottes
- **Montmains**
- Foret

- Vaux Ragons
- **Vaucoupin**
- **Vosgros**
- Vaugiraut
- **Les Fourneaux**
- Morein

- Vaupulent
- Côte de Fontenay
- L'Homme Mort
- Vaulorent
- **Vaillons**
- Chatains
- Sechet
- Beugnons

- Butteaux
- **Côte de Lechet**
- **Beauroy**
- Troësme
- Côte de Savant
- **Vauligneau**
- **Vaudevey**

- Côte de Pres Girots
- **Côte de Vaubarousse**
- **Berdiot**
- **Chaume de Talvat**
- **Côte de Jouan**
- **Les Beauregards**
- Côte de Cuissy

Of the 40 Premier Cru vineyards 17 are better known and perceived as more prestigious and the other 23 Premier Cru vineyards are now allowed to label their wine with the name of one of these so called 'umbrella' vineyards (denoted in bold type face)

B – THE GRAND CRU VINEYARDS OF THE CÔTE D'OR, THEIR VINEYARD AREAS AND WINE PRODUCTION

CÔTE DE BEAUNE

THE GRAND CRU VINEYARDS OF LADOIX SERRIGNY, ALOXE—CORTON, AND PERNAND VERGELESSES

| GRAND CRU | VINEYARD AREA (HECTARES) | WINE PRODUCTION | | |
| | | RED | WHITE | TOTAL |
		(HECTOLITRES)		
Corton*	97.8	2822	162	**2984**
Corton-Charlemagne*	52.4	-	2237	**2237**
Charlemagne**	4.5	-	135	**135**
TOTALS	154.7	2822	2534	**5356**

*   *Shared by the communes of Ladoix-Serrigny, Aloxe-Corton, and Pernand Vergelesses*
** *Shared by the communes of Aloxe-Corton and Pernand Vergelesses*

NOTE: The 'Charlemagne' Grand Cru is entitled to label its wine 'Corton-Charlemagne' which it invariably does.

THE GRAND CRU VINEYARDS OF PULIGNY-MONTRACHET AND CHASSAGNE MONTRACHET

GRAND CRU	VINEYARD AREA (HECTARES)	WINE PRODUCTION		
		RED	WHITE	TOTAL
		(HECTOLITRES)		
Bienvenues-Batard-Montrachet *	3.6	-	163	163
Chevalier-Montrachet *	7.4	-	305	305
Montrachet **	8	-	310	310
Batard Montrachet **	11.2	-	502	502
Criots-Batard-Montrachet ***	1.6	-	73	73
TOTALS	31.8	-	1353	1353

* Shared by both communes
** Puligny Montrachet
*** Chassagne Montrachet

CÔTE DE NUIT

THE GRAND CRU VINEYARDS OF GEVREY CHAMBERTIN

GRAND CRU	VINEYARD AREA (HECTARES)	WINE PRODUCTION		
		RED	WHITE	TOTAL
		(HECTOLITRES)		
Chambertin	14.0	454	-	454
Chambertin-Clos-De-Bèze *	14.6	444	-	444
Charmes-Chambertin **	30.0	1112	-	1112
Mazoyeres-Chambertin **	2.0	67	-	67
Chapelle-Chambertin	5.5	159	-	159
Griotte-Chambertin	2.7	92	-	92
Latricieres- Chambertin	7.0	308	-	308
Maziz-Chambertin	9.2	322	-	322
Ruchottes-Chambertin	3.1	102	-	102
TOTALS	88.1	3060	-	3060

* Has the right to be labelled 'Chambertin'
** Have the right to interchange their names

NOTE: Chambertin and Chambertin-Clos-de-Bèze are considered slightly superior and have a lower allowable yield (35 hectolitres/hectare) compared with the seven other Grand Cru vineyards which are allowed 37.

THE GRAND CRU VINEYARDS OF MOREY-SAINT-DENIS AND CHAMBOLLE-MUSIGNY

GRAND CRU	VINEYARD AREA (HECTARES)	WINE PRODUCTION		
		RED	WHITE	TOTAL
		(HECTOLITRES)		
Clos de Tart *	7.5	218	-	**218**
Clos des Lambrays *	7.0	236	-	**236**
Clos Saint-Denis *	6.0	200	-	**200**
Clos de la Roche *	13.4	448	-	**448**
Bonnes-Mares ***	16.2	522		**522**
Musigny **	10.3	284	23	**307**
TOTALS	**60.4**	**1908**	**23**	**1931**

*   *Morey-Saint-Denis Grand Cru*
** *Chambolle Musigny Grand Cru*
*** *Shared by both communes.*

THE GRAND CRU VINEYARDS OF VOSNE-ROMANÉE

GRAND CRU	VINEYARD AREA (HECTARES)	WINE PRODUCTION		
		RED	WHITE	TOTAL
		(HECTOLITRES)		
La Tache	5.0	151	-	151
La Grand Rue	1.7	52	-	52
La Romanée	0.9	28	-	28
Romanée-Conti	1.6	42	-	42
Romanée-Saint-Vivant	9.3	237	-	237
Richebourg	7.4	198	-	198
Echézeaux *	34.8	1240	-	1240
Grand Echézeaux *	7.5	240	-	240
TOTALS	**68.2**	**2188**	-	**2188**

* *Located in Flagey Echézeaux*

THE GRAND CRU VINEYARD OF VOUGEOT

Vougeot has one Grand Cru vineyard, Clos de Vougeot, and its 50.6 hectares produces 1770 hectolitres of red wine

C – THE PRINCIPAL WINE COMMUNES OF THE CÔTE D'OR, THEIR PREMIER CRU AND VILLAGES VINEYARD AREAS, RED AND WHITE WINE PRODUCTION AND THE NUMERICAL DISTRIBUTION OF THE GRAND CRU AND PREMIER CRU VINEYARDS

CÔTE DE BEAUNE

COMMUNE	GRAND CRU VINEYARDS	PREMIER CRU VINEYARDS	PREMIER CRU AND VILLAGES VINEYARD AREA (HECTARES)	WINE PRODUCTION		
				RED	WHITE	TOTAL
				(HECTOLITRES)		
Ladoix-Serrigny		11	94	3021	1042	4063
Aloxe-Corton	3 *	14 **	117.78	4301	81	4382
Pernand-Vergelesses		8	135.32	2958	2680	5638
Savigny-lès-Beaune	-	22	347.82	11443	1916	13359
Chorey-des-Beaune	-	-	133.65	4913	324	5237
Beaune	-	42	411.7	13319	2333	15652
Pommard	-	27	321.69	12892	-	12892
Volnay	-	29	206.7	7733	-	7733
Monthélie	-	15	119.34	4148	597	4745
Auxey-Duresses	-	9	134.61	3919	1919	5838
Saint-Romain	-	-	96.25	1779	2118	3897
Meursault	-	19	394.05	365	18171	18536
Puligny-Montrachet	2 *** 2 1	17	207.98	52	10792	10844
Chassagne-Montrachet		50	301.43	5262	10398	1 5660
Saint Aubin	–	20	162.81	2017	6247	8264
Santenay	–	11	329.31	11719	2321	14040
TOTALS:	**8**	**294**	**3514.44**	**89841**	**60939**	**150780**

*   *Shared with Ladoix Serrigny and Pernand Vergelesses*
**   *Six are located in Ladoix Serrigny but labelled Aloxe-Corton*
*** *Two in Puligny Montrachet one in Chassagne Montrachet and two shared by the two communes*

CÔTE DE NUITS

COMMUNE	GRAND CRU VINEYARDS	PREMIER CRU VINEYARDS	PREMIER CRU AND VILLAGES VINEYARD AREA (HECTARES)	WINE PRODUCTION (HECTOLITRES)		
				RED	WHITE	TOTAL
Marsannay	–	–	227	6455	3195 *	9650
Fixin	–	5 **	96.01	3797	161	3958
Geverey Chambertin	9	26	409.65	17282	–	17282
Morey St Denis	4 1 shared	20	96.4	3679	143	3822
Chambolle Musigny	1	25	152.23	6044	–	6044
Vougeot	1	4	65.73	2111	154	2265
Vosne Romanée	8 ***	15	153.6	5955	–	5955
Nuits St Georges	–	41	306.33	11703	328	12031
TOTALS:	24	136	1506.95	57026	3981	61007

* Includes 1481 hectolitres of Rosé
** One located in the commune of Brochon
*** Two located partly in the commune of Flagey Echezaux

NOTE: *The foregoing provide the Premier Cru and Villages vineyard areas and wine production. The figures for the Grand Cru vineyards are given in (B).*

D – THE CONFRÉRIE DES CHEVALIERS DU TASTEVIN

Burgundy, as one of the most famous wine regions of the world, has, in keeping with its international status, established a brotherhood, the Confrérie des Chevaliers du Tastevin, based in France's most famous vineyard château – Clos Vougeot. It has a worldwide membership of 12,000 dedicated to Burgundy and its wine.

The founding of the Confrérie and its international acclaim is eloquently described by Jean-Robert Pitte:-

"On 16th November 1934, a time of plunging wine sales, a group of growers and merchants in Nuits led by Georges Faiveley and Camille Rodier created the Confrérie des Chevaliers du Tastevin. This merry band has since become an institution. Its neo-medieval style (mocked everywhere else, but a source of delight to the some five hundred guests invited to the banquets of the various chapters) has served to effectively promote the wines and gastronomy of Burgundy among celebrities and dignitaries from around the world. There is hardly a great film actor or opera singer, or an ambassador of the United States, the Netherlands, Great Britain, or Japan, or a member of a royal family who has not been honoured as a special guest of the Confrérie, and who has not taken immense pride in beating the famous Burgundian drum with his hands while singing 'la-la-la-la-la-la-la-lalère'!"

Its ancient predecessor was the 'Ordre de la Boisson' originally founded in 1703. The present Confrérie was established in 1934. Its primary goals are:-

"To hold in high regard and encourage the use of the products of Burgundy, particularly her great wines and her regional cuisine. To maintain and revive the festivities, customs and traditions of Burgundian folklore," and *"To encourage people from all over the world to visit Burgundy."*

And its ethos:-

"Because wine is more than wine, a gift from Heaven and the fruit of man's work, it expresses the beautiful, the great, and the true. The words of the Universal language of Brotherhood sing the joy of living and the happiness of encounters, with a sense of balance and good measure. To raise one's glass, indeed, but not just to drink it! 'He is not good, who strives not to be better', said Saint Bernard. Such is the ethos of the Tastevin."

CONFRÉRIE DES CHEVALIERS DU TASTEVIN

CONFRÉRIE DES CHEVALIERS DU TASTEVIN

Each year is marked by a series of formal black tie dinners celebrating the various 'Chapitres' – Spring, Summer, Autumn, the Equinox, Flowers, Saint Vincent and Saint Hubert. The dinners are held in the Cistercian cellars of the Château of Clos Vougeot which can seat up to 600. These memorable occasions with members and guests have over the years included heads of state, ministers, ambassadors, royalty, Nobel prize-winners, famous military or business leaders, sport champions, singers or actors, all have come or will come one evening or another to the Cistercian cellar to have the moving experience of going through the 'Cercles du Vin'.

Another annual event celebrated by the Confrérie is the festival of St Vincent. Each year a Burgundy village is selected and honoured with the celebration. In 2011 the village was Corgoloin. According to a long-established tradition the festival has a very formal aspect with the Saints' parade, the religious service and the induction of veteran winegrowers, as well as a more festive aspect with the opening of the cellars for wine tasting in a musical atmosphere including a varied entertainment pro-gramme. Various banquets are organised to which many are invited.

The Confrérie has a formal system of governance through a Grand Conseil of Chevaliers. Its president is called the Grand Maître and its secretary is called the Grand Connetable. In the US the organisation del-egates authority to a Grand Pilier, who is assisted by a Grand Connetable. Candidates for membership are approved by the Grand Pilier or Grand Connetable, and are confirmed by the Grand Conseil.

Members are hierarchically ranked (in descending order) as Grand Officiers, Officiers Commandeurs, Commandeurs, and Chevaliers. The Confrérie des Chevaliers du Tastevin is a private club. It may have 12,000 members but it has no desire for a noticeable increase of membership, so that the quality of reception facilities at the Château du Clos de Vougeot can be maintained. Yet, the 'Tastevin' does not just receive 'anyone' no matter how successful he or she may be. It appreciates merit as well as talent, it likes to honour courage, personal endeavour, scientific intel-ligence, the love of France and fulfilment of human values.

An important role which the Confrérie fulfils is the tasting and quality evalutation each year of Burgundy wines submitted to it through a process known as TASTEVINAGE which was first established in June 1950. Those vineyards which submit their wines and meet the exacting standards of the Confrérie are allowed to display on their wine labels the Tastevinage emblem which is readily recognisable.

The wine tasting, evaluation, and quality control are described by the Confrérie:-

> The Tastevinage aims to be of use to all lovers of Burgundy's wines: as an invaluable landmark in the complex landscape of the region's terroirs, it provides the consumer with a guarantee of unmitigated enjoyment. The Tastevinage consists of a rigorous test of wines from every corner of the Burgundy wine region, from Chablis to the Beaujolais crus, with the purpose of selecting those that come up to the standard of their appellation and vintage. These are then awarded the seal of the Confrérie des Chevaliers du Tastevin, allowing the consumer to identify those wines which, because of their integrity, personality and indisputable quality, have shown themselves worthy of this distinction.
>
> Each year, the Confrérie des Chevaliers du Tastevin organises two Tastevinage sessions at the Château du Clos de Vougeot: the first in spring for red burgundy; the second in autumn for white burgundy and the Beaujolais crus. Burgundy's sparkling wines are represented at both sessions.
>
> In this way, the Tastevinage confirms the role of the Confrérie in championing the reputation and quality of Burgundy's great wines.
>
> In the great Cistercian cellar at the Château du Clos de Vougeot, a jury of more than 250 wine-tasters chosen from an elite of connoisseurs and fine palates are gathered together: famous winegrowers, wine merchants, leaders of the viticulture associations, brokers, oenologists, restaurateurs, government officials working in partnership with the wine industry, enthusiastic and knowledgeable wine lovers, all surrounded by key Confrérie officials and journalists, present as 'disinterested observers'.
>
> At each table, a score of wines, presented anonymously with no mention of the grower or negociant, are subjected to a

rigorous organoleptic examination, lasting almost two hours.

The questions the judges have to ask themselves are very precise. "Does the wine conform to its appellation and vintage? Is it really typical and will it improve with age? In other words, is it a wine I would be happy to have in my cellar and proud to serve to my friends?".

Absorbed in their work the tasters evaluate the wines in religious silence under the watchful but strictly neutral eyes of the Confrérie organisers, whose task it is to see that all runs smoothly.

To keep track of the wines as they pass through the distribution process, the Confrérie des Chevaliers du Tastevin has introduced a quality guarantee monitoring system that assures the complete and individual traceability of each bottle of tastevinéwine.

In tandem with the wine-tasting, the wine is sent to the Centre Oenologique de Bourgogne where each lot is ana-lysed. The analysis is based on eight set criteria (voluminal mass, alcoholic degree, LMF, acidities, etc.) which provide the data for an analysis identity card for each wine.

These analyses, carried out by a COFRAC accredited lab-oratory, can be used together with the control samples held by the Tastevinage organisers, to check the authenticity of a tastevinébottle at any point in its shelf-life.

The Confrérie des Chevaliers du Tastevin regularly takes wines from wine-shops and the wine-departments of large supermarkets which are then compared with the analysis data and the control samples kept at the Château du Clos de Vougeot.

With this double guarantee of authenticity, the customer can be confident he is making the right choice when he opts for a tastevinéwine.

At the first Tastevinage on the 28th June 1950, of 133 wines presented to the thirty wine-tasters for evaluation, 114 were selected to display the Tastevinage seal.

In 2010, more than 1,500 wines were put to the test.

In sixty years of wine selecting, the Tastevinage has

successfully managed to adapt to the changing requirements of wine-drinkers. The constant improvements in the organisation of the selection test, the inclusion of new appellations, official recognition by the European Union – these changes have all been introduced in conformity with the Confrérie's abiding concern with maintaining quality.

The selection criteria are strict: roughly only a third of the lots submitted pass the selection test.

More than 100 million bottles have displayed the Tastevinage label since its creation.

The twin aims of the Tastevinage have been achieved: to reward the producer for the quality of his wine, and to give the consumer a guaranteed assurance of enjoyment.

The results of the tastings and evaluation are published each year in the 'Guide des Vins de Bourgogne'. The views of Robert Parker who has pioneered the objective evaluation and quality ranking of wine worldwide are very interesting:-

"In their efforts to promote only the highest quality burgundy, the Confrérie instituted a wine competition in 1950 wherein the very best wines would be entitled to carry a very distinctive label called Tastevin. This elaborate, colourful label is supposed to be given only to those wines that reflect their appellations and are irrefutably of high quality. This procedure has been maligned, but I am unpersuaded that it is not just simply jealousy or ignorance that has caused the criticism, as virtually every wine I have ever tasted with the Tastevin label has been at least good. In most cases, the wines are very good to excellent. No doubt the Confrérie, given their power, high profile, and promotion-oriented philosophy, are easy targets for criticism. However, the fact remains that they have served an extremely valuable purpose in seeing that their Tastevin labels are only bestowed on good examples of Burgundy wines. One further point to consider is that many producers do not submit wines, so the fact that a wine does not have a Tastevin label does not mean that the wine is not of high quality."

PRINCE ALBERT DE MONACO IN FINE VOICE

THE CELLARS OF CLOS VOUGEOT – A TASTEVIN BLACK TIE DINNER

THE CELLARS OF CLOS VOUGEOT – A TASTEVIN BLACK TIE DINNER

APPENDIX 2

BORDEAUX

A – THE CLASSIFICATIONS OF THE CHÂTEAUX OF BORDEAUX

1. THE MÉDOC CLASSIFICATION OF 1855

The background to this classification and its formulation, which featured in the 'Exposition Universelle' in Paris in 1855, are included in Appendix 3.

FIRST-GROWTHS

Château Lafite-Rothschild	Pauillac
Château Latour	Pauillac
Château Margaux	Margaux
Château Haut Brion	Pessac, Graves
Château Mouton-Rothschild	Pauillac

SECOND-GROWTHS

Château Rauzan-Ségla	Margaux
Château Rauzan-Gassies	Margaux
Château Léoville-Las Cases	St-Julien
Château Léoville-Poyferré	St-Julien
Château Léoville-Barton	St-Julien
Château Durfort-Vivens	Margaux
Château Lascombes	Margaux
Château Gruaud-Larose	St-Julien
Château Brane-Cantenac	Cantenac-Margaux
Château Pichon-Longueville Baron	Pauillac
Château Pichon Lalande	Pauillac
Château Ducru-Beaucaillou	St-Julien
Château Cos d'Estournel	St-Estèphe
Château Montrose	St-Estèphe

THIRD-GROWTHS

Château Giscours	Labarde-Margaux
Château Kirwan	Cantenac-Margaux
Château d'Issan	Cantenac-Margaux
Château Lagrange	St-Julien
Château Langoa-Barton	St-Julien
Château Malescot St-Exupéry	Margaux
Château Cantenac-Brown	Cantenac-Margaux
Château Palmer	Cantenac-Margaux
Château La Lagune	Lludon-Haut-Médoc
Château Desmirail	Margaux
Château Calon-Ségur	St-Estèphe
Château Ferriere	Margaux
Château Marquis d'Alesme-Becker	Margaux
Château Boyd-Cantenac	Cantenac-Margaux

FOURTH-GROWTHS

Château St-Pierre	St-Julien
Château Branaire	St-Julien
Château Talbot	St-Julien
Château Duhart-Milon	Pauillac
Château Pouget	Cantenac-Margaux
Château la Tour-Carnet	St-Laurent-Haut-Médoc
Château Lafon-Rochet	St-Estèphe
Château Beychevelle	St-Julien
Château Prieuré-Lichine	Cantenac-Margaux
Château Marquis-de-Terme	Margaux

FIFTH-GROWTHS

Château Pontet-Canet	Pauillac
Château Batailley	Pauillac
Château Grand-Puy-Lacoste	Pauillac
Château Grand-Puy-Ducasse	Pauillac
Château Haut-Batailley	Pauillac
Château Lynch-Bages	Pauillac
Château Lynch Moussas	Pauillac

Château Dauzac	Labarde-Margaux
Château Mouton-Baronne-Philippe (now d'Armhailac)	Pauillac
Château du Tertre	Barsac-margaux
Château Haut-Bages-Liberal	Pauillac
Château Pédesclaux	Pauillac
Château Belgrave	St-Laurent-Haut-Médoc
Château de Camensac	St-Laurent-Haut-Médoc
Château Cos Labory	St-Estèphe
Château Clerk-Milon-Rothschild	Pauillac
Château Croizet-Bages	Pauillac
Château Cantemerle	Macau-Haut-Médoc

The following shows how the six appellations in the 1855 classification fared:-

	GROWTHS					
APPELLATION	1st	2nd	3rd	4th	5th	**TOTALS**
Margaux	1	5	10	3	2	**21**
Pauillac	3	2	-	1	12	**18**
St Estèphe	-	2	1	1	1	**5**
St Julien	-	5	2	4	-	**11**
Graves	1		-	-	-	**1**
Haut Médoc	-	-	1	1	3	**5**
TOTALS:	**5**	**14**	**14**	**10**	**18**	**61**

2. THE SAUTERNES – BARSAC CLASSIFICATION OF 1855

At the time (1855) that the red wines of Médoc (plus one Graves) were classified the sweet white wines of Sauternes – Barsac were also officially classified.

FIRST GREAT GROWTH
Château d'Yquem

FIRST-GROWTHS
Château Guiraud

Château la Tour Blanche

Château Lafaurie-Peyraguey

Château de Rayne-Vigneau

Château Sigalas Rabaud

Château Rabaud-Promis

Clos Haut-Peyraguey

Château Coutet

Château Climens

Château Suduiraut

Château Rieussec

SECOND-GROWTHS
Château d'Arche

Château Filhot

Château Lamoth Guignard

Château de Myrat

Château Doisy-Védrines

Château Doisy-Daëne

Château Doisy Dubroca

Château Suau

Château Broustet

Château Caillou

Château Nairac

Château de Malle

Château Romer du Hayot

Château Lamoth Despujols

3. GRAVES CLASSIFICATION OF 1953
1959 UPDATE NOW IN EFFECT

CLASSIFIED RED WINES OF GRAVES
Château Haut-Brion — Pessac

Château Bouscaut — Cadaujac

Château Carbonnieux — Léognan

Domaine de Chevalier — Léognan

Château de Fieuzal — Léognan

Château Haut-Bailly — Léognan

Château La Mission-Haut-Brion — Pessac

Château La Tour-Haut-Brion	Talence
Château La Tour-Martillac	Martillac
Château Malartic-Lagravière	Léognan
Château Olivier	Léognan
Château Pape-Clement	Pessac
Château Smith-Haut-Lafitte	Martillac

CLASSIFIED WHITE WINES OF GRAVES

Château Bouscaut	Cadaujac
Château Carbonnieux	Léognan
Domaine de Chevalier	Léognan
Château Couhins	Villenave-d'Ornon
Château Laville-Haut-Brion	Talence
Château Malartic-Lagravière	Léognan
Château Oliver	Léognan
Château La Tour-Martillac	Martillac

4. ST ÉMILION CLASSIFICATION OF 1955

St Émilion wines were first classified in 1955 with a view to updating every 10 years. The 2006 update was legally challenged and the 1996 version remained in effect until the 2006 version was reinstated in a complex legal ruling in 2009 and extended to 2012 classification which was undertaken by French wine experts from outside Bordeaux in an attempt to introduce impartiality and avoid controversy and challenge. It did not work as four châteaux filed complaints, but at present the following 2012 classification remains in effect.

FIRST GREAT GROWTHS (ST-ÉMILION – PREMIERS GRANDS CRUS CLASSÉS)

(A) Château Angèlus
   Château Ausone
   Château Cheval Blanc
   Château Pavie

(B) Château Beau-Séjour Bécot
   Château Beauséjour
    (Duffau-Lagarrosse)
   Château Bélair-Monange
   Château Canon
   Château Canon-la-Gaffelière

(B) *Continued*
Château Clos Fourtet
Château Figeac
Château La Gaffelièr
Château Larcis Ducasse

Château La Mondotte
Château Pavie-Macquin
Château Troplong Mondotte
Château Trotte Vielle
Château Valandraud

GREAT GROWTHS (ST ÉMILION - GRANDS CRUS CLASSÉS)

Château l'Arrosée
Château Balestard-La-Tonnelle
Château Barde-Haut
Château Bellefont-Belcier
Château Bellevue
Château Berliquet
Château Cadet-Bon
Château Côte de Baleau
Château Chauvin
Château La Commanderie
Château La Couspaude
Château La Clotte
Château Corbin
Château Grand Corbin
Château Grand Corbin-Despagne
Château Dassault
Château Cap de Moulin
Château Destieux
Château La Dominique
Château Faugères
Château Jean Faure
Château Faurie-de-Souchard
Château de Ferrand
Château Fleur-Cardinale
Château La Fleur Morange
Château Fombrauge
Château Fonplégade
Château Fonroque
Château Franc Mayne

Château Guadet
Château Clos des Jacobins
Château Couvent des Jacobins
Château Larmande
Château Laniote
Château Laroque
Château Laroze
Château La Madelaine
Château La Marzelle
Château Grand Mayne
Château Monbousquet
Château Moulin du Cadet
Château Mourlin
Château Les Grandes Murailles
Château Clos de l'Oratoire
Château Pavie-Decesse
Château Péby Faugères
Château Grand Pontet
Château de Pressac
Château Le Prieuré
Château Quinault l'Enclos
Château Ripeau
Château Rochebelle
Château Clos Saint-Martin
Château Saint-Georges-Côte-Pavie
Château Sansonnet
Château Clos de Sarpe
Château Haut Sarpe
Château La Serre

Château Soutard   Château Tertre Daugay
Château Petit Faurie de Soutard   Château Villemaurine
Château La Tour Figeac   Château Yon Figeac

5. THE CRU BOURGEOIS CLASSIFICATION OF THE MÉDOC 1978
THE 1978 SYNDICATE'S CLASSIFICATION NOW IN EFFECT

The first classification was in 1932 when 444 châteaux were classified compared with 127 for the following 1978 classification

CRUS GRANDS BOURGEOIS EXCEPTIONNELS

D'Agassac (Ludon)   Dutruch Gand-Poujeaux
                                   (Moulis)

Andron-Blanquet (St-Estèphe)   Fourcas-Dupre (Listrac)
Beau-Site (St-Estèphe)   Fourcas-Hosten (Listrac)
Capbern-Gasqueton (St-Estèphe)   du Glana (St Julien)
Caronne-St-Gemme (St-Laurent)   Haut-Marbuzet (St-Estèphe)
Chasse-Spleen (Moulis)   de Marbuzet (St-Estèphe)
Cissac (Cissac)   Meyney (St-Estèphe)
Citran (Avensan)   Phelan-Ségur (St-Estèphe)
Le Crock (St-Estèphe)   Poujeaux (Moulis)

CRUS GRANDS BOURGEOIS

Beaumont (Cussac)   Lamothe-Cissac (Cissac)
Bel-Orme (St-Seurin-de-Cadourne)   Larose-Trintaudon (St-Laurent)
Brillette (Moulis)   Laujac (Begadan)
La Cordonne (Blaignan)   Liversan (St-Saveur)
Colombier-Monpelou (Pauillac)   Looudenne (St-Yzans-de-Médoc)
Coufran (St-Seurin-de-Cadourne   De Malleret (Le Pian)
Coutelin-Merville (St-Estèphe)   Martinens (Margaux)
Duplessis-Hauchecorne (Moulis)   Morin (St-Estèphe)
La Fleur Milon (Pauillac)   Moulin a Vent (Moulis)
Fontesteau (St-Saveur)   Le Meynieu (Vertheuil)
Greysac (Begadan)   Les-Ormes-de-Pez (St-Estèphe)
Hanteillan (Cisac)   Les-Ormes-Sorbet (Couqueques)
Lafon (Listrac)   Patache d'Aux (Begadan)
de Lamarque (Lamarque)   Paveil-de-Luze (Soussans)

Peyrabon (St-Saveur)

Pontoisc-Cabarrus
    (St-Seurin-de-Cadbourne)

Potensac (Potensac)

Reysson (Vertheuil)

Ségur (Parempuyre)

Sigognac (St-Yzans de Médoc)

Sociando-Mallet
    (St-Seurin-de-Cadbourne)

Du Taillan (Le Taillan)

La Tour de Bu (Begadan)

La Tour du Haut-Moulin (Cussac)

Tronquoy-Lalande (St-Estèphe)

Verdignan (St-Seurin-de-Cadbourne)

CRUS BOURGEOIS

Aney (Cussac)

Balac (St-Laurent)

La Becade (Listrac)

Bellerive (Valeyrac)

Bellerose (Pauillac)

Les Bertins (Valeyrac)

Bonneau (St-Seurin-de-Cadourne)

Le Bosq (St-Christoly)

Du Breuilh (Cissac)

La Bridane (St-Julien)

De By (Begadan)

Cailloux De By (Begadan)

Cap Leon Veyrin (Listrac)

Carcanieux (Queyrac)

Castera (Cissac)

Chambert (St-Estèphe)

La Clare (St-Estèphe)

Clarke (Listrac)

La Closerie (Moulis)

De Conques (St-Christoly)

Duplessis-Fabre (Moulis)

Fonpiqueyre (St-Saveur)

Fonreaud (Listrac)

Fort Vauban (Cussac)

La France (Blaignan)

Gallais-Bellevue (Potensac)

Grand-Duroc-Milon (Pauillac)

Grand-Moulin
    (St-Seurin-de-Cadourne)

Haut-Bages-Monpelou (Pauillac)

Haut-Canteloup (Couqueques)

Haut-Garin (Begadan)

Haut-Padargnac (Pauillac)

Houbanon (Prignac)

Hourton-Ducasse (St-Saveur)

De Labat (St-Laurent)

Lamothe-Bergeron (Cussac)

Le Landat (Cissac)

Landon (Begadan)

Lavalière (Blaignan)

Lartigue-de-Brochon
    (St-Seurin-de-Cadourne)

Lassalle (Pontensac)

Lavalière (St-Christoly)

Lestage (Listrac)

MacCarthy (St-Estèphe)

Monthil (Begadan)

Moulin de la Roque (Begadan)

Moulin-Rouge (Cussac)

Panigon (Civrac)

Pibran (Pauillac)

Plantey de la Croix
    (St-Seurin-de-Cadourne)

Pontet (Blaignan)

Ramage la Batisse (St-Saveur)
Romefort (Cussac)
La Roque de by (Begadan)
De La Rose Marechale
　　(St-Seurin-de-Cadourne)
St-Bonnet (St-Christoly)
St-Roch (St-Estèphe)
Saransot (Listrac)
Sourdars (Avensac)
Tayac (Soussans)

La Tour Blanche (St-Christoly)
La Tour du Haut-Caussan
　　(Blaignan)
La Tour du Mirail (Cissac)
La Tour St-Bonnet (St Christoly)
La Tour St-Joseph (Cissac)
Des Tourelles (Blaignan)
Vernous (Lesparre)
Vieux-Robin (Begadan)

6. ROBERT PARKER'S BORDEAUX CLASSIFICATION

FIRST-GROWTH QUALITY

Angèlus (St-Émilion)
Ausone (St-Émilion)
Cheval Blanc (St-Émilion)
Cos d'Estournel (St-Estèphe)
Ducru-Beaucaillou (St-Julien)
L'Eglise-Clinet (Pomerol)
L'Evangile (Pomerol)
Haut-Brion (Graves)
Lafite Rothschild (Pauillac)
Lafleur (Pomerol)

Latour (Pauillac)
Léoville-Las Cases (St-Julien)
Margaux (Margaux)
La Mission Haut-Brion (Graves)
Montrose (St-Estèphe)
Mouton Rothschild (Pauillac)
Palmer (Margaux)
Pavie (St-Émilion)
Pétrus (Pomerol)
Le Pin (Pomerol)

SECOND-GROWTH QUALITY

Beauséjour-Duffau (St-Émilion)
Bellevue (St-Émilion)
Bellevue-Mondotte (St-Émilion)
Calon-Ségur (St-Estèphe)
Canon-La-Gaffelière (St-Émilion)
Certan de May (Pomerol)
Clerc Milon (Pauillac)
Clinet (Pomerol)
Clos l'Église (Pomerol)
Clos St-Martin (St-Émilion)

La Conseillante (Pomerol)
Figeac (St-Émilion)
La Fleur de Gay (Pomerol)
La Gomerie (St-Émilion)
Grand-Puy-Lacoste (Pauillac)
Gruaud Larose (St-Julien)
Hosanna (Pomerol)
Léoville Barton (St-Julien)
Léoville Poyferré (St-Julien)
Lynch-Bages (Pauillac)

THE WINES OF BURGUNDY AND BORDEAUX

Magrez-Fombrauge (St-Émilion)
Malescot St-Exupéry (Margaux)
Monbousquet (St-Émilion)
La Mondotte (St-Émilion)
Marojallia (Margaux)
Nenin (Pomerol)
Pape-Clément (Graves)
Pavie Decesse (St-Émilion)
Pavie Macquin (St-Émilion)
Péby Faugères (St-Émilion)
Pichon-Longueville Baron (Pauillac)

Pichon-Longueville-Comtesse
   de Lalande (Pauillac)
Quinault-L'Enclos (St-Émilion)
Rauzan-Ségla (Margaux)
Rol Valentin (St-Émilion)
Smith-Haut-Lafite (Pessac-Léognan)
Le Tertre-Rôteboeuf (St-Émilion)
Troplong Mondot (St-Émilion)
Trotanoy (Pomerol)
Valandraud (St-Émilion)
Vieux-Château-Certain (Pomerol)

THIRD-GROWTH QUALITY

Beau-Séjour Bécot (St-Émilion)
Bon Pasteur (Pomerol)
Branaire-Ducru (St-Julien)
Brane Cantenac (Margaux)
Les Carmes Haut-Brion (Graves)
Chauvin (St-Émilion)
Domaine de Chevalier (Graves)
Clos des Lunelles (Côtes de Castillon)
Croix St-Georges (Pomerol)
Duhart-Milon (Pauillac)
La Fleur-Pétrus (Pomerol)
La Gaffelière (St-Émilion)
Gracia (St-Émilion)
Grand Mayne (St-Émilion)

Les Grandes Murailles
   (St-Émilion)
Haut-Bailly (Graves)
Haut-Bergey (Pessac-Léognan)
L'Hermitage (St-Émilion)
d'Issan (Margaux)
Kirwan (Margaux)
Lagrange (St-Julien)
Larrivet-Haut-Brion
   (Pessac-Léognan)
Latour à Pomerol (Pomerol)
Magdelaine (St-Émilion)
Pontet-Canet (Pauillac)

FOURTH-GROWTHS QUALITY

D'Armailhac (Pauillac)
L'Arrosée (St-Émilion)
Barde-Haut (St-Émilion)
Chasse-Spleen (Moulis)
La Clémence (Pomerol)
La Couspaude (St-Émilion)
La Dominique (St-Émilion)

Ferrand-Lartigue (St-Émilion)
de Fieuzal (Graves)
La Fleur de Boüard
   (Lalande-de-Pomerol)
Les Forts de Latour (Pauillac)
Gazin (Pomerol)
Giscours (Margaux)

Gloria (St-Julien)
Lafon-Rochet (St-Estèphe)
La Lagune (Ludon)
La Louvière (Graves)
St-Domingue (St-Émilion)

St-Pierre (St-Julien)
Sociando-Mallet (Médoc)
Soutard (St-Émilion)
Talbot (St-Julien)

FIFTH-GROWTHS QUALITY

Domaine l'A (Côtes de Castillon)
D'Aiguilhe (Côtes de Castillon)
d'Angludet (Margaux)
Bahans Haut-Brion (Graves)
Balestard La Tonnelle (St-Émilion)
Batailley (Pauillac)
Belair (St-Émilion)
Berliquet (St-Émilion)
Beychevelle (St-Julien)
Cadet-Piola (St-Émilion)
Canon (St-Émilion)
Canon-de-Brem (Canon-Fronsac)
Cantemerle (Macau)
Cantenac-Brown (Margaux)
Chambert-Marbuzet (St-Estèphe)
De Chambrun (Lalande-de-Pomerol)
Charmail (Médoc)
Citran (Médoc)
Clos des Jacobins (St-Émilion)
Clos la Madeleine (St-Émilion)
Clos René (Pomerol)
Couvent-des-Jacobins (St-Émilion)
La Croix du Casse (Pomerol)
La Croix de Gay (Pomerol)
Croque Michotte (St-Émilion)
La Dauphine (Fronsac)
Destieux (St-Émilion)
Dufort-Vivens (Margaux)
Domaine de l'Eglise (Pomerol)

Feytit-Clinet (Pomerol)
La Fleur de Jaugue (St-Émilion)
Fombrauge (St-Émilion)
Fontenil (Fronsac)
Fougas Maldorer (Côtes de
   Bourg)
Le Gay (Pomerol)
Grand Pontet (St-Émilion)
Grand-Puy Ducasse (Pauillac)
La Grave à Pomerol (Pomerol)
Jean de Gué-Cuvée Prestige
   (Lalande-de-Pomerol)
Haut-Bages Libéral (Pauillac)
Haut-Batailley (Pauillac)
Haut-Marbuzet (St-Estèphe)
Labégorce Zédé (Margaux)
Lanessan (Haut-Médoc)
Langoa Barton (St-Julien)
Larcis Ducasse (St-Émilion)
Larmande (St-Émilion)
Lascombes (Margaux)
Pierre de Lune (St-Émilion)
Lynsolence (St-Émilion)
Marquis de Terme (Margaux)
Maucaillou (Moulis)
Meyney (St-Estèphe)
Moulin-Haut-Laroque (Fronsac)
Moulin-Pey-Labrie
   (Canon-Fronsac)

Les Ormes de Pez (St-Estèphe)
Pavillon Rouge du Château Margaux
(Margaux)
Petit Village (Pomerol)
Potensac (Médoc)
Poujeaux (Moulis)
Prieuré-Lichine (Margaux)
Roc des Cambes (Côtes de Bourg)
Rouget (Pomerol)
de Sales (Pomerol)

Sanctus (St-Émilion)
Siran (Margaux)
du Tertre (Margaux)
La Tour-Figeac (St-Émilion)
La Tour Haut-Brion (Graves)
Tour Haut-Caussan (Médoc)
Tour du Haut-Moulin (Haut-Médoc)
Trotte Vieille (St-Émilion)
La Vieille-Cure (Fronsac)

B – SUPER SECONDS AND THE WINES NOW CONSIDERED EQUAL IN QUALITY TO FIRST GROWTHS

This is not a classification but arises from the fact that the 1855 classification has never been updated (with a single exception) and therefore does not reflect the significant improvement in the quality of certain wines from the lower growths over the years. Furthermore the 1855 classification was confined to Médoc wines (plus only one other – Haut Brion) and great wines from other Bordeaux sub-regions should now be formally acknowledged in the modern world. In recognition of this anomalous situation the wine trade has adopted the term 'super seconds' for wines from the original 1855 lower growths and those from non-Médoc sub-regions which now exhibit exceptional quality. The list of 'super seconds' is not static and will continue to be revised to recognise wines which achieve the highest standards of excellence irrespective of their original classification or exclusion.

THE CURRENT SUPER SECONDS

Angélus
Calon Ségur
Clinet
Cos d'Estournel
Ducru Beaucaillou
Eglise Clinet
Evangile
Figeac
Grand Puy Lacoste

La Clusière
La Conseillante
Larcis Ducasse
Léoville Barton
Léoville Las Cases
Léoville Poyferre
Lynch-Bages
Montrose
Palmer

Pavie
Pichon Baron
Pichon Lalande
Tertre Rôteboeuf
Troplong Mondot
Trotanoy
Valandraud
Vieux Château Certan

THE WINES OMITTED FROM THE 1855 CLASSIFICATION WHICH ARE NOW CONSIDERED EQUAL IN QUALITY TO FIRST GROWTHS:-

In addition to the adoption of the 'super second' categorisation it was also apparent that certain wines, not originally classifed, achieved the standards of excellence of first growths. These exceptional wines have been recognised and listed by the wine trade.

Ausone	Le Pin
Pétrus	Lafleur
Cheval Blanc	La Mission Haut Brion

C – THE GRAPE VARIETIES AND TYPICAL WINE BLENDS OF BORDEAUX

GRAPE VARIETIES

The red wines of Bordeaux are blended from four grape varieties – Cabernet Sauvignon, Merlot, Cabernet Franc, and Petit Verdot (very small quantities of the Malbec grape are also used on the right bank). The dominant grape of the right bank, St Émilion and Pomerol, is Merlot. On the left bank, Pauillac, Margaux, St Estèphe, St Julien, and the red wines of Graves, Cabernet Sauvignon dominates although in modern times there has been an increase in the amount of Merlot used on the left bank. The blends vary from year to year depending on the affect of variable climatic conditions on the different grape varieties.

For the white wines of Bordeaux, produced in Graves and Sauternes/Barsac, the main grape varieties are Semillon, Sauvignon Blanc, and small quantities of Muscadelle.

THE WINES OF BURGUNDY AND BORDEAUX

TYPICAL WINE BLENDS

<u>RED</u>

RIGHT BANK		CABERNET SAUVIGNON	MERLOT	CABERNET FRANC	PETIT VERDOT
1	Pétrus	-	95%	5%	-
	La Conseillante	-	70%	25%	5% Malbec
2	Cheval Blanc	-	34%	66%	-
	Ausone	-	50%	50%	-

LEFT BANK					
3	Lafite	70%	25%	3%	2%
	Latour	80%	15%	5%	-
4	Margaux	75%	20%	5%	-
	Palmer	55%	40%	5%	-
5	Calon Ségur	45%	40%	15%	-
	Haut Marbuzet	50%	40%	10%	-
6	Léoville Barton	72%	20%	8%	-
	Léoville Lascases	65%	19%	13%	3%
7	Haut Brion	45%	37%	18%	-
	La Mission Haut Brion	48%	45%	7%	-

1 - POMEROL	2 - ST ÉMILION	3 - PAUILLAC
4 - MARGAUX	5 - ST ESTÈPHE	6 - ST JULIEN
7 - GRAVES		

WHITE

SAUTERNES	SEMILLON	SAUVIGNON BLANC	MUSCADELLE
D'Yquem	80%	20%	-
Suduiraut	90%	10%	-
BARSAC			
Climens	100%	-	-
Coutet	75%	23%	2%
GRAVES DRY WHITE			
Domaine de Chevalier	30%	70%	-
Laville Haut-Brion	27%	70%	3%

D – THE PRINCIPAL CHÂTEAUX OF THE MAIN SUB-REGIONS AND COMMUNES OF BORDEAUX AND THEIR QUALITY RANKING BY ROBERT PARKER

THE RIGHT BANK
(The north bank of the river Dordogne)

ST ÉMILION

The wines of St Émilion were first officially classified in 1955 into two groups – Premier Grand Cru Classés and Grand Cru Classé with the intention of updating every ten years. Following the 1996 classification there were legal challenges to the 2006 version which was invalidated and the 1996 classification remained in effect. The 2006 version was subsequently reinstated and then replaced by the 2012 classification. Details of this classification are included in Appendix 2.

QUALITY RANKING
OUTSTANDING

Angélus, Ausone, Canon-la-Gaffelière, Cheval Blanc, Clos St-Martin, La Gomerie, Magrez-Fombrauge, La Mondotte, Pavie (since 1998), Pavie Decesse (since 1998), Péby Faugères, Le Tertre-Rôteboeuf, Troplong Mondot, Valandraud

THE WINES OF BURGUNDY AND BORDEAUX

EXCELLENT
L'Arrosée, Barde-Haut, Beau-Séjour Bécot, Beauséjour, Bellevuc,
Bellevue-Mondotte, Clos Dubreuil, Clos de l'Oratoire, Clos de Sarpe,
La Couspaude, Croix de Labrie, La Dominique, Ferrand Lartigue, Figeac,
Gracia, Grand-Mayne, Larmande, Monbousquet (since 1994),
Moulin St.Georges, Pavie Macquin, Quinault, Rol Valentin, Soutard

VERY GOOD
Balestard La Tonnelle, Bellefont-Belcier, Cadet-Piola, Canon,
Chauvin, Clos Fourtet, Clos des Jacobins, La Clotte, La Confession,
Corbin-Michotte, Faugères, Fombrauge, La Gaffelière, Grand Corbin-
Despagne, Grand-Pontet, Laplagnotte-Bellevue, Pierre de Lune,
Lusseau, Magdelaine, Saint-Dominigue, Yon-Figeac

GOOD
Berliquet, Cap de Mourlin, Chante Alouette Cormeil, Clos la Madeleine,
Corbin, Couvent des Jacobins, Croque Michotte, Curé-Bon, Dassault,
Daugay, Destieux, Faurie de Souchard, Château de Ferrand, Fleur
Cardinale, La Fleur-Pourret, Fonplégade, Fonroque, Franc-Mayne,
Godeau, Haut Brisson, Haut-Corbin, Haut-Sarpe, Jean-Faure, Le Jurat,
Larcis Ducasse, Laroze, Mauvezin, Petit-Faurie-de-Soutard, Ripeau,
Rocher Bellevue Figeac, Rolland-Maillet, Saint-Georges-Côte Pavie,
Tertre-Daugay, La Tour-Figeac, La Tour du Guetteur,
La Tour-du-Pin-Figeac, Trotte Vielle

POMEROL
The wines of Pomerol have never been officially classified

QUALITY RANKING
OUTSTANDING
Clos l'Église, La Conseillante, L'Eglise-Clinet, L'Evangile, La Fleur de
Gay, Hosanna, Lafleur, Pétrus, Le Pin, Trotanoy, Vieux Château Certan

EXCELLENT
Le Bon Pasteur, Certan de May, Clinet, La Coix du Casse, La Fleur-Pétrus,
Gazin, Latour à Pomerol, Nenin (since 1998), Petit Village

VERY GOOD
Beauregard, Bourgueneuf, La Croix de Gay, Domaine de L'Eglise,
L'Enclos, Le Gay, Gombaude Guillot, La Grave à Pomerol
(formerly La Grave-Trigant-de-Boisset)

GOOD
Bellegrave, Bonalgue, Clos du Clocher, Clos René, La Croix,
Feytit-Clinet (since 2001), Haut-Maillet, Rouget, de Sales, La Violette,
Vraye-Croix-de-Gay

THE LEFT BANK

To the south of the Gironde estuary, the left bank, is the Médoc peninsular.
It has the Médoc and Haut Médoc AOC's and is particularly famous for the
communes, of St Estèphe, Pauillac, St Julien, and Margaux and also has the
other lesser-known communes of Listrac and Moulis. Further inland on the
south bank of the Garonne river is the Graves and Sauternes and Barsac.

MÉDOC
PAUILLAC

Although many of its wines were included in the 1855 classifications
including two of the original four First Growths (there are now five as
a further Pauillac, Château Mouton Rothschild, was added in 1973)
Pauillac does not have a classification.

QUALITY RANKING
OUTSTANDING
Lafite Rothschild, Latour, Lynch-Bages, Mouton Rothschild,
Pichon Longueville, Pichon Longueville Comtesse de Lalande

EXCELLENT
Clerc Milon, Grand-Puy-Lacoste, Pontet-Canet (since 1994)

VERY GOOD
Duhart-Milon, Les Forts de Latour, Haut-Batailley

GOOD

d'Armaihac (known as Mouton-Baronne-Philippe from 1956–1989),
Batailley, Carruades de Lafite, Grand Puy Ducasse

MARGAUX

Margaux wines, although dominating the 1855 official classification
together with Pauillac, (together they have 39 wines classified out of an
overall total of 61), the Margaux appellation does not have a separate
official classification.

QUALITY RANKING

OUTSTANDING

Margaux, Palmer

EXCELLENT

Brane-Cantenac (since 1998), d'Issan, Kirwan, Lascombes (since 2000),
Malescot St-Exupéry (since 1990), Rauzan-Ségla (since 1983)

VERY GOOD

d'Angludet, Cantemerle, Giscours, La Lagune, Marquis de Terme,
Prieuré-Lichine, du Tertre

GOOD

Boyd-Cantenac, Cantenac-Brown, Charmant, Dauzac, La Gurgue,
Labégorce Zédé, Marsac Séguineau, Monbrison, Siran

ST ESTÈPHE

Generally considered the least prestigious of the four great appellations
of Médoc and in the 1855 classification only 5 St Estèphe wines were
included. Nevertheless a number of outstanding wines are now produced
led by Cos d'Estournel and Montrose. A characteristic of the modern St
Estèphe wines is the recent increased use of Merlot (up to 40%)

QUALITY RANKING

OUTSTANDING

Calon-Ségur, Cos d'Estournel, Montrose

EXCELLENT

None

VERY GOOD

Haut-Marbuzet, Lafon-Rochet, Les Ormes de Pez

GOOD

Chambert-Marbuzet, Cos Labory, Coutelin-Merville, Lavillotte,
Meyney, Petit Bocq, de Pez, Phelan Ségur, Tronquoy-Lalande

ST JULIEN

Another left bank appellation now producing a number of superb world-class wines and also maintaining throughout the highest standards of winemaking and quality. Unlike its illustrious neighbours Pauillac and Margaux, St Julien achieved only a modest inclusion in the 1855 classification of only 11 wines.

QUALITY RANKING

OUTSTANDING

Ducru-Beaucaillou, Gruaud Larose, Léoville Barton,
Léoville Las Cases, Léoville Poyferré

EXCELLENT

Branaire Ducru, Lagrange, Saint Pierre, Talbot

VERY GOOD

Beychevelle, Gloria, Hortevie, Langoa Barton

GOOD

Lalande Borie, Terrey-Gros-Cailloux

GRAVES

The sub-region, in addition to the area designated 'Graves', also encompasses the sub-regions of Pessac-Léognan, Sauternes/Barsac and uniquely for Bordeaux produces both red and white wine.

Graves has historical significance as it was the first 'claret' exported to England. Pope Clement V established Château Pape Clement in the 14th C. This famous château was inexplicably left out of the 1953 Graves Classification but was included in the 1959 update. In 1663 Samuel Pepys mentioned Haut Brion in London – the first specific mention of Claret in the city.

The 1855 official classification included only wines from the Médoc with the one single exception of Haut Brion produced in Pessac-Léognan and classified as a first growth. The wines of Graves were officially classified in 1953 and updated in 1959 and details are included in Appendix 2.

QUALITY RANKING
OUTSTANDING
Domaine de Chevalier (white only), Haut-Brion (red and white), Laville Haut-Brion (white only), La Mission Haut-Brion, Pape Clément (red and white)

EXCELLENT
Branon (since 2000), Les Carmes Haut-Brion, Couhins-Lurton (white only), de Fieuzal (red and white), Haut-Bailly, Haut-Bergey (since 1998), Larrivet-Haut-Brion (red and white), La Louvière (red and white), Malartic-Lagravière, Smith Haut Lafitte (red and white since 1991)

VERY GOOD
Bahans Haut-Brion, Clos Floridene (white only), Domaine de Chevalier (red only), La Garde, Roqueaillaide (white only), La Tour Haut-Brion

GOOD
Archambeau, Baret, Carbonnieux, Chantegrive, Cheret-Pitres, Cruzeau, Ferrande, Graville-Lacoste, Haut-Gardère, Olivier, Picque Caillou, Pontac Monplaisir, Rahoul, Rochemorin, La Tour-Martillac, La Vieille-France

BARSAC AND SAUTERNES
The sweet white wines of Barsac and Sauternes are quite unique in just about every way in comparison to the red (and limited dry white wines) of their neighbours.

In practically all wine making healthy ripe grapes are harvested and undergo a scientifically based winemaking process which in modern times is carried out in high tech wineries. Providing climatic conditions, up to and during the harvesting of the grapes are favourable, then, with modern winemaking techniques, an excellent wine will be produced with almost complete certainty.

The very opposite is true for the complex process involved in producing high quality sweet white wines which depends on natural changes in the grapes before harvesting. This natural process continues for up to two months after the grapes in the rest of Bordeaux have been picked and this greatly increases the risk of adverse and possibly catastrophic climatic conditions.

The eventual winemaking depends on the natural formation of a mould on the grape called *Botrytis cinerea* commonly known as 'noble rot'. The mould attacks and shrivels the skin of the Semillon grape, consumes up to half of its sugar content, forms glycerol, decomposes the tartaric acid and greatly reduces the volume of the grape the juice of which now has a very high sugar content.

This natural process is not consistent and the mould does not form on all the grapes and when it does its effect is also variable. This means only those grapes which have been fully affected by the 'noble rot' can be used for winemaking which means the picking of individual grapes and not bunches. This tedious and time consuming operation goes on through October and November and is then only successful if the climatic conditions are favourable for the formation of the mould. The grapes of Sauternes/Barsac are Semillon, Sauvignon Blanc, and Muscadelle. Semillon dominates in the range 80% to 100%. Muscadelle is used in very small quantities usually less than 5%.

Over the centuries one château has been pre-eminent in the production of exceptional sweet wine and that is Château d'Yquem. In the 1855 Sauternes/Barsac classification the wines were ranked as first and second growth that is except Château d'Yquem which was ranked alone above all other wines as a First Great Growth. The 1855 official classification of Barsac-Sauternes is included in Appendix 2.

THE WINES OF BURGUNDY AND BORDEAUX

QUALITY RANKING

OUTSTANDING

Climens, Coutet Cuvée Madame, Gilette, Rieussec, Suduiraut, Yquem*

EXCELLENT

D'Arche-Pugneau, Coutet, de Fargues, Guiraud, Lafaurie-Peyraguey,
Raymond-Lafon, La Tour Blanche

VERY GOOD

Doisy Dubroca, Doisy-Védrines, Haut-Claverie, Rabaud-Promis,
Sigalas Rabaud

GOOD

D'Arche, Bastor Lamontagne, Broustet, Clos Haut-Peyraguey, Doisy-
Daëne, Filhot, Les Justices, Lamothe Guignard, Liot, de Malle, Nairac,
de Rayne Vigneau, Romer du Hayot, Roumieu-Lacoste

---

* Yquem, despite the existence of other outstanding estates, rarely has any competition and must be considered to be the only Bordeaux wine in a class by itself.

APPENDIX 3

GOVERNMENTAL QUALITY CONTROL FOLLOWING THE PHYLLOXERA DISASTER – THE APPELLATIONS (AOC'S) OF BURGUNDY AND BORDEAUX

A – QUALITY CONTROL THROUGH THE APPELLATION ORIGINE CONTRÔLÉE (AOC) REGULATIONS AND ITS TURBULENT INTRODUCTION FOLLOWING THE PHYLLOXERA DISASTER

Wine selection and the role which the governmental regulations, in the form of the Appellation Origine Contrôlée (AOC's) and official classifications, play in this has been dealt with in the main text covering the selection of the wines of Burgundy and Bordeaux. There it has been concluded that the regulations are not particularly helpful in the selection process as they only provide a very broad guide to quality. As a result of this the selection of Burgundy and Bordeaux wine has been progressively based on the quality ratings of the international wine experts now using a numerical rating system and Burgundy 'best producers'.

And so if the official AOC's and classifications cannot be effectively used for wine selection on the basis of quality what purpose do they serve? The answer is a very important purpose as the AOC's provide central quality control and, in particular, they ensure that what is on the label of the bottle accurately describes what is in it. Nevertheless the 'policing' of this through the INAO's fraud squad is clearly a monumental task.

Although the selection of wine on the basis of quality has firmly passed to the wine experts and their legendary noses and palates it is nevertheless important to have a basic understanding of the legally binding quality regulations that are in force in the wine regions of France and again to have confidence that the label on the bottle accurately describes what is in it.

France in the mid-19th century recognised the need for the introduction of some degree of orderliness in its production of fine wine and the

1855 Official Classification of Bordeaux was an important watershed in the formal ranking of wine quality. It had in fact been preceded by several informal, personal classifications starting with Thomas Jefferson's of 1787 which was followed by Lawton (1815), Andre Julien (1830), and Wilhelm Franck (1845).

The mid 19th century was a time for great exhibitions. The first was Crystal Palace held in Hyde Park, London in 1851. Not to be outdone the newly proclaimed French Emperor, Napoleon III, commissioned 'The Exposition Universelle de Paris' for 1855. It was decided to display the fine wines of Bordeaux at the exhibition and a classification of these wines was undertaken. It was based on the market price of the wines combined with expert blind tasting. The preparation of the classification was the responsibility of the 'courtiers' or 'brokers' of Bordeaux. The classification covered the wines of Médoc plus Château Haut Brion and separately the sweet, white wines of Sauternes/Barsac. The Médoc classification included 61 châteaux. The wines of St Émilion, Pomerol, and all of Graves except Haut Brion were excluded on the basis that they were deemed to be of lower quality. The classification was divided on a quality basis into five groups or 'growths'. The châteaux in each group were also listed in order of quality and not alphabetically as they are in the modern classifications. The only change from 1855 to the present day was the elevation of Château Mouton Rothschild from second to first growth in 1973 by Presidential decree. Château Cantemerle was also classified as a fifth growth but was initially omitted by error and added later. The 1855 classification of the wines of Sauternes/Barsac designated Château d'Yquem as the only 'First Great Growth' followed by 11 'First Growths' and 14 'Second Growths' all grouped and listed in order of quality.

Burgundy also started with early classifications but unlike Bordeaux it did not continue with official classification of its wines.

In 1831 Denis Morelot published an important book on the wines of Burgundy – *La Vigne et Le Vin en Côte d'Or*. This was followed in 1855, the year of the Bordeaux Official Classification, by the publication of an influential book by Dr Jules Lavalle *Histoire et Statistique de la Vigne de Grands Vins de la Côte d'Or* which provided an unofficial classification of Burgundy vineyards developed from Morelot's earlier book.

Lavalle had five classes – hors ligne, tête de cuvée, 1er cuvée, 2eme cuvée, and 3eme cuvée. Lavalle's 'classification' was adopted in modified form by the Beaune Committee of Agriculture in 1861 based on three classes. The 'top' class vineyards were made Grand Cru when the AOC regulations were introduced in 1936.

A catastrophic event in the history of French wine and certainly the Burgundy and Bordeaux wine regions started around 1863. The disaster was phylloxera. This plant louse which burrows into the root of the vine and kills it, was brought to Europe through vines imported from America where the vines were resistant to it but not in Europe. Practically every vine in Europe was wiped out and the recovery was through the expensive grafting of imported vines (many from Chile) onto phylloxera resistant rootstock generally of American origin. This process continues throughout most of Europe to the present day.

Following this terrible period there was an urgent need for effective quality control to ensure that the reputation of French wine was maintained both at home and in particular in the international market. The post phylloxera period was an extremely difficult time for the French wine producers whose livelihoods and cash flow had been virtually wiped out overnight. The understandable reaction was to use the limited cash available to generate the maximum and quickest return and that could only mean sacrificing quality.

Vineyards were re-planted with hybrid vines on the basis of quantity before quality. The result was wines which were harsh and thin and totally inferior to the great wines produced before the crisis.

At this point the French Government decided to act to restore the quality and reputation of the nation's wine which was economically important.

The legislations of 1905 and 1908 proved, unfortunately, to be ineffective as those who drafted the laws had only a limited knowledge of viniculture and the wine producers could, if they wished, drive a proverbial 'horse and cart' through them, and the situation was exacerbated rather than improved.

The fundamental problem of the early legislation was that it concentrated only on the geographical location where the wine was produced. If for instance the wine was produced in Pomerol or Pauillac then this had to be displayed on the bottle label and providing this was complied with then the producer was acting within the law. What was put in the bottle was not controlled.

What the legislatures failed to understand and act on was that the quality of the wine depended on the control of grape variety, yield, vinicultural practice, minimum alcohol content, and chaptalisation.

The failure of the 1905 and 1908 legislations was accepted and they were withdrawn and in 1911 an attempt was made to introduce laws which would go a long way to enforcing wine quality. It failed as the vineyard owners who had been free to plant whatever grape variety they wished in the 'sacred' soil of a once great vineyard opposed the proposed regulations with the rallying cry '*can you contest the right of a cultivator to make what use he pleases of the name of his property and the fruit of his soil.*'

A further unsuccessful attempt was made in 1914 when Deputy Jenouvrier pointed out that the reputation of the great vineyards and the fine wines which they had produced should not be sullied by individual materialistic practices. '*The reputation attached to these products is the result of the sustained effort of successive generations; the fruit of their combined labour became famous, and the proprietorial right was thus established for the whole commune or region.*'

After the war new legislation was passed in 1919. It was again opposed as in modern terminology it contravened the human rights of the wine producers who were prepared to litigate to protect what they perceived to be their 'God given rights'.

The courts also eventually ruled that the new laws indeed only applied to the control of geographical location and the legislation had again failed to impose any order in the production of wine.

The only thing that could bring about a change in this disastrous situation was a major consumer backlash and this is exactly what happened.

The recalcitrant wine producers who had opposed the imposition of governmental regulations, to control quality, realised that 'the game was up'. Nevertheless many years rolled by before regulations became enforceable.

On 30th July 1935 the Institut National des Appellations d'Origine (INAO)*** was created by decree. This organisation issues Appellation d'Origine Contrôlée (AOC) which define the regulations which the wine

---

*** now Institut National de l'Origine et de la Qualite, but remains as the acronym INAO

producers are required to comply with.

Clearly the stringency of the regulations vary considerably as for instance in Burgundy between those that apply to a Grand Cru and those for a generic Bourgogne AOC. On this basis the AOC's cover the complete quality spectrum for each wine region. It is also important to note that in drawing up the AOC's the INAO does so only after detailed consultation with the wine producer to whom the regulations will apply.

And so finally there was effective governmental control over the principal aspects of wine production namely the defining of geographical area, grape variety, vinicultural practice, yield, and chapalization. It is important to note at this point that although the AOC regulations ensure that basic quality requirements are complied with they do not influence the level of excellence of the wine produced. This, of course, depends entirely on the expertise, skill and dedication of the winemaker.

The governmental action through the INAO did indeed have the desired affect and French wines, and in particular those of Burgundy and Bordeaux, regained their international reputation for exceptional quality.

B – THE AOC'S OF BURGUNDY AND THE CLASSIFICATION SYSTEM (AND AOC'S) OF BORDEAUX

BURGUNDY

There is no classification of Burgundy wines. There is however a comprehensive AOC system which, in ascending order of quality and stringency of regulations which have to be met are:

I – THE APPELLATIONS

1. Bourgogne AOC – This is the generic or commercial wine of Burgundy and providing the wine is made from Burgundy grapes, which can be blended from different locations, and the INAO regulations are met the 'Bourgogne AOC' can be displayed on the bottle label. The maximum yield for the AOC is 55 hl/ha.

2. *Sub-Region AOC's*

Burgundy has six sub-regions:-

Beaujolais***	*Côte de Beaune**
Mâconnais	*Côte de Nuit**
Côte de Châlonnaise	*Chablis***

* *together the Côte d'Or*
** *Chablis has a different appellation structure and is dealt with separately at the end of*
   this section
*** *Beaujolais is <u>officially</u> not part of the Burgundy wine region but is generally treated as a*
   Burgundy sub-region

Each sub-region has its own AOC and any wine produced from grapes from within the boundaries of a sub-region from a single vineyard or blended from several can use that sub-region's AOC providing it satisfies the regulations which apply to it. These are slightly more demanding than those of Bourgogne AOC.

3. *Commune AOC's*

Each sub-region is divided into a number of wine producing communes (viticultural areas) and each commune has its own AOC. The Burgundy wine sub-regions and their communes are:-

BEAUJOLAIS	MÂCONNAIS	CÔTE DE CHÂLONNAISE
Saint Amour	Mâcon	Bouzeron
Juliénas	Saint Véran	Rully
Chénas	Pouilly Fuissé	Mercurey
Moulin-à-Vent		Givrey
Fleurie		Montagny
Chiroubles		
Morgon		
Régnié		
Brouilly		
Côte de Brouilly		
These communes are		
designated Cru Beaujolais		

CÔTE DE BEAUNE	CÔTE DE NUIT	CHABLIS
Aloxe Corton	Fixin	In Chablis the
Pernand-Vergelesses	Geverey	appellations are
	Chambertin	not by vineyard
Savigny-lès-Beaune	Morey St Denis	which are clas-
Chorey-Les-Beaune	Chambolle-	sified as Grand
	Musigny	Cru, Villages,
		and Petit Chablis
Beaune	Vougeot	and are dealt with
Pommard	Flagey Echézaux	separately at the
Volnay	Nuits St Georges	end of this section
Monthélie		
Auxey-Duresses		
Saint Roman		
Meursault		
Puligny-Montrachet		
Chassagne-Montrachet		
Saint Aubin		
Santenay		

Again the wine from a single vineyard or blends from several from within the boundaries of a commune can use the commune AOC for its wines providing it meets those AOC regulations which in the ascending quality regulations are more stringent than those of the sub-region AOC. With regard to commune AOC's the communes of one sub-region, Beaujolais, differs from all the others in the Burgundy wine region. There are ten named communes of Beaujolais located in the northern part of the sub-region, and they are, designated 'Cru Beaujolais'. Most of the vineyards outside these communes would qualify as Beaujolais-Villages AOC or Beaujolais AOC. The latter would mainly finish up as Beaujolais Nouveau which is disallowed for the 'Cru' vineyards and generally not used as such by the Beaujolais-Villages vineyards through choice. The vineyards of the Cru Beaujolais communes are allowed to label their wines with the name of the vineyard and the commune and are not obliged to mention 'Beaujolais' which none do as they prefer not to be identified with the other wines of the sub-region. The vineyards of Beaujolais are not able to aspire to the highest designations, Grand Cru and Premier Cru as these are confined to wines from the Pinot Noir and Chardonnay grapes and Beaujolais wine is produced mainly from the Gamay grape. In Chablis there are 27 communes but they are not designated as AOC viticultural areas and individual vineyards qualify for the designations in highest to lowest quality order – Grand Cru, Premier Cru, Villages, Petit Chablis.

4. Villages AOC

As we ascend the quality hierarchy the Villages AOC is next and there are 42 in Burgundy (which is exactly the same number as those for the whole of Bordeaux).

A Villages AOC applies to the wines produced from grapes from within a delineated viticultural area around a wine commune. The villages areas can be large (Gevrey-Chambertin Villages – 360 hectares) or smaller (Morey-St-Denis Villages – 64 hectares).

The wines can be produced from grapes from a single vineyard or blended from those from several within the designated Villages area.

If the wine is produced from a single vineyard then the name of the vineyard and that of the commune and the appellation – Villages AOC are displayed on the label.

Where a wine is produced by blending from several vineyards from within the Villages area then only the name of the commune and appellation are displayed on the label.

From the foregoing it can be seen that a wide range of wines of differing quality and price have almost identical labels.

5. Premier Cru

We are now at the penultimate quality level – Premier Cru of which Burgundy has 669, details of these are provided in Appendix I, and all are restricted to the Pinot Noir and Chardonnay grapes.

The Premier Cru appellations are granted to a number of climats located in the delineated Premier Cru areas of the principal wine communes.

As with the villages appellations the Premier Cru wines can be from a single vineyard or blended from wines from a number of Premier Cru vineyards from within the same commune. For instance Chambolle-Musigny has 25 Premier Cru vineyards and a Premier Cru wine blended from a number of these vineyards would state on the label *Chambolle-Musigny Premier Cru* whereas when the wine is from a single vineyard the name of the vineyard would <u>also</u> be displayed on the label – *Chambolle-Musigny, Premier Cru, Les Charmes*.

It is at this level in the Burgundy quality hierarchy that there is multiple vineyard ownership and all are allowed to display 'Premier Cru' on their labels, providing they meet the INAO regulations, but the quality of the wine in the bottle does not depend solely on this but the dedication and expertise of the individual winemakers and the variations in the quality of the terroir within the vineyard particularly where the vineyard covers a large area as it does for instance at Clos Vougeot. The right to blend from several Premier Cru vineyards combined with multiple vineyard owner-ship and producers results in a wide range in quality and price of wines which are similarly labelled.

6. *Grand Cru AOC*

This is the pinnacle of the quality hierarchy and was granted to vineyards of special historical renown and reputation. The selection of certain vineyards of exceptional standing goes back to 1831 when Denis Morelot published his book *La Vigne et le Vin en Côte d'Or* and in 1855 Dr Jules Lavalle followed up Morelot book with *Histoire et Statistique de la Vigne de Grands Vins de la Côte-d'Or* which provided an unofficial classification of the Burgundy vineyards in five classes – *hors ligne, tete de cuvée, 1ere cuvée, 2eme cuvée, and 3eme cuvée*. This was adopted in modi-fied form by the Beaune Committee of Agriculture in 1861. When the INAO decided on the Grand Cru vineyards in 1936 they were based on the cuvée of the old classification. Burgundy has 39 Grand Cru vineyards (Côte-de-Beaune 8, Côte-de-Nuit 24, Chablis 7).

Details of the distribution of the Grand Cru vineyards across the Burgundy sub-regions and communes is given in Appendix I. The fol-lowing is an alphabetical listing of the Grand Crus of the Côte de Beaune and the Côte de Nuits.

THE WINES OF BURGUNDY AND BORDEAUX

Bâtard-Montrachet	*Criots-Bâtard-Montrachet*
Bienvenues-Bâtard-Montrachet	Échezeaux
Bonnes-Mares	Grand Échezeaux
Chablis Grand Cru	Griotte-Chambertin
Chambertin	La Grande Rue
Chambertin-Clos de Bèze	La Romanée
Chapelle-Chambertin	La Tâche
Charlemagne	Latricières-Chambertin
Charmes-Chambertin	Mazis-Chambertin
Chevalier-Montrachet	Mazoyères-Chambertin
Clos de la Roche	*Montrachet*
Clos de Tart	Musigny
Clos de Vougeot	Richebourge
Clos des Lambrays	Romanée-Conti
Clos Saint denis	Romanée-Saint-Vivant
Corton	Ruchottes-Chambertin
Corton-Charlemagne	

The Grand Cru vineyards of the Côte de Beaune are shown in italics.

The Chablis sub-region has 7 Grand Cru vineyards (one unofficial) – details are given section III Chablis.

The multiple ownership of vineyards is very much a feature of Burgundy and the background to it, the selling off of the church's vineyards by the state and the enactment of the Napoleonic Code of Inheritance is addressed in the main text. The end result is wines of a significant range in quality being labelled identically except for the name of the producer or negociant. The focal point for this has been the great and historically famous Grand Cru vineyard of Clos Vougeot. It has around 80 individual owners who produce wine individually, collectively or through négociants.

II – THE GRAND CRU VINEYARDS AND THE PREMIER CRU CLIMATS OF BURGUNDY – AN OVERVIEW

SUB-REGION	GRAND CRU VINEYARDS	PREMIER CRU CLIMATS
Beaujolais	0	0
Mâconnais	0	0
Côte Châlonnaise	–	132*
Côte de Beaune	8	303
Côte de Nuit	24	145
Chablis	7	89
	39	**669**

*The commune of Montagny which produces white wine from the Chardonnay grape is uniquely allowed to qualify for Premier Cru status if its wines exceed 11.5% alcohol which results in this commune having 49 Premier Cru vineyards.

III – CHABLIS

Chablis has four appellations which in order of quality and stringency of regulations, from lowest to highest, are:-

Petit Chablis AOC
Chablis AOC (which is the equivalent of a 'Villages' AOC)
Premier Cru AOC
Grand Cru AOC

a. Petit Chablis AOC
The AOC was created in 1944 and is the 'generic' or 'commercial' Chablis wine. The vineyards are located on the plateau above the Premier Cru and Grand Cru viticultural areas and have a less favourable 'terroir'. The wines are generally light and fragrant but do not have the same depth and complexity of the wines of their illustrious neighbours.

b. Chablis AOC
This is the 'villages' appellation of Chablis and was introduced in 1938. It is by far the largest producer of Chablis with more than 60% of total

production. The quality lies between the wines of Petit Chablis and the exceptional Premier and Grand Cru wines.

c. Premier Cru AOC

This is an exceptional appellation insofar as the Premier Cru delineated areas are not around principal wine communes as they are elsewhere in the Burgundy sub-regions of Côte Châlonnaise, Côte de Beaune, and Côte de Nuits but in delineated areas around a number of designated 'principal' vineyards of which there are 17 (and these are referred to as the 'umbrella vineyards'). The other vineyards within these delineated areas also qualify as Premier Cru vineyards providing they meet the relevant INAO regulations.

Furthermore these vineyards <u>may</u> label their wines, not with the name of the vineyard where they were produced, but the name of their 'principal' or 'umbrella' vineyard. There are 72 of these 'umbrella related' Premier Cru vineyards which results in a total number of 89 Chablis Premier Cru vineyards.

THE 89 PREMIER CRU VINEYARDS OF CHABLIS – THE 17 'UMBRELLA' VINEYARDS ARE IN BOLD TYPE

♦ **Mont de Milieu** –
Vallée de Chigot

♦ **Montée de Tonnerre** –
Chapelot, Les Chapelots, Pied d'Aloup, Sous Pied d'Aloup, Côte de Bréchain

♦ **Fourchaume** –
Vaupulent, Vau Pulan, Les Vaupulans, La Fourchaume, Côte de Fontenay, Dine-Chien, L'Homme Mort, La Grande Côte, Bois Seguin, OL'Ardillier, Vaulorent, Les Quatre chemins, La ferme couverte, Les Couvertes

- **Vaillons** –
Sur les Vaillons, Chatains, Les Grands Chaumes, Les Chatains, Sécher, Beugnons, Les Beugnons, Les Lys, Champlain, Mélinots, Les Minos, Roncières, Les Epinottes

- **Montmains** –
Les Monts Mains, Forêts, Les Forêts, Butteaux, Les Bouts des Butteaux, Vaux Miolot, Le Milieu des Butteaux, Les Ecueillis, Vaugerlains

- **Côte de Léchet** –
Le Château

- **Beauroy** –
Sous Boroy, Vallée des Vaux, Benfer, Troesmes, Côte de Troesmes, Adroit de Vau Renard, Côte de Savant, Le Cotat-Château, Frouquelin, Le Verger

- **Vauligneau** –
Vau de Longue, Vau Girault, La Forêt, Sur la Forêt

- **Vaudevey** –
La Grande Chaume, Vaux Ragons, Vignes des Vaux Ragons

- **Vaucoupin** –
Adroit de Vaucopins

- **Vosgros** –
Adroit de Vosgros, Vaugiraut

- **Les Fourneaux** –
Morein, Côte des Près Girots, La Côte, Sur la Côte

- **Côte de Vaubarousse**
- **Berdiot**
- **Chaume de Talvat**

- ◆ **Côte de Jouan**
- ◆ **Les Beauregards –**
  Hauts des Chambres du Roi, Côte de Cuissy, Les corvées, Bec d
  Oiseau, Vallée de Cuissy

d. Grand Cru AOC

This is the appellation which is at the top of the Chablis quality hierarchy.
Chablis has seven Grand Cru vineyards which produce only 3% of the
total Chablis production. One of the seven vineyards, La Moutonne, is
'unofficial' as it is recognised by the Burgundy Syndicate (BIVB) but not
the INAO and declares this status on its label.

   The seven Chablis Grand Cru vineyards:-

- ■ Les Preuses
- ■ Vaudésir
- ■ Grenouilles
- ■ Valmur
- ■ Les Clos
- ■ Blanchot
- ■ (unofficial) La Moutonne

An important development in Chablis in respect of the Grand Crus was the
founding of the L'Union des Grand Crus de Chablis (UGCC), launched in
March 2000, this syndicate is restricted to Grand Cru proprietors and has
a single purpose: 'To defend and promote the quality of Chablis Grand
Cru wines'. All members are bound to abide by a charter which covers
all aspects of wine making and sales (e.g. density of new plantings, limit-
ing yields and selling dates). Grand Cru makers must submit their wines
to a tasting committee of other Union members to ensure they meet the
required quality.

BORDEAUX

Bordeaux, unlike Burgundy, has persisted with the official classification
of the châteaux of a number of its sub-regions.

   It started in 1855 with the official classification of the Châteaux of

Médoc (plus Haut Brion) and those of Sauternes/Barsac. These classifications, although not updated, have nevertheless retained their prestigious status to the present day.

The sub-regions of St Émilion, Graves, and the Cru Bourgeois of the Médoc have modern classifications.

Details of the foregoing are included in Appendix 2.

The Bordeaux sub-regions and their appellations and classifications are:-

1. POMEROL

Pomerol has no classification and no commune AOC's. The great wines of Pètrus and La Conseillante down to the simplest wines of Pomerol all use the designation on their bottle labels the sub-region AOC '*Appellation Pomerol Contrôlée*'.

2. ST ÉMILION

In 1955 the principal châteaux of St Émilion were classified in two groups:-

Thirteen châteaux were designated First Great Growths – *Premier Grand Cru Classé*. Fifty-five châteaux designated Great Growths – *Grand Cru Classé*. The listing within these two groups is in alphabetical order and not in order of quality. This approach to quality classification is not at all helpful in wine selection as clearly there is a considerable quality variation in the first group of 13 and certainly in the second large group of 55 but as the listing of both groups is in alphabetical order it follows that the wines in each group are designated equal in quality which of course is not the case. This policy applies to all the current official classifications.

The intention was to update the 1955 classification every 10 years. The last update in 2006 was legally challenged and suspended and the 1996 version remained in effect. The 2006 version was subsequently reinstated and then replaced by a 2012 version, details of which are given in Appendix 2(A).

3. MÉDOC CRU BOURGEOIS

In 1855 sixty châteaux of the Médoc were classified and as a result of this became internationally famous and remain so to the present day.

Those châteaux not classified at that time remained in the shadows of these great châteaux and still do although many have now reached, and in some cases exceeded the wine quality of their illustrious neighbours. They are known as Cru Bourgeois and for knowledgeable wine enthusiasts often represent outstanding quality and value.

As part of the move in the earlier part of the 20th century to centralise the quality control of wine production through governmental regulations attempts were made to classify the Cru Bourgeois châteaux of the Médoc.

This was finally achieved in 1932 when 444 Cru Bourgeois château were classified as follows:

Crus Bourgeois Superieurs Exceptionnels	6
Crus Bourgeois Superiors	99
Crus Bourgeois	339

In 1966 an organisation was formed by the Bourgeois châteaux – the Syndicat des Cru Bourgeois. In 1978 the Syndicat issued a new classification of 127 châteaux as follows:-

Cru Grand Bourgeois Exceptionnel	18
Grand Cru Bourgeois	41
Crus Bourgeois	68

This classification is considered by a number of wine experts as unrepresentative as only members of the Syndicat are eligible for inclusion. A number of outstanding wine producers refused to join the Syndicat and were excluded.

4. MÉDOC

The great châteaux of Médoc do not have a modern classification and the famous communes of Pauillac, Margaux, St Estèphe and St Julien each have their own commune AOC's which they display on their bottle labels. These châteaux, with a single exception, made up the entire 1855 Official Classification, for red wine, and 3 of the 5 first growths are from the commune of Pauillac. And so the label of one of the world's most famous wine, Château Lafite, simply displays on the labels of its bottles 'Appellation Pauillac Contrôlée'. They do however continue to retain the right to display their 1855 classification status – Premier Grand Cru (first growths) and Grand Cru (other growths) and a number of châteaux choose to do so.

5. GRAVES

The wines of Graves were first classified in 1953 and confirmed in 1959 since when it has not been updated. It is the only Bordeaux classification which covers both red and dry white wines. All the classified Graves wines are from the northern part of Graves and immediately adjacent to the city of Bordeaux – an area referred to as Pessac-Léognan which has six important wine producing communes – Pessac, Léognan, Cadaujac, Talence, Mortillac and Villenave d'Ornon.

The oldest and one of the most famous wine estates of Bordeaux, Château Haut Brion, is located in the commune of Pessac. From the time of King Henry II and his wife, Eleanor of Aquitaine, the 12th century England was a major export market for Bordeaux's 'claret'. Its first written mention however was in the diary of Samuel Pepys in 1663 *'to the Royal Oake Tavern and here drank a sort of French wine called Ho Bryen, that hath a good and most peculiar taste that I have never met with'*. It was John Evelyn who in 1683 refers to the owner of the vineyard as 'O'Brien' with Haut Brion being the French version of that name but there is no valid historical record of this.

The 1959 Official Classification of Graves has 13 châteaux producing red wine and 9 producing dry white wine. This red wine classification is topped by Château Haut Brion (described on its bottle label as Premier Grand Cru Classé based on its first growth status of the 1855 classification) and the other 12 are listed in alphabetical order as are the 9 white wines. This is again very little help to wine selection on the basis of quality except that the classified wines are presumed to be superior to those which are not.

6. SAUTERNES/BARSAC

At the southern end of Graves this is the most southerly of the Bordeaux sub-regions and is world famous for its sweet white wines. The complex and costly wine making process is described in Appendix 2(D). At the time of the 1855 Official Classification of the red wines of the Médoc (plus Haut Brion) the sweet white wines of Sauternes/Barsac were also officially classified in respect of quality. Château d'Yquem tops the classification as the only 'First Great Growth' and is a 'Premier Grand Cru Classé'. The second grouping of 11 First Growths châteaux are designated 'Premier Cru Classé.' The third grouping of 14 'Second Growths' châteaux are 'Deuxieme Cru Classé'. The 1855 Official Classification has not been updated although changes have occurred through the demise, portioning, and merging of vineyards.

BURGUNDY AND BORDEAUX

SIZE, WINE PRODUCTION AND THE NUMBER OF AOC'S OF BURGUNDY AND BORDEAUX – AN OVERVIEW

Of all the wine regions of France Burgundy has the greatest number of AOC's. If Beaujolais is included Burgundy has almost three times the number of AOC's than Bordeaux although it is less than half the size in terms of viticultural area and wine produced.

	HECTARES UNDER VINE	HECTOLITRES PRODUCED ANNUALLY	BOTTLES PRODUCED ANNUALLY	NUMBER OF AOC'S
BORDEAUX	120,000	5 MILLION	670 MILLION	42
BURGUNDY	27,700	1.5 MILLION	200 MILLION	99
BEAUJOLAIS	19,000	0.825 MILLION	110 MILLION	14
BURGUNDY + BEAUJOLAIS	46,700	2.325 MILLION	310 MILLION	113

APPENDIX 4

WINE TASTING

"An old wine-bibber having been smashed in a railway collision, some wine was poured on his lips, to revive him. 'Pauillac, 1873,' he murmured and died."
AMBROSE BIERCE
Enlarged Devil's Dictionary.

The tasting of wine to determine its characteristics and quality (and therefore, inevitably, its market price) has an important role to play in the wine trade. The wine experts with their superior noses and palates (which are often heavily insured) guide those of us who are not so blessed. Wine tasting is also used in 'blind tasting' to try and identify the region, vineyard, and vintage of a wine whose label is covered or has been removed, which is also an important part of the examinations for the prestigious 'Master of Wine' qualification.

Wine over the centuries has always been viewed, inhaled, tasted and commented upon as an important part of its enjoyment. Many of the 'great and the good' participated and their comments recorded for posterity.

Talleyrand, an important figure in revolutionary France, enjoyed his wine and Chambertin in particular:-

"Sir, when one is served such a wine, one takes the glass respectfully, looks at it, inhales it, then having put it down once discusses it."

King Edward VII of England also described his approach to wine tasting:

"Not only does one drink wine, but one inhales it, one looks at it, one tastes it, one swallows it…and one talks about it."

188/600   Stewed Cabbage

203/600   Dull & Oily

Clearly wine tasting is not a simple process and a great deal has been written on the subject. Michael Broadbent has published an informative, landmark book on the subject and many other wine writers offer expert advice.

There is however a basic order in which this fascinating and enjoyable experience proceeds.

The first step is visual as the wine is first defined by its colour which varies for both red and white wine, over a wide spectrum. The white wines of Chablis, Meursault, and Sauternes have quite different colours (basically yellow-green, straw, and gold). The colour of red wine varies from purple to brick red. The colour of wine changes with age some of which are beneficial like the darkening and progression to a red-orange hue of fine red wines to the undesirable colour of daffodils in dry white wines which usually signals their demise. Clarity is also of great importance as a cloudy wine is generally unsatisfactory in both appearance and taste.

However the most important part of wine tasting is smell and taste or in more polite 'winespeak' terms (humourously depicted by Ronald Searle) 'nose' and 'palate'.

The nose comes first and what it receives is the evaporation of the complex esters and ethers contained in the wine. The smell changes from that of the initial opening of the wine referred to as 'bouquet' to a different lingering smell which is called the 'aroma'. This important event will of course only be successful if the wine is properly prepared. This means that it should not be too cold and has had sufficient time for the contact with the air, after the removal of the cork, to create evaporation known as 'breathing' and some wines are decanted to accelerate this.

A characteristic of younger wines is that they have a bouquet of 'fruit' and are described as such (raspberries, strawberries, cherry, plum, etc.) which are also detected in the taste. Just as the nose detects the initial 'bouquet' and the subsequent 'aroma' the palate also identifies an immediate taste and then a sensation known as 'aftertaste', and the length of time this taste remains is referred to as 'finish'. Furthermore as wine changes colour with age so does, of course, the nose and the taste and this is why great red wines are 'laid down' for many years and fine white wines also but for a much shorter period. This process is often colourfully described by the wine experts:-

"Strawberry, cherry, raspberry, and plum predominant in the young wine, but as it ages, the cherry becomes more scented, the plums turn to prunes, chocolate and wood smoke and figs mingle with truffles and over-hung game and the decayed stink of old vegetables."

Oz Clarke
Sainsbury's Regional Wine Guide

Another important feature of wine detected through tasting is 'body' and wines are described as light, medium or full bodied.

The key to a great wine is 'balance' of its differing characteristics – acidity, fruit, alcohol, body, and tannin and when this is achieved there is the sensation of smoothness, finesse, and harmony.

Like many other aspects of the modern wine trade the tasting and evaluation of fine wines and the sophisticated and colourful notes which follow is very much the territory of the international wine experts and not surprisingly Robert Parker leads the way:-

"I agree that among the first growths, this wine is showing surprising forwardness and complexity in its aromatics. It possesses an exuberant, flamboyant bouquet of roasted coffee, cassis, smoky oak, and soy sauce. The impressive 1996 Mouton-Rothschild offers impressive aromas of black currants, framboise, coffee, and new saddle leather. This full-bodied, ripe, rich, concentrated, superbly balanced wine is paradoxical in the sense that the aromatics suggest a far more evolved wine than the flavours reveal."

Although having the greatest respect for the undoubted expertise, integrity, and venerable noses and palates of the eminent wine experts nevertheless a degree of light hearted cynicism is inevitable, and particularly so when they are, imitated by 'claret man' who, declares that the "club red has a touch of absinthe combined with liquorice and old leather." And so wine tasting has also become fertile ground for the cynics:-

JOHN STEED – THE AVENGERS
'SOUTHERN END OF THE VINEYARD'

- *'Wine tasting is the last refuge of the wine snob'*
- *'Wine tasting notes evolved in the school for horoscope writers'*
- *'I am sure that it will be possible to load the equivalent of a kaleidoscope with wine tasting terms and give it a shake after each tasting'*

For the second part of wine tasting, that of identifying a wine, details of which are not divulged to the taster, has an important role to play in the 'Master of Wine' exams but otherwise is usually a fun social occasion.

Even the eminent, Michael Broadbent, introduces a little entertaining cynicism here:-

"A sight of the label is worth fifty years experience."

However a favourite story comes from the television series 'The Avengers'. John Steed is the quintessential English 'gent' – bowler hat, pinstripe suit, rolled umbrella and of course always understated. He together with his usual beautiful colleague (I believe Diana Rigg on this occasion) are invited to a French Château and the host announces a pre-dinner wine tasting. It went like this:-

'Steed you will take part?'

'No not really, not my subject you know.'

'Oh, come on Steed at least try, be a sport.'

Steed takes a tentative sip and says, *'Ah, a lovely Chambertin.'*

'That is amazing Steed, it is indeed a Chambertin so please continue'

'No, no I was probably a little lucky.'

Nevertheless another sip and, *'1959 was indeed a great vintage.'*

'That is quite amazing, Steed, it is indeed a 1959 Chambertin.'

By this time the whole room was clamouring for Steed to continue. He diffidently took another sip and *'Clos St Jacque produces a wonderful Chambertin.'*

The whole room was now silenced as indeed the 1959 Chambertin was from the vineyard of Clos St Jacque.

A lone voice calls out, 'Come on Steed one more try.'

With a wry smile Steed takes one more sip and pronounces, *'Southern end of the vineyard.'*

APPENDIX 5

VINTAGE CHARTS

When the wine list or carte des vin arrives and the sommelier briefly departs then it is time for a furtive look at the vintage chart. Unfortunately the light is poor and the all important scores are small and the selection of the better vintage is once more a stab in the dark. Vintage selection also clearly depends on the climatic conditions of each wine region. Burgundy and Bordeaux have seasons ranging from glorious to wipe-out whereas Chile, Australia, and South Africa are not so highly weather sensitive and vintage choice becomes less critical.

Vintage charts exist in profusion as all the diaries seem to have them and wine merchants, hoping to influence choice, hand out pocket size vintage cards. Different methods of scoring are used. Robert Parker of course scores out of 100 and embellishes his chart with three colours. Others score out of 10, 5 or even 7. Wine glasses are depicted filled to different levels with some upright and others at a 45° angle. Michael Broadbent, the recognised authority on wine vintages, uses stars. So, why not create another presentation without numbers, colours, or stars and simply list the years under *'exceptional'*, *'great'*, *'excellent to good'*, and *'avoid'*.

Here is the idea and you can always make up your own version and include Rhône, Tuscan, Spanish wines etc.

BURGUNDY AND BORDEAUX VINTAGES
BORDEAUX 1990–2013
BURGUNDY 1990–2012

VINTAGE RANKING				
SUB-REGION	EXCEPTIONAL 96–100	**GREAT** **90–95**	**EXCELLENT** **TO GOOD** **85–89**	AVOID -84%
BORDEAUX ST JULIEN PAUILLAC ST ESTÈPHE	10, 09, 00, 96, 90 21%	08, 05, 03, 95 17%	12, 11, 07, 06, 04, 02, 01, 99, 98, 94 41%	13, 97, 93, 92, 91 21%
MARGAUX	09, 05 8%	10, 08, 00, 90 17%	12, 11, 07, 06, 04, 03, 02, 01, 99, 98, 96, 98, 96, 95, 94 54%	13, 97, 93, 92, 91 21%
GRAVES	10, 09, 05, 00 17%	08, 98, 90 13%	12, 11, 07, 06, 04, 03, 02, 01, 99, 97, 96, 95, 94, 93 57%	13, 92, 91 13%
POMEROL	09, 08, 00, 98 17%	12, 10, 06, 05, 01, 95, 90 29%	11, 07, 04, 02, 99, 97, 96, 94, 93 37%	13, 03, 92, 91 17%
ST ÉMILION	05, 00, 98, 90 17%	10, 09, 08, 03, 01 21%	12, 11, 07, 06, 04, 02, 99, 97, 96, 95, 94 45%	13, 93, 92, 91 17%
BARSAC-SAUTERNES	09, 05, 01, 90 17%	13, 11, 10, 07, 03 21%	12, 08, 06, 02, 00, 99, 98, 97, 96, 95 41%	94, 94, 93, 92, 91 21%
BURGUNDY CÔTE DE NUIT (RED)	10, 05 9%	12, 11, 09, 03, 02, 99, 97, 96, 95, 90 43%	08, 06, 04, 00, 93, 91 26%	07, 01, 98, 94, 92 22%
CÔTE DE BEAUNE (RED)	05 4%	12, 11, 10, 09, 02, 99, 97, 96, 90 40%	08, 07, 06, 03, 02, 00, 98, 97, 96, 95, 92, 91 13%	07, 06, 04, 01, 00, 98, 94, 93, 92, 91 43%
CÔTE DE BEAUNE (WHITE)	 0%	12, 11, 10, 09, 08, 07, 06, 05, 04, 02, 96, 95, 92 56%	01, 00, 99, 97, 90 22%	03, 98, 94, 93, 91 22%

APPENDIX 6

<u>MODERN WINEMAKING</u>

INTRODUCTION

The basic process of making wine from the grape was not created by man but has always existed in nature. The grape is unique insofar as its juice has a high level of sugar (around 30%) and as it ripens yeast collects on its skin and if the skin is split the yeast acts on the sugar of the juice and converts it into alcohol and carbon dioxide (the modern term for this process is fermentation). If the effect of the yeast expires before all the sugar is converted the result is a sweet low alcohol content wine (port is an example of this but its alcohol level is then raised by fortifying it with brandy). If the sugar is completely converted then a 'dry' wine results. This natural process was used by the ancient civilisations going back some 5000 years.

What modern man has now achieved is an in-depth scientific understanding of the basic process of converting the sugar in the grape juice into alcohol to create wine. As a result of this winemakers of today are more able to effectively understand and control the winemaking operation. This has been a major contributory factor in wines of quality being consistently produced in many countries around the world, and, particularly, those of the new world, Chile, South Africa, Australia and New Zealand. It should of course be emphasised that the scientifically based approach to winemaking does not mean that fine wine can be simply produced by a qualified chemist. Present day winemakers although using scientifically based techniques and equipment still need vast experience and a comprehensive understanding of the extensive and important nuances which apply to winemaking which will mean the difference between the wine being of the highest standard of excellence or a wine which is not so. This fundamental change in the approach to winemaking is encapsulated by one of the most distinguished and prolific modern writers on wine,

Hugh Johnson, in the foreword to the 1974 edition of his landmark book 'Wine':-

> *"Far more significant than commercial, legal or even social change has been the revolution in wine technology. Eight years ago there were a few individuals, mostly in universities, who fully understood the controls necessary to make thoroughly good wine. Today wine-science is almost universal. Eight years ago good wine was the exception: the bulk of the world's wine was mediocre. Today good wine is the rule: a real old-fashioned bad wine is getting hard to find."*

WINEMAKING

Winemaking has its own distinctive vocabulary which is used and defined in the following outline of the winemaking process.

After the harvesting of the grapes (*VENDANGE*) the first operation is to ensure that only undamaged healthy, ripe grapes pass on to the winemaking process. The next is to remove and reject all or part of the stems. The benefit of retaining stems for the making of red wine is that they contain tannin which is necessary for the longevity of red wine. The winemakers who oppose the use of stems argue that the tannin present in the skins of the grape is sufficient to ensure longevity and is preferable to the inferior 'vegetal' tannin of the stems which also absorb colour. For white wine, longevity is achieved through the retention of the natural acids of the grape. Tannin in white wine is undesirable as it spoils the taste and total de-stemming is undertaken before the grapes are crushed. However some winemakers re-introduce stems into the press to improve and increase the flow of the juice. De-stemming (*EGRAPPAGE*) policy differs between Burgundy and Bordeaux. This is partly due to the use of different grape varieties which of course have different characteristics. In particular skin thicknesses vary as does the level of tannin in the skins.

For Bordeaux, Cabernet Sauvignon is a late ripening thick skinned grape the skins of which contain a relatively high level of tannin. The Merlot grape has almost exactly the opposite characteristics. This grape variety, used primarily on the right bank, is now being used more extensively in the blends of the left bank. In Bordeaux a total de-stemming policy is adopted by most of the châteaux.

In Burgundy the red wine is produced from the Pinot Noir grape which has a thin skin which is relatively low in tannin. Partial de-stemming is used in most of the Burgundy vineyards which is also related to the vintage (the general rule being the better the vintage the higher the retention of stems). Romanée Conti, one of the greatest of the great wines of Burgundy, did not de-stem for the excellent 1999 and 2005 vintages and, for lesser vintages, 50–80% of the stems are retained. However for most Burgundy wineyards lower levels of stems are retained normally in the range 20–30%.

After grapes, suitable for processing, have been selected and de-stemmed either partially or completely the grapes are initially crushed to split the skin and release the juice. The resulting mixture of juice (and young red wine after the start of fermentation) and the solid parts of the grape is known as '*MUST*'. The solid part (skins, stems, and seeds) is known as '*POMACE*'. The transfer to and the absorption by the white wine fruit juice or the young red wine of elements contained in the pomace is known as '*MACERATION*' and what is extracted is known as '*MATTIERE*'.

The maceration time *('CUVAISON')* for white wines is very short as the winemaker must avoid the juice absorbing tannin and colouring from the skins which would result in an undesirable taste and a greyish discolouration of the wine. The longevity of white wine, in the absence of tannin, has to be through the natural acidity of the grape which has to be retained and carefully balanced against alcohol and fruit. This process eliminates most of the natural anti-oxidants and prevention of oxidation throughout the winemaking has to be carefully managed. This has to be achieved through scrupulous hygiene and the use of sulphur dioxide as a disinfectant the use of which has to be kept to an absolute minimum. It also follows that harvesting of the grapes has to be carried out with special care and any split or unhealthy grapes eliminated.

During and after maceration of the red wine and after the extraction of juice for white wine the primary fermentation takes place (natural and cultured yeast causing sugar to be converted to alcohol and carbon dioxide). At some point in the winemaking process a secondary malolactic fermentation occurs (certain bacteria causing malic acid to be converted to lactic acid and carbon dioxide). The winemaker needs to ensure that this occurs before bottling where it has no deleterious affect except a small reduction in acidity (and is beneficial in many red wines) or controls it or prevents it through the use of sulpur dioxide. If it occurs in the bottle the carbon dioxide generated is trapped and a 'gassy' or turgid wine results.

For red wine the longer maceration period means that the fermentation process also occurs simultaneously due to the presence of natural yeast often together with the addition of cultured yeast which is used to control and maintain the fermentation. At this point the winemaker also has to decide whether to add sugar ('*CHAPTALISE*'). This is necessary where the natural sugar content would result in an alcohol level of less than 12%. Chaptalisation is used extensively in both Burgundy and Bordeax. It is however not permitted in a number of wine producing countries including Austria, Italy, South Africa and Australia. As carbon dioxide is generated the gas pushes the pomace to the surface of the fermenting vessel forming what is referred to as a '*CAP*' which reduces contact with the juice now being converted into alcohol. To increase contact the juice is either pumped over the cap ('*REMONTAGE*') or it is pushed down depending on the degree of maceration which the winemaker requires. The fermentation process generates considerable heat and the temperature must be carefully controlled by the winemaker. Modern fermentation vats are stainless steel which simplifies cooling as cold water can be run over the outside surface of the vat. For red wine fermentation temperatures are usually controlled in the range 25–30°C. The higher the temperature the greater the extraction of tannin and colour from the grape skins and where this is of particular importance for the winemaker temperatures can be allowed to rise to 33°C but not without the considerable risk of a ruined wine as the yeasts are 'killed' by the temperature and the fermentation stops and is almost impossible to restart. For white wine much lower fermentation temperatures of 15–20°C are used.

Once this process has been completed the wine is 'free run' ('*VIN DE GOUTTE*') into the maturing vat and the pomace transferred to a press to extract the remaining wine. The modern press consists of a rotating perforated drum which causes the pomace to line its inner surface. A heavy duty 'balloon' is then inflated in the drum which presses the pomace against its perforated sides which squeezes out the remaining wine ('*VIN DE PRESSE*') which is coarse and tannic and the winemaker has to decide whether to blend it with the free run wine either entirely or partially or reject it.

For white wine the brief maceration process (now normally using a vinimatic) is followed by the separation of the pomace and the juice which is free run into the fermentation vat. The pomace is then pressed (in the same manner as red wine) and the last juice extracted which is blended with the free run juice in the fermentation vat, again to the extent adopted by different winemakers.

With the red wine having completed its time in the maturing vat and the wine juice having been transformed into wine in the fermentation vat (both having been earlier blended with wine or juice from their respective presses) then the next requirement is to remove the solid particles to ensure that the final wine is clear. Many of the particles, particularly the larger heavier ones, will of course automatically sink to and settle to the bottom of the vat which is known as '*DEBOURBAGE*'. What is separated from the wine is known as '*LEES*' Any particles remaining are removed through filtering and fining. The extent to which this is carried out varies considerably between different winemakers, many of whom are proud to pronounce that their wine is unfiltered or unfined or both. It is important to note, in fact, that the carry over of solid particles is also greatly reduced by the modern cylindrical presses employing a central inflatable heavy duty balloon. It is also important for limited contact to be maintained between the wine and the lees which can contribute to the body, aroma and complexity of the wine. In fact the lees at the bottom of the vat are stirred up by some winemakers, a process known as '*BATONNAGE*'. In the past there was often concern that filtration would damage or adversely change the characteristics of the wine. To a great extent this concern has been eliminated by the use of modern high tech filtering equipment. Both red and white wines are fined by adding substances, for instance egg white, bentonite etc. which sink to the bottom of the vat carrying any small particles, present in the wine, with them. The wine is finally '*RACKED*' which is the removal of the clear wine from the lees which have accumulated at the bottom of a vat or barrel into a clean barrel where the wine is then ready for bottling. Before this final step the winemaker must ensure the wine is stable. It is for instance essential that no active yeast cells and sugar remain in the bottled wine as their reaction would create carbon dioxide resulting in a 'gassy' not a still wine. Another phenomenon which the winemaker has to deal with is the crystalisation of tartaric acid present in the wine, which look like small shards of glass, which although harmless, are clearly undesirable. The solution to this problem is cold stabilisation where the wine is subjected to freezing temperatures which results in any tartrates present crystalising and settling out of the wine.

In Burgundy none of the wines are blended and in modern terminology are known as 'varietals'. In Bordeaux all the wines, both red and white, are blended. The wines from the different grape varieties are made separately and blending takes place at the end of the winemaking process when the affect of the climatic conditions on the different grape varieties in a particular year and therefore the quality of the wine which they produce is known.

The blending decision of the winemaker, in order to create the '*ENSEMBLE*', and the final blend which is bottled, is one which affects both the characteristics and quality of the wine and it also has important commercial implications.

Clearly the most successful commercial outcome would be to include in the ensemble all the wines produced from the different grape varieties of the vineyard in the 'top label' wine.

On the right bank, St Émilion and Pomerol, there are only two principal grape varieties, Merlot and Cabernet Franc. On the left bank, St Estèphe, Pauillac, St Julien, and Margaux a further important grape variety dominates – Cabernet Sauvignon. In both, minute quantities of Petit Verdot and Malbec are included. These grapes respond differently to varying climatic conditions. Merlot ripens readily whereas Cabernet Sauvignon is a slow ripening grape and in a poor summer certainly does not reach optimum ripeness for winemaking.

1998 for instance was one of the greatest vintages for Merlot based wines whereas those based primarily on Cabernet Sauvignon, on the left bank, were less distinguished and the winemakers would have maximised Merlot wine in their ensemble where it was available to them (some left bank châteaux now regularly blend around 40% Merlot in their wines).

In Sauternes/Barsac the wines are blended from Semillon (which dominates), Sauvignon Blanc, and minute amounts of Muscadelle.

The wines included in the blend of one of the great châteaux of Bordcaux would achieve very high prices (some astronomic!) whereas those wines not included would finish up in the moderately priced 'second label' wines of the châteaux or even sold off to produce very modest 'table wine'.

And so there is the temptation to include the maximum quantities of wines produced from the different grape varieties of the vineyard in the ensemble which would only be at the expense of quality. Fortunately it is almost certain that for most Bordeaux winemakers quality is the first priority.

Another major decision which the winemaker has to make is the use of oak in the winemaking process which will have an important influence on the style and characterics of the final wine which is bottled. This is not a simple decision but is multi-faceted:-

- At which stage of the winemaking process (fermenting, maturing, ageing) is the wine placed in contact with oak?

- What type of oak – French, American, Balkans – is to be used as each has special characteristics which have different affects on the wine?

- To what extent should the cooper 'toast' the barrels?

- Should new barrels or old (used) barrels be used?

- How long should the wine remain in contact with the oak?

- How large should the barrels be as the smaller the barrel the greater the oak surface contact area is in relation to the volume of wine in the barrel?

- Where the wine is in an inert (say stainless steel) container should the wine be oaked and if so should oak staves or chips (usually in porous fabric bags) be used?

In modern winemaking the wine comes into contact with oak at sometime during the production process and is essential for the creation of a wine with the style and characteristics which the winemaker sets out to achieve. The oak when expertly used results in enhanced aromas, flavours, and increased tannin. Unfortunately there was a period in the past where many wines were excessively oaked, mainly white wines made from the Chardonnay grape. This created an adverse consumer reaction and oak is now used in a more discrete manner.

It is clear from the foregoing that winemaking is a highly complex and laborious process. To produce great or excellent wine requires winemakers of vast experience, total dedication and widely versed in both the practical and scientific aspects of their profession. For all of us who enjoy and appreciate the wines which they produce we are truly indebted.

DIAGRAMMATIC
THE BASIC WINEMAKING
PROCESSES

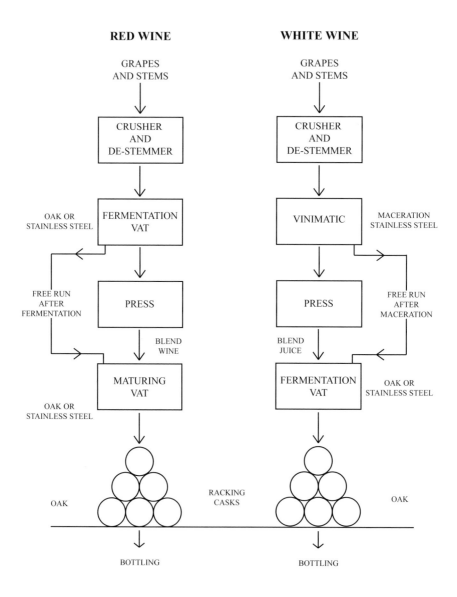

RED WINE

GRAPES
AND STEMS

CRUSHER
AND
DE-STEMMER

OAK OR
STAINLESS STEEL — FERMENTATION
VAT

FREE RUN
AFTER
FERMENTATION — PRESS

BLEND
WINE

MATURING
VAT

OAK OR
STAINLESS STEEL

OAK

BOTTLING

WHITE WINE

GRAPES
AND STEMS

CRUSHER
AND
DE-STEMMER

VINIMATIC — MACERATION
STAINLESS STEEL

PRESS — FREE RUN
AFTER
MACERATION

BLEND
JUICE

FERMENTATION
VAT — OAK OR
STAINLESS STEEL

OAK

BOTTLING

RACKING
CASKS

APPENDIX 7

A WINE MISCELLANEA

This is a collection of items and information on wine which are necessary for a fuller understanding of the subject but which cannot be readily fitted into the main text.

For instance 'yield' is an important issue in controlling wine quality and is therefore specified and controlled through the AOC regulations. Yield is expressed as hectolitres/hectare which for most conveys no meaningful understanding of this very important wine parameter and is addressed in this miscellanea.

Wine prices are particularly important to everyone involved in the wine trade whether producer, merchant, speculator, or consumer. In the main text the prices of certain exceptional wines are referred to as 'astronomical' which simply leaves the question of 'how much' unanswered. Although wine pricing is clearly a major subject in its own right a general overview is included in this miscellanea together with a number of other subjects of interest.

CONTENTS

1. YIELD

Yield is an important parameter in the production of fine wine. It is the volume (or basically the number of bottles) of wine which can be produced from a defined unit of vineyard surface area. For high quality fine wine the yield is restricted to lower levels and specified and controlled through AOC regulations. For wines of lower quality the allowable yield is higher. Yield is expressed as hectolitres/hectare (hl/ha) which is not a unit which readily conveys anything meaningful unless you are producing the wine in a vineyard. The following is intended to provide a more 'visual' understandable meaning of yield.

Hectolitre:	is	100 litres
		(133 standard 0.75 litre bottles of wine)
Hectare:	is	10,000 sq. metres

For a visual image of this we can take a typical international soccer pitch. The size of this would be 115 x 75 yards or 105 x 69 metres. And so as a vineyard (or a part) it would be 7212 sq metres or 0.7212 hectares. Such a vineyard with a controlled yield of say 40 hl/ha would be allowed to produce 2885 litres of wine (or 3846 standard 0.75 litre bottles). Not quite the return of a premiership football club but nevertheless quite significant.

It is of interest to note that one of the worlds most famous and prestigious vineyards, Romanée Conti, is only 1.8 hectares. Yields are also well below the maximum allowable for a Grand Cru vineyard with annual production around 500 cases. This would mean a yield of 25 hl/ha.

Although there is a clear link between yield and wine quality the reality is much more complex as quality is certainly not solely dependent on yield. The other essential factors relating to wine quality are the excellence (or otherwise) of the terroir, the careful and dedicated application of advanced, modern, scientific vinicultural practice, the age of the vines, the climatic conditions for a particular vintage, and the dedication and expertise of the winemaker.

The foregoing has been clearly demonstrated by the 'garage' vineyards of Pomerol and St Émilion (and now beyond). These started as tiny plots of indifferent terroir but through the dedicated application of all aspects of modern, scientific viniculture and winemaking practice, together with tightly controlled low yields, many of these vineyards are producing wine rated at the same level of quality as their world famous neighbouring châteaux. Yield is certainly important in this case but no matter how low the yields are a high quality wine could not be produced solely on the basis of yield.

The old famous and established vineyards with exceptionally fine terroir and many old vines have also demonstrated in the past that they can produce great wines with high yields.

Nevertheless the INAO regulations in respect of yields (hectolitres/hectare – hl/ha) are particularly important. Before 1974 the yield control was based on a 'Cascade System' where for instance the maximum yield for a Grand Cru wine was 30 hectolitres/hectares (hl/ha) but that of the vineyard was not. And so a vineyard could produce say 50 hl/ha 'Grand Cru' and the balance of the production would be labelled with lower designations. This was clearly unsatisfactory as a vineyard yielding 50 hl/ha cannot produce a Grand Cru quality wine. This was changed to a maximum vineyard yield (rendement de base) with an allowable over production of 20% (Plafonde Limite de Classement or PLC), subject to tasting, a highly subjective form of quality control to say the least. As part of this process the rendement de base was increased.

The changes in the regulations can be summarised as follows:-

	YIELD (HL/HA) GRAND CRU	YIELD (HL/HA) PREMIER CRU
Pre 1974	30	35
Post 1974	35	40
Plc – 20%	7	8
Total post 1974	**42**	**48**

Many wine experts question whether wines of Grand Cru and Premier Cru quality can be produced with these higher yields.

Finally how are yields controlled in order to meet those specified and controlled through the AOC regulations? This is achieved through:-

- Severe pruning in the early season.
- 'Green' pruning (eclaircissage/vendange en vert) in July/ August.
- Passage de nettoyage before harvest to remove substand-ard grapes.
- Examination of the grapes on triage tables to eliminte damaged or defective grapes before the start of winemaking.

2. WINE PRICES

From the 1970's onwards there was a fundamental change in the inter-national wine market as wines of excellent quality became available at modest prices. This was led by the so called 'New World' (Chile, South Africa, Australia and New Zealand). This in turn led to the 'Old World' vineyards (France, Italy and Spain) raising their standards and lowering their prices to compete. The days of an old fashioned bottle of 'plonk' were over.

So it is now possible to buy a perfectly decent bottle of wine for around 10 to 15 euros and an excellent bottle for 20 to 30 euros. However if you or your esteemed guests want the 'best' then a first growth Bordeaux of a good year and more than 10 years old will cost 500 to 1000 euros a bottle. If you are really 'flush' and wish to be very extravagant then an 'old' Pètrus from at least a decent vintage will set you back around 3000 euros for a bottle. Even more dramatic would be a 1996 Romanée Conti as a single bottle would cost 10,000–12,000 euros.

So if there is clearly a vast range of fine prices it is important to examine the factors which influence and determine these prices. The main ones are as follows:-

A – QUALITY

Clearly this ranges from the old fashioned 'plonk' (if you can find it) to the exquisite wines produced by the old well established vineyards.

Great wines which command high prices are produced from old vines, in an ideal 'terroir'****, which are cared for to the highest vinicultural

---

**** The essential characteristics of a vineyard including soil, effective drainage, and excellent climate.

standards combined with low yield and consummate winemaking skills. Lower priced wines although excellent are from vineyards which are unable to achieve these exceptional standards.

B – OLD WELL PROVEN RELIABILITY AND CAPABILITY

The internationally famous vineyards have an established reputation, sustained over many centuries, for the consistent creation of great wines. As a result of this these vineyards have a prestigious position in the market and this is reflected in the high prices which these wines command. It follows that vineyards which do not have this acclaim are obliged to price their wines on the stature they have (or lack of it) in the market.

C - EXCEPTIONAL PRESTIGE

Many vineyards have achieved an acclaimed status in the international wine trade and command high prices for their wine. However a very small number have an international status which can be described as 'exceptional prestige' and this has a dramatic effect on the 'astronomical' prices which they achieve. Two in particular, Pètrus and Romanée Conti are such 'iconic' wines and command prices which are three to five times greater than a Bordeaux first growth.

D – NUMERICAL QUALITY RATING

A 'phenomenon' of the modern world of fine wine was the extensive adoption of the numerical quality rating system.

The concept was first introduced by Robert Parker and eventually other experts followed with many rating out of 100 and others out of 20. These ratings have a significant impact on wine prices particularly at the 'top end' of the market. For instance if a wine from a particular vintage is numerically rated at say just below 90 then a modest wine price is achieved whereas had it been rated say above 95 then a much higher market price would result. Each vintage is also numerically rated and clearly the two ratings are linked, the poorer the vintage the lower the wine rating and vice versa. The following example demonstrates this principle:-

WINE – LYNCH BAGES (PAUILLAC)

YEAR	VINTAGE RATING	WINE RATING	PRICE RANGE (EUROS)
1999	90	90	80 – 150
2000	98	94	180 – 230

E – AGE AND PROVENANCE

Fine wines, particularly those from a good vintage, improve in quality and increase in value with age. That is providing that the wine is kept in a manner which allows it to progressively improve and not deteriorate. The way in which the wine has been kept over a period of time is known in the wine trade as 'provenance'.

The following need to be carefully controlled in the storage of fine wine:-

LIGHT – The storage area needs to be dark or with only subdued light as exposure to bright light will cause the wine to deteriorate.

TEMPERATURE – This is a particularly important parameter in wine storage. The general consensus is that a temperature in the range 10–15°C is ideal which allows the wine to develop at a safe rate. Lower temperatures would suppress development and higher ones cause damage.

HUMIDITY – The concern here is that if wine is stored at a low humidity there is a risk that the cork would dry out and allow oxygen to enter the bottle which would cause serious damage to the wine. Most 'top' wine cellars maintain humidity of up to 70%.

VIBRATION – There is only limited scientific evidence on the effect of vibration on stored wine. However the general conclusion is that it is detrimental and should be avoided.

F – BUYING WINE

Wine can be bought from a wine shop, a supermarket, a wine club, a wine merchant, or at auction. The key factors are price and provenance. For excellent but relatively lowly priced wines your wine shop or supermarket is satisfactory. However these wines will almost certainly have been subjected to bright light, fairly high temperatures, and often displayed vertically which for wines with a fairly rapid turnover there is no real cause for concern. These conditions are not however satisfactory for older expensive wines.

Wine clubs have become increasingly popular as they offer excellent wines at competitive prices. This is because their wine selection process is generally of a very high standard and their bulk buying capability enables them to offer very favourable prices.

Established wine merchants generally offer a full range of wines and their storage and display facilities are usually professionally sound. They also offer wines which are retained in bond. For great and expensive wines which need around ten years to mature and 'open' a bonded wine offers the best possible provenance as the bonded warehouses have a reputation for maintaining almost ideal conditions, in a permanent fixed location, for the long term storage of expensive fine wines. The VAT on the wine is only payable when the wine is released from bond.

In buying at auction the ideal purchase would be a wine in bond as it has a guaranteed provenance. Auction houses are highly reputable professional institutions and the large ones employ internationally recognised wine experts. They would be able to provide details of the provenance provided by the seller which should be examined before purchase.

G – A LIMITED OVERVIEW OF WINE PRICES

BORDEAUX

Bordeaux is a very large wine producer and covers the full range of wines from table wine (vin de table) to very expensive classified growths.

So an excellent but modest 'claret' can be bought for 15–20 euros whereas at the very 'top', Pètrus, a single bottle from a good vintage and more than 10 years old would cost more than 3000 euros.

The following is a range of Bordeaux wines and vintages at the 'top end' of the market (prices in euros for one standard 0.75 litre bottle)

	1990	*	2000	*	2009	*
PÈTRUS	1800–3500	97	2500–4500	98	2500–4500	98
CHEVAL BLANC	600–1300	97	500–900	95	700–1300	98
LATOUR	400–650	98	550–900	98	900–1600	97
LAFITE	400–850	95	650–1400	98	600–1000	97
LYNCH BAGES	200–400	95	100–200	94	90–160	94
MONTROSE	250–600	95	100–200	94	150–280	96

SOURCE: Internet Wine Searcher System
MID 2016 PRICES
* AVERAGE NUMERICAL QUALITY RATINGS

BURGUNDY

The wine of a Bordeaux château is a unique product, there is only one Lafite, Cheval Blanc or Montrose and likewise for all the châteaux. Where there is multiple ownership of a château it is based on financial investment and not on the right of an investor to produce wine from a share in ownership. There is only one winemaker for a Bordeaux château.

The situation is totally different in Burgundy where multiple ownership of a vineyard results in multiple producers. Furthermore it has been described in the main text that the disposal of sequestered Burgundy vineyards by the state was based on the sale of vineyard lots mainly to local families. If this is followed over a very long period of time by the continuing change in ownership as a result of the Napoleonic Code whereby parents are required to bequeath their estate equally between their children then the extent of ownership progressively increases. Furthermore many owners assign their 'plots' to established wine producers who produce wine from plots which they have acquired or which have been assigned to them.

The Grand Cru vineyard of Clos Vougeot is often used as an example of multiple ownership and producers as the vineyard has more than 80 owners. The vineyard is also the largest Grand Cru vineyard in the

Côte de Nuits being 50 hectares (124 acres). This also means that there are significant differences in terroir of individual plots from one that is ideal on the upper slopes to a plot that is not, down near the road with alluvial soil. Even with the combining of plots by a producer there is still in excess of 25 individual winemakers in Clos Vougeot. This situation applies extensively to Burgundy vineyards particularly to those which are Grand Cru and Premier Cru. For these vineyards the result is that for each vintage there is a wide range of quality and prices from the multiple producers who have differing terroirs and winemaking expertise.

There are a small number of exceptions the most notable being Romanée Conti which although it has joint owners is operated as a 'monople' with a single control and winemaker.

The following are examples of the impact on wine prices resulting from the multiple ownership of Burgundy vineyards:

Prices in euros for one standard 0.75 litre bottle.

CLOS VOUGEOT – 2009		EUROS	*
DOMAINE	LEROY	950–1600	97
	JEAN GRIVOT	100–170	93
	JOSEPH DROUHIN	120–200	91
	VADOT	80–150	92

LE CHAMBERTIN – 2009			
DOMAINE	LEROY	3300	98
	DUGAT PY	1700–2500	95
	PONSOT	600–700	93
	TORTOCHOT	100–125	91

MONTRACHET – 2009			
DOMAINE	LEFLAIVE	5000–5600	96
	LEROY	1400–2000	94
	PIERRE YVES COLIN MOREY	650–750	98
	THENARD	275–300	95

NOTES: SOURCE: *Internet Wine Searcher System*
MID 2016 PRICES
THE ABOVE ARE ALL GRAND CRU VINEYARDS
* AVERAGE NUMERICAL QUALITY RATINGS

ROMANÉE CONTI

This Grand Cru Burgundy wine is quite unique as it is, by far, the worlds most prestigious and expensive wine. Pètrus far exceeds the cost of the Bordeaux first growths but Romanée Conti is in an entirely different league in respect of prestige and cost.

The following table demonstrates this:-

PRICES IN EUROS FOR A 0.75 L STANDARD BOTTLE

YEAR	ROMANÉE CONTI	*	PÈTRUS	*	LATOUR	*
2010	11,000–15,000	94	2,500–4,000	98	1,000–1,800	99
2005	13,000–25,000	99	2,000–3,500	98	600–1,000	97
1996	12,000–14,000	97	1,000–2,000	93	350–450	96
1990	12,000–20,000	99	1,800–3,800	97	400–650	98

SOURCE: Internet Wine Searcher System
MID 2016 PRICES
* AVERAGE NUMERICAL QUALITY RATINGS

3.   WINE BOTTLES AND STOPPERS

There is a very wide range of wine bottles in respect of size and shape. Also less than twenty years ago all wine bottles were stoppered with the traditional cork produced from the bark of the oak tree but now there are a number of wine bottle stoppers.

A – WINE BOTTLE SHAPE

It has been demonstrated in the main text that the Burgundy and Bordeaux wine regions are known from their differences and not there similarities and that certainly extends to wine bottle shapes. Burgundy adopted a bottle with sloping shoulders whereas the Bordeaux bottles has straight sides and high shoulders.

The Burgundy Style Bottle   The Bordeaux Style Bottle

The recess as the base of all wine bottles is known as the 'Punt'. Burgundy bottles have a small punt whereas that for the Bordeaux bottle is much larger

B – WINE STOPPERS

The traditional cork stopper has now been extensively replaced by other types of stoppers. The case against the cork stopper is that it is expensive and there is a risk that the wine can be tainted by only minute contamination of the cork. The dreaded expression 'corked' is known to all wine lovers as a bottle of a favourite wine is opened. The case for cork is that it has been tried and tested over centuries and in particular, for term laying down of wine it has been fully proven and effective.

The most widely used alternative to cork is a screw cap. They have been widely adopted by New Zealand and Australian wineries. The wines produced are excellent but are not intended for a long lay down period which would normally be less than ten years. In fact an experiment was carried out by Haut Brion where one hundred bottles were sealed by screw cap and laid down. The conclusion was that they worked satisfactorily for slightly more than ten years but after that the progressive deterioration of the plastic used in the screw cap allowed ingress of oxygen and the inevitable decline of the wine. However the opposite conclusions were reached by Domaine Laroche (a Premier Cru Chablis vineyard) which decided to use screw caps.

The other type of stopper is an extruded plastic 'bung'. Scientific experiments carried out have shown that short term results are satisfactory but the plastic stopper has potentially a higher progressive rate of oxygen ingress than with screw caps.

C – WINE BOTTLE SIZES

The international wine trade has 23 bottle sizes. Some of these are rather obscure and those which are widely used and well known are the twelve principal bottle sizes which are listed here.

BURGUNDY has ten bottle sizes eight of which are from the principal list and two which are not.

BORDEAUX has twelve bottle sizes ten of which are from the principal list and two which are not.

The foregoing is shown in the following tables

PRINCIPAL BOTTLE SIZES

LITRES	NUMBER OF STANDARD BOTTLES	NAME
0.1875	0.25	PICCOLO[1]* OR SPLIT[2]+
0.375	0.5	DEMI
0.75	1	STANDARD
1.5	2	MAGNUM
3.0	4.	DOUBLE MAGNUM
4.5	6	JEROBOAM*
6.0	8	IMPERIAL*
9.0	12	SALMANAZAR
12.0	16	BALTHAZAR
15.0	20	NEBUCHADNEZZAR
18.0	24	MELCHIOR
25.5	34	*SOVEREIGN +

* NOT USED IN BURGUNDY
+ NOT USED IN BORDEAUX

ADDITIONAL BURGUNDY BOTTLE SIZES
(NOT ON THE PRINCIPAL LIST)

4.5 LITRES	SIX STANDARD BOTTLES	REHOBOAM
6.0 LITRES	EIGHT STANDARD BOTTLES	METHUSELAH

ADDITIONAL BORDEAUX BOTTLE SIZES
(NOT ON THE PRINCIPAL LIST)

40.25 LITRES	ONE THIRD STANDARD BOTTLE	CHOPINE
2.25 LITRES	THREE STANDARD BOTTLES	MARIE JEANE

4.   BASIC WORLD AND BURGUNDY AND BORDEAUX WINE STATISTICS

Wine is produced in 60 countries worldwide. Production is however dominated by three countries, Italy, France, and Spain, which together produce 50% of the worlds wine. At the other end of the scale we have tiny producers such as Malta which has excellent wine but contributes only 0.01% to world production.

THE TOP TEN WINE PRODUCING NATIONS
(MILLION HECTOLITRES)

	2010	2011	2012	2013
ITALY	48	43	40	45
SPAIN	36	33	32	43*
FRANCE	45	50	41	42
USA	22	22	20	22
ARGENTINE	16	16	12	15
CHILE	9	10	13	13
AUSTRALIA	11	11	12	13
CHINA	13	12	14	12
SOUTH AFRICA	9	10	11	11
GERMANY	7	9	9	8

WORLD PRODUCTION

	2010	2011	2012	2013
WORLD	266	270	268	277

*This remarkable increase in Spanish wine production was indeed achieved and there are claims that it reached 50 million hectolitres

The world's three principal wine producers Italy, Spain and France produce 50% of the world's wine.

The top ten producers produce 81% of the world's wine

BURGUNDY WINE PRODUCTION

Officially Beaujolais is not part of the Burgundy wine region. However the practical perception is that when referring to Burgundy Beaujolais is included. For instance the Confrérie du Chevalier des Tastevin includes the Beaujolais 'Cru' vineyards in their wine tastings and have awarded tastevinage labels to these vineyards. Robert Parker in his book 'Burgundy' includes Beaujolais.

BASIC BURGUNDY STATISTICS

	SURFACE AREA (HECTARES)	%	ANNUAL PRODUCTION		%
			HECTOLITRES	BOTTLES	
BURGUNDY +	27,700	59	1.5 MILLION	200 MILLION	65
BEAUJOLAIS	19,000	41	0.825 MILLION	110 MILLION	35
TOTALS	46,700	100	2.325 MILLON	310 MILLION	100

+ CHABLIS   CÔTE CHALONAISE
   CÔTE DE NUIT   MÂCONNAISE
   CÔTE DE BEAUNE

BORDEAUX WINE PRODUCTION
BASIC BORDEAUX STATISTICS

VINEYARD SURFACE AREA   -   120,000 Hectares
ANNUAL WINE PRODUCTION   -   5 MILLION hectolitres
    670 MILLION bottles

5.   THE JUDGEMENT OF PARIS

The top Californian vineyards always aspired to match or even surpass the quality of the great wines of France. To finally put this to the test Steven Spurrier, a British wine merchant, organised a blind tasting of Californian and French wines by a panel of eleven distinguished specialists from the world of fine wine (nine French, one English, and one American).

The event took place in Paris on the 24th May 1976. Ten red (Cabernet Sauvignon) and ten white (chardonnay) wines were tasted (six Californian and four French in each case).

Each wine was scored out of 20 and the detail scoring for the red wines is given in the order to see the pattern of scores by the eleven judges. The final ranking of both the red and white wines are given with the dramatic result that Californian wines came first for both the red and white wines.

THE ELEVEN JUDGES

A	Pierre Brejoux (French) of the Institute of Appellations of Origin
B	Claude Dubois-Millot (French) (Substitute to Christian Millau)
C	Michel Dovaz (French) of the Wine Institute of France
D	Patricia Gallagher (American) of l'Academie du Vin
E	Odette Kahn (French) Editor *of La Revue du vin de France*
F	Raymond Oliver (French) of the restaurant Le Grand Véfour
G	Steven Spurrier (British)
H	Pierre Tari (French) of Château Giscours
I	Christian Vanneque (French) the sommelier of Tour D'Argent
J	Aubert de Villaine (French) of the Domaine de la Romanée-Conti
K	Jean-Claude Vrinat (French) of the Restaurant Taillevent

RED WINE – CABERNET SAUVIGNON SCORES

	Vintage	A	B	C	D	E	F	G	H	I	J	K
Stag's Leap Wine Cellars	1973	14	16	10	14	15	14	14	13	16.5	15	14
Ridge Vineyards Monte Bello	1971	13	7	12	16	7	12	14	17	15.5	9	11
Heitz Wine Cellars Martha's Vineyard	1970	12	8	11	17	2	10	13	15	10	7	9
Clos Du Val Winery	1972	14	9	11	13	2	10	11	13	16.5	5	7
Mayacamas Vineyards	1971	7	9.5	8	9	13	14	9	12	3	12	13
Freemark Abbey Winery	1969	5	9	15	15	5	8	13	14	6	7	7

	Vintage	A	B	C	D	E	F	G	H	I	J	K
Château Mouton-Rothschild	1970	16	16	15	15	12	12	14	11	16	14	14
Château Montrose	1970	12	17	11	14	12	14	14	14	11	16	15
Château Haut-Brion	1970	17	13.5	12	12	12	10	8	14	17	15	15
Château Léoville Las Cases	1971	10	11	10	14	12	12	12	12	8	10	12

THE RANKING OF THE RED WINES

Rank	Grade	Wine	Vintage
1.	14.14	Stag's Leap Wine Cellars	1973
2.	14.09	Château Mouton-Rothschild	1970
3.	13.64	Château Montrose	1970
4.	13.23	Château Haut-Brion	1970
5.	12.14	Ridge Vineyards Monte Bello	1971
6.	11.18	Château Léoville Las Cases	1971
7.	10.36	Heitz Wine Cellars Martha's Vineyard	1970
8.	10.14	Clos Du Val Winery	1971
9.	9.95	Mayacamas Vineyards	1971
10.	9.45	Freemark Abbey Winery	1969

242

THE RANKING OF THE WHITE WINES

Rank	Wine	Vintage
1.	Château Montelena	1973
2.	Meursault Charmes Roulot	1973
3.	Chalone Vineyard	1974
4.	Spring Mountain Vineyard	1973
5.	Beaune Clos des Mouches Joseph Drouhin	1973
6.	Freemark Abbey Winery	1972
7.	Batard-Montrachet Ramonet-Prudhon	1973
8.	Puligny-Montrachet Les Pucelles Domaine Leflaive	1972
9.	Veedercrest Vineyards	1972
10.	David Bruce Winery	1973

The results of the tasting caused both disbelief and outrage in France and both Le Figaro and Le Monde dismissed the results in terms such as 'laughable' and 'cannot be taken seriously'.

But an even more serious reaction was from those who considered the methodology of the tasting fundamentally flawed. In particular the statistical interpretation of the results by simply adding the eleven scores and then dividing by eleven was considered unsound. The scoring in some case was also seen as bizarre particularly where a taster used the dubious precision of a half digit in a score or rated a wine 'plonk' by scoring it 2 whereas another judge scored the same wine 17.

Although the tasting had a major impact on the world of fine wine the event may have eventually been lost in the 'mists of time' had it not been granted virtual 'immortality' through it being described as 'The Judgement of Paris', a famous event in ancient mythology, by a journalist, George Taber, in fact the only journalist to attend the tasting. The original event changed the course of history and had a major and lasting influence on great art where Botticelli, Raphael, Rubens, Renoir and other distinguished artists have depicted the Judgement in great masterpieces.

The original Judgement was a contest between the three most beautiful goddesses of Olympus – Aphrodite, Hera, and Athena. Zeus appointed Paris, a Trojan prince, as judge to decide who was the fairest. He chose Aphrodite as she promised him Helen, the most beautiful woman in the world, and the wife of Menelaus the Spartan King. Paris abducted Helen and this led to the Trojan war.

And so the 'Judgement of Paris' was followed by a number of similar events.

In January 1978 the wines tasted in Paris were again tasted in San Francisco where the first three ranked in both red and white wines were Californian.

In 1986 on the 10th anniversary of the Paris tastings the French Culinary Institute conducted tastings of nine of the original ten red wines. The first two ranked were Californian and the third Château Montrose. The Wine Spectator also arranged a tasting of all ten of the original red wines where Californian wines were ranked in the first five places.

On 24th May 2006, the 30th anniversary of the 'Judgement of Paris' the original red wines were again tasted simultaneously at Berry Bros and Rudd in London and in Napa California. This finally confirmed the superiority of the Californian wines in comparison to those of Bordeaux as they were ranked in the first five places.

6.   SERVING WINE

Wine can be considered to be one of nature's greatest benefits to mankind and brings pleasure to a vast number of people throughout the world. Nevertheless whether your wine is carefully selected, excellent and affordable or expensive prestigious and from a great vintage it is essential that it is served correctly. To not to do so immeasurably detracts from its true natural potential for superb taste and exquisite bouquet.

A pedantic approach is not uncommon to many aspects of wine and the term 'wine snob' is often applied to those who seek to socially impress in this way. Strangely the importance of serving wine in a correct manner is generally omitted from their 'repertoire' and also many of those who prepare and serve wine both domestically and professionally fail to recognise and respect and in fact blatantly disregard the need to follow very simple and basic but essential principles in the serving of wine.

How often have you been served a warm tepid and insipid white wine or one close to freezing having been dumped in an ice bucket for half an hour or more resulting in no taste of delicious fruit and no exquisite bouquet. Also a red wine delivered directly to the table from a cold cellar or eurocave and immediately opened and served with no chance to warm up or breathe. Also particularly in restaurants, red wine is often displayed in wall racks as part of the décor but at a 'room temperature' above 20°C and served without cooling.

All this, despite the fact, that serving wine, such that its full potential is realised and enjoyed is in fact simple and easily achievable if the following basic principals are recognised and implemented.

1. White wine should be served at 5°C–10°C which is the temperature range of most refrigerators. If stored in a warm place then the bottle can be placed in a freezer or a bucket of ice for around 15 to 20 minutes. It should not be forgotten and taken down to freezing or close to it. White wine can be served upon opening but should not be left unopened for a long time as it would become oxidised.

2. Red wines should be served at 15°C–20°C. If they have been stored at 'room temperature' (18°C–22°C) they should be placed in a refrigerator for 30 to 45 minutes. If they have been stored in a cool cellar or eurocave they should be immersed in warm (not hot) water for 15 to 20 minutes. They should not be warmed by placing them near the fire or on a radiator.

   Full bodied red wines (Bordeaux) need to be opened 30 to 60 minutes before serving whereas lighter red wines (Burgundy) should not be opened more than 30 minutes before serving.

3. Certain red wines, of significant age, deposit sediment in the bottle and these should ideally be decanted before serving. These wines are normally full bodied and the decanting also allows them to breathe more quickly. The rule generally adopted is that older Bordeaux red wines should be decanted but not those of Burgundy.

4. White wines retained after opening can generally be maintained in a drinkable condition by either pumping out the air from the bottle, using a special pump and bung, or injecting an inert gas which is heavier than air and covers the surface of the wine preventing any oxygen coming into contact with it.

Opened red wines are generally difficult to maintain in drinkable condition even with pumps or inert gas. There are some where it is possible but they are the exception not the rule.

APPENDIX 8

THE AOC OF PETIT CHABLIS

There is probably a general misconception that an AOC (Appellation Origine Contrôlée) issued by the INAO is a relatively simple directive setting out a range of quality standards which a wine producer is required to meet if the AOC is to be displayed on the labels of the wine bottles. This translation of an AOC is included by way of example to demonstrate that the INAO regulations are far from a simple directive. They are in fact comprehensive, detailed, and complex a great deal of which is unfortunately lost in translation.

A TRANSLATION OF THE AOC (APPELLATION ORIGINE CONTRÔLÉE) FOR PETIT CHABLIS

Specification of controlled designation of origin 'PETIT CHABLIS'
APPROVED BY decree No. 2011–1791 of December 5, 2011,
Official Gazette of December 7, 2011

SPECIFICATION OF DESIGNATION OF ORIGIN CONTRÔLÉE 'PETIT CHABLIS'

CHAPTER 1
I – Label Name

Only entitled to the controlled designation of origin 'Petit Chablis' initially recognised in the Decree of 5th January 1944, the wines answering the specific provisions as set out below.

II – Geographical names and additional comments

No special provision

III – Colour and product types
The AOC 'Petit Chablis' is reserved for white still wines

IV – Areas and zones in which different operations are carried out
1 – Geographical area
The grape harvest, and wine making are carried on the territory of the following communes of the department of Yonne: Beine, Beru, Chablis, La Chapelle-Vaupelteigne, Chemilly-sur-Serein, Chichee, Collan, Courgis, Fleys, Fontenay-pres-Chablis, Lignorelles Ligny-le-Chatel, Maligny, Poilly-sur-Serein, Prehy, Villy and Viviers.

2 – Parcel area bounded
The wines are made exclusively from vineyards located in the parcel area of production as approved by the Institut National de l'origine et de la Qualite at the meeting of the national committee jurisdiction of January 31, 1978.

The National Institute for Origin and Quality file with the town halls of the communes mentioned at 1 are graphic documents establishing the parcel boundaries of the production area as approved.

3 – Close area
The close proximity to areas defined by the exemption for wine and winemaking consists of the following municipalities:

Department of Côte-d'Or:
Agencourt, Aloxe-Corton, Ancey, Arcenant, Argilly, Autricourt, Auxey-Duresses, Baubigny, Beaune, Belan-sur-Ource, Bevy, Bissey-la-Côte, Bligny-les-Beaune, Boncourt-le-Bois, Bouix, Bouze-lès-Beaune, Brion-sur-Ource, Brochon, Cerilly, Chamboeuf, Chambolle-Musigny, Channay, Charrey-sur-Seine, Chassagne-Montrachet, Chatillon-sur-Seine, Chaumont-le-Bois, Lime, Chenove, Chevannes, Chorey Lès Beaune, Clemencey Collonges-lès-Bévy, Combertault, Comblanchien, Corcelles-les-Arts, Corcelles-les-Monts, Corgoloin, Cormot-le-Great, Corpeau, Couchey, Curley, Curtil-Vergy, Daix, Dijon, Ebaty, Echevronne, Eperney-sub-Gevrey, L'Etang-Vergy, Etrochey, Fixin, Flagey-Echézeaux, Flavignerot, Fleurey-sur-Ouche, Fussey, Gerland, Gevrey Chambertin,

Gilly-lès-Cîteaux, Gommeville, Grancey-sur-Ource, Griselles, Ladoix-Serrigny, Lantehay, Larrey, Levernois, Magny-lès-Villers, Malain, Marcenay, Marey-les-Fussey, Marsannay-la-Côte, Massigny, Mavilly-Mandelot, Meloisey, Merceuil, Messanges, Meuilley, Meursanges, Meursault, Molesme, Montagny-lès-Beaune, Monthélie, Montliot-et-Courcelles, Morey-Saint-Denis, Mosson, Nantoux, Nicey, Noiron-sur-Seine, Nolay, Nuits-Saint-Georges, Obtree, Pernand-Vergelesses, Perrigny-lès-Dijon, Plombieres-lès-Dijon, Poincon-lès-Larrey, Pommard, Pothieres, Premeaux-Prissey, Prusly-sur-Ource, Puligny-Montrachet, Quincey, Reulle-Vergy, The Rochepot, Ruffey-lès-Beaune, Saint-Aubin, Saint Bernard, Saint-Philibert Saint-Romain, Saint-Colombe-sur-Seine, Saint-Marie-la-Blanche, Santenay, Savigny-lès-Beaune, Segrois, Tailly, Talant, Thoires, Vannaire, Vauchignon, Velars-sur-Ouche, Vertault, Vignoles, Villars-Fontaine, Villebichot, Villedieu, Villers-la-Faye, Villers-Patras, Villy-le-Moutier, Vix, Volnay, Vosne- Romanée and Vougeot:

Rhône:
Alix, Anse, L'Arbresle, Les Ardillats, Arnas, Bagnols, Beaujeu, Belleville, Belmont d'Azergues, Blace, Le Bois-d'Oingt, Le Breuil, Bully, Cercie, Chambost-Allieres, Chamelet, Charentay, Charnay, Chatillon-d'Azergues Chazay, Chénas, Chessy, Chiroubles, Cogny, Corcelles-en-Beaujolais, Dareize, Denice, Drace, Emerignes, Fleurie, Frontenas Gleize, Jarnioux, Juliénas Jullie, Lacenas, Lachassagne, Lancie, Lantignie, Legny, Letra, Liergues, Limas, Lozanne, Lucenay Marchampt, Marcy, Moire, Montmelas-Saint-Sorlin, Morance, Nuelles, Odenas, Oingt, Les Olmes, The Perreon, Apples, Pouilly-le-Monial, Quincie-en-Beaujolais, Régnié-Durette, Rivolet, Saint Clement-sur-Valsonne, Saint-Cyr-le-Chatoux, Saint-Didier-sur-Beaujeu, Saint-Etienne-des-Oullieres, Saint-Etienne-la-Varenne, Saint-George-de-Reneins, Saint-Germain-sur-l'Arbresle, Saint John of Ardieres, Saint-Jean-des-Vignes, Saint-Julien, Saint-Just-d'Avray, Saint-Lager, Saint-Laurent Oingt, Saint-Loup, Saint-Paule, Saint-Romain-de-Popey, Saint-Verand, Salles-Arbuissonnas-en-Beaujolais, Sarcey, Taponas, Ternand, Theize, Vaux-en-Beaujolais, Vauxrenard, Vernay, Villefranche-sur-Saône, Ville-sur-Jarnioux and Villie-Morgon;

Department of Saône-et-Loire:

Aluze, Ameugny, Aze, Barizey, Beaumont-sur-Grosne, Berze-la-City, Berze-le-Chatel, Bissey-sous-Cruchaud, Bissy-la-Mâconnaise, Bissy-sous-Uxelles, Bissy-sur-Fley, Blanot Bonnay, Bouzeron, Boyer, Bray, Bresse-sur-Grosne, Burgy, Burnand, Bussieres, Buxy, Cersot, Chagny, Chaintre, Chalon-sur-Saône, Chamilly, Champagny-sous-Uxelles, Champforgeuil, Chanes, Currency Exchange, Chapaize, La Chapelle-de-Bragny, La Chapelle-de-Guinchay, La Chapelle-sur-Brancion, Charbonnieres, Chardonnay, The Charmed, Charnay-lès-Mâcon, Charrecey, Chasselas, Chassey-le-Camp, Castle, Chatenoy-le-Royal, Chaudenay, Cheilly-lès-Maranges, Chenoves, Chevagny-les-Chevrières, Chissey-lès-Mâcon, Clessé, Cluny Cormatin Cortambert, Cortevaix, Couches, Creches-sur-Saône, Creot, Cruzille, Culles-les-Roches, Curtil-sous-Burnand, Davaye, Demigny, Dennevy, Dezize-lès-Maranges, Donzy-le-National, Donzy-le-Pertuis, Dracy-le-Fort, Dracy-lès-Couches, Epertully, Etrigny, Farges-lès-Chalon, Farges-lès-Mâcon, Flagy, Fleurville, Fley, Fountains, Fuissé, Genouilly, Germagny, Givry, Granges, Grevilly, Hurigny, Ige, Jalogny, Jambles, Jugy, Jully-lès-Buxy, Lacrost, Laives, Laize, Lalheue, Leynes, Lournand La Loyere, Lugny, Mâcon, Malay, Mancey, Martailly-lès-Brancion, Massilly Massy, Mellecey, Mercurey, Messey-sur-Grosne, Milly-Lamartine, Montagny-lès-Buxy, Montbellet, Montceaux-Ragny, Moroges, Nanton, Ozenay, Paris-l'Hopital, Peronne, Pierreclos Plottes, Prety, Prisse, Pruzilly, Remigny, La Roche-Vineuse, Romaneche-Thorins, Rosey, Royer, Rully Saint-Albain, St, Ambreuil, Saint-Amour-Bellevue, St Boil, Saint-Clement-sur-Guye, Saint-Denis-de-Vaux, Saint-Desert, Saint-Gengoux-de-Scisse, Saint-Gengoux-le-National, Saint-Germain-lès-Buxy, Saint-Gervais-sur-Couches, Saint-Gilles, Saint-Jean-de-Trezy, Saint-Jean-de-Vaux, Saint-Leger-sur-Dheune, Saint-Mard-de-Vaux, Saint Martin-Belle-Roche, Saint-Martin-du-Tartre, Saint-Martin-sous-Montaigu, Saint-Maurice-de-Satonnay, Saint Maurice-des-Champs, Saint-Maurice-lès-Couches, Saint-Pierre-de-Varennes, Saint-Rémy, Saint-Sernin-du-Plain, Saint-Symphorien-d'Ancelles, Saint Vallerin, Saint-Verand, Saint-Ythaire, Saisy, The Room, Salornay-sur-Guye, Sampigny-lès-Maranges, Sance, Santilly, Sassangy, Willows, Savigny-sur-Grosne, Sennecey-le-Grand, Senozan, Sercy, Serrieres, Sigy-le-Châtel, Sologny, Solutre-Pouilly, Taize

Tournus, Uchizy, Varennes-lès-Mâcon, Vaux-en-Pre, Vergisson, Worms, Verze, The Villars, La Vinous, Vinzelles and Vire;

Department of Yonne:
Accolay, Aigremont, Annay-sur-Serin, Arcy-sur-Cure, Asquins, Augy, Auxerre, Avallon, Bazarnes, Bernouil, Bessy-sur-Cure, Bleigny-le-Carreau, Censy, Champlay, Champs-sur-Yopnne, Champvallon, Chamvres, Charentenay, Chatel-Gerard, Cheney, Chevannes, Chitry, Coulangeron, Coulanges-la-Vineuse, Cravant, Cruzy-le-Chatel, Dannemoine, Dye, Epineuil, Escamps, Escolives-Saint-Camille,Gy l'Eveque, Hery, Irancy, Island, Joigny, Jouancy, Junay, Jussy, Licheres-pres-Aigremont, Licy-sur-Cure,Mensey, Merry-Sec,Mige, Molay, Molosmes, Monugny-la-Resle, Mouffy, Moulins-en-Tonnerois, Nitry, Walnut, Ouanne, Paroy-sur-Tholon, Pasilly, Pierre-Perthuis, Pontigny, Quenne, Roffey, Rouvray, Sacy, Saint-Bris-le-Vineux, Saint-Cyr-les-Colons, Pallaye Holy, Holy Father, Sainte-Vertu, Sarry, Senan, Serrigny, Tharoiseau, Tissey, Thunder, Tronchoy, Val-de-Mercy, Vallan, Venouse, Venoy, Vermenton, Vezannes, Vezelay Vezinnes, Villeneuve-Saint-Salves, Villiers-sur-Tholon, Vincelles, Vincelottes, Volgre and Yrouerre.

V – Grape Varieties
The wines are exclusively from Chardonnay B.

VI – Vineyard Management
1 – Driving Modes
a) – Density
  – The vines have a minimal density planting 5,500 vines per hectare, with a spacing between the row, less than or equal to 1.20 metres, with the exception of vines planted on slopes greater than or equal to 40% for which this distance is less than or equal to 1.60 metres;
  – The vines have a spacing between feet on the same row, greater than or equal to 0.80 metres.

b) – size Rules
  – The wines come from vines cut according to following provisions:

GENERAL PROVISIONS

The vines are pruned with a maximum of 14 eyes per foot and a maximum of 10 eyes francs per square metre:
- Either by short stature (pipes Royat crodon vines);
- Either longwall (single and double Guyot size and size Chablis).

SPECIAL PROVISIONS

Whatever the size mode, the vines can be pruned with frank eyes provided that additional phenological stage corresponding to 11 or 12 leaves, number of fruiting branches of the year by foot is less than or equal to the number of frank eyes defined rules for size.

c) – Rules of trellising and leaf height
- The trellised foliage height is at least equal to 0.6 times the spacing between the rows, the trellised foliage height being measured between the lower limit of the established foliage 0.30 metres less above the ground and the upper limit of trimming;
- The vines are trellised and compulsorily tying met.

d) – Average Maximum Load at parcel
- The maximum average charge to the plot is set at 10,500 kg per hectare.

e) – missing Threshold
- The percentage of dead or missing vines, referred to in Article D. 645–4 of the Code rural and sea fishing, is 20%.

f) – cultural state of the vine
- The plots are to be conducted to ensure a good overall cultural condition of the vine which is reflected in particular by:
- Maintenance of the soil, namely the control of the weed by weed height of less than half the height of trellising (height from the ground to the top trellis wire), and control erosion by an apparent lack of root.

2 – Other cultural practices

a) – In order to preserve the characteristics of the physical and biological environment, which is an element of the fundamental terroir:
  – The permanent grass cover headlands and slopes is mandatory; the destruction of the canopy plant is tolerated occasionally during earth works;
  – Any substantial change in morphology, subsoil, topsoil or elements to ensure the integrity and sustainability of a parcel of land for the production of the appellation of origin is prohibited, excluding classic work.

b) – vine plantations and replacements are made with healthy plant material which is subject to a hot water treatment or other method to fight against golden flavescence.

3 – Irrigation

Irrigation is prohibited.

VII – Harvest, transport and grape maturity

1 – Harvest

a) – The wines come from grapes with good maturity.

b) – Special provisions for transporting the harvest
  – The harvest is protected from rain during transport and when delivered

2 – Grape Maturity

The sugar content of the grapes and the natural alcoholic strengths wines meet the following characteristics:

MINIMUM GRAPE SUGAR (grams per litre of wort)	ALCOHOLIC STRENGTH
153	9.5%

VIII – Yields – Production Entry

1 – Efficiency and output stop

Performance and output stop referred to in Article D. 645–7 of the Rural Code and Maritime Fishing shall be:

NORMAL YIELD (hectolitres per hectare)	MAXIMUM YIELD (hectolitres per hectare)
60	70

2 – Entry into production of young vines

Detailed regulations are provided for the introduction of young vines

IX – Transformation, development, farming, packaging, storage

1 – General Provisions

The wines are vinified in accordance with local procedures.

a) – Analytical Standards

The finished wine, ready to be released for consumption within the meaning of Article D. 645-18-1 of the Code rural and sea fishing, have a maximum content of fermentable sugars (glucose + fructose) to:
  – 3 grams per litre, or:
  – 4 grams per litre, if the total acidity is greater than or equal to 55.10 milliequivalents per litre, or 4.13 grams per litre expressed as tartaric acid (or 2.7 grams per litre expressed as H_2SO_4).

b) – oenological practices and physical treatments
  – The use of pieces of wood is forbidden;
  – After enrichment, the wines should not exceed the total alcoholic strength by volume of 12.5%.

c) – banned Equipment

Continuous presses are prohibited.

d) – fermenting capacity

Any operator has an overall capacity of the winery (wine making and storage) equivalent to at least the volume of wine vinified for the harvest of the previous year.

e) – Maintenance of chai and equipment

The winery and equipment are properly maintained; this is reflected in particular by:
- General hygiene with a state of general cleanliness, manicured land, adequate drainage and avoiding stagnation;
- Separation and specificity of premises: premises not having the same functions should be such as separate storage areas for pesticides, cleaning products or hydrocarbons with local wine, livestock and storage of dry materials (plugs, cartons);
- An absence of risk or odorants in local winemaking, livestock and storage (smell).

f) – Breeding

The temperature of the containers during the fermentation phase is controlled at less than or equal to 25°C.

2 – Provisions on packaging

For batch conditioning, the operator makes available to the inspection body:
- The information in the register of handling referred to in Article D. 645–18 of the Rural Code and marine fisheries;
- The results of the analysis carried out before or after.These bulletins are kept for a period of six months from the packing date.

3 – Provisions relating to storage

The operator completes a storage place protected for wines in bulk and cylinders.

4 – Provisions on the movement of products and marketing to the consumer.

The wines are marketed to the consumer under the provisions of Article 645–D.17 of the Code rural and maritime fishing.

THE WINES OF BURGUNDY AND BORDEAUX

X – Link with the geographical area

1 – Information on geographical area

a) – Description of natural features.

The geographical area occupies a cluster of hills nestled in the heart of the plates of the '*Auxerrois*' in the Paris Basin. The '*Chablis*' is a small well-defined region corresponding to reliefs along the Serein valley, a tributary of the Yonne, in its crossing of the '*Côte des Bars*'. The geographical area thus extends the territory of 17 municipalities in the department of Yonne, east Auxerre.

The cuesta of the 'Côte des Bars' great geomorphological structure that flush sediments Upper Jurassic age, is a relief formed of hard limestone, the '*Limestone Barrois*' forming cornice above a long side in the basement marl (calcareous clay) and compact raincoats, '*Marls with Exogyra virgula*' rich in small comma-shaped oysters that have given their name to the formation.

Under the marl, limestone topographic level forms a small jump near the bottom of the valley ('*Limestone Astartes*'). Marl up the slopes are usually masked by coat screen combining fine materials and coarser limestone elements. The elevation of the front side reached 120 metres to 130 metres, remaining moderate altitudes; the highest point of the plate does not exceed 320 metres. Northeast of the geographical area, the limestone plateau is topped by of Cretaceous formations, represented by clays and marl oysters.

Chablis landscape is very original. Large slightly concave slopes occupied by the vine, are dominated by a wooded limestone cornice, closing prospects, only open in the axis the Serein valley. A multitude of small valleys, often dry, cut to the slopes various orientations. These valleys are generally received and woodlands on their steepest sides leaving room for the vines on the best exposed slopes. Plots demarcated for the grape harvest occupy various situations:

– The slopes, mainly on marl slopes with well-drained soil;
– But locally, the foothills on '*limestone Astartes*' or colluvium slope down;
– The edges of the plates, shallow and very stony limestone soil, ensuring good warming climate compensates deficit due to lack of shelter.

The soils are varied, though still limestones. Lean and very stony, well-drained on limestone plateau (known locally as '*small lands*'), they are richer in clay on the bank marl and its foothills.

Northwest of the geographical area, some wine sectors are developed on clays Cretaccous covering the '*limestone Barrois*'. The floors are waterproof and so drainage is provided by the slope.

The '*Chablis*' is bathed in a slightly modified oceanic climate influences Continental. This climate is characterised by a moderate and regular rainfall regime (650 annual millimetres in Auxerre), affirmed without summer drought and temperatures rather fresh with an annual average of 10.8°C.

The climate is characterised by a relatively high risk of winter and spring frosts that can be catastrophic for the vine. The relatively cashed terrain increased the risk in the galleys while the trays are exposed to winter cold winds.

b) – Description of human factors to the link
The culture of the vine is attested in the '*Chablis*' early Middle ages. A monastery created Chablis in 510, and then transferred in 867, the monks of Saint Martin of Tours fleeing the Viking invasion in the Loire Valley. It seems that they have developed a vineyard near the village.

In 1114, founded the Cistercians, near Chablis, the Pontigny Abbey and gradually developed a vineyard, and then installed in the town of Chablis, a pantry, the '*Petit Pontigny*' whose buildings still exist. Besides the ecclesiastical areas which continued to the French Revolution, prosperous secular viticulture, also turned to foreign trade. Paris and Northern Europe provided regular opportunities.

During its history, the wine '*Chablis*' remains remarkably stable in its type of white dry wine. In 1186, donations to the abbey of Pontigny for a vineyard located near Chablis, giving a '*white, and long aging*' wine. The authors of the 19th century also describe this feature making '*Chablis*' an exception in a world dominated by red wines and 'claret'.

Phylloxera, downy mildew and powdery mildew seriously affected 'Chablis' which took several decades to recover. During the second half of XXth century alone, supported by the advances in viticulture, mechanisation and protection against freezing, the reconstition of the vineyard actually restarted. This reconstruction is realised in respect of vineyards for the production of dry white wines.

The use of the name 'Petit Chablis' is proved from the beginning of XX century, when producers created their first union, in 1908 to fight effectively against the usurpations of the name. The name 'Petit Chablis' is in various appellation of origin recognition judgments controlled 'Chablis' or to designate dry white wines produced in the Chablis region, from grapes other than *'Beaune'* (local name Chardonnay B – Judgment 1920) or from the vine *'Beaune'*, but not originating in plots with the *'nature soil kimmeridgienne'* (1923).

The AOC 'Petit Chablis' is recognised by decree in 1944.

The 'Petit Chablis' is derived from a single grape variety, Chardonnay B, reputed to give great white wines of Burgundy.

The wines are produced mainly from vines planted on the plateaus with calcareous soils, in the northwest, on slopes of the Cretaceous clays. The bottom of the slopes are heavier soils also planted locally.

The vineyards of 'Petit Chablis' are traditionally small. The traditional size called 'size Chablis' is well adapted to harsh climatic conditions, while ensuring regular and moderate production.

The Guyot, single or double, extended to all the Burgundy vineyards in the 19th century, is also practiced in 'Chablis'. The development of an efficient plant material by clonal selection favours the development of a short size for a proper regulation of vegetation. The vines are trellised, generally planted in the direction of the slope. If this arrangement facilitates ressuyage clay soils, it also poses problems of erosion, offset with a return to tillage and cover crops.

The vineyards cover, in 2009, an area of about 850 hectares, with an annual production approximately 50000 hectolitres.

2 – Information on the quality and characterises of produces
The 'Petit Chablis' is a dry white wine, lively and fruity, characterised by its lightness and minerality. The acidity and minerality gives it a freshness and character that makes it a wine asking not to grow old but pleasant to drink.

3 – Casual Interactions

The wines, exclusively white, profiting from the controlled label of origin 'Petit Chablis' owe their lively and mineral character in the geographical area. The terms mesoclimatiques mark the wine-growing potential and expression of wines particularly sensitive to the conditions of the vintage.

The *'Chablis'* holds a special place in the Burgundian together by its relative isolation from other great vineyards of Burgundy, and by the apparent simplicity of its 'Terroir' with a simple geological context, a single grape variety, only one type of wine. The producers have developed over generations, specific know-how enabling them to make the most of Chardonnay B, in this difficult environment. They, for example, favoured cutting techniques regulating the best performance and ensuring a maturity optimal, and developed ways to fight against frost.

The *'Petit Chablis'* is mainly produced from vines planted on plots located on the bottom of slopes, or with clay soils. These natural situations promote a controlled ripening of the grapes, which is the guarantee of sufficient acidity that characterises the wines.

The AOC 'Petit Chablis' is a component of the Chablis vineyards. 'Chablis' and 'Chablis Grand Cru', which is a range of wines reflecting the environmental conditions and know how of the producers. However each has its own character. The 'Petit Chablis' appears as the lightest and most vivid.

XI – Transitional measures

1 – Driving Modes

The plots of vines in place before 28 March 2003 does not respect the provision on planting density and row spacing, specified in this specification, continue to benefit, for their crop, the rights to AOC until complete tear.

2 – Transformation, development, farming, packaging, storage

The following provisions shall apply from 1st November 2014;
– Provision for the winery capacity;
– Provision for temperature control containers during the fermentation phase;
– Provision for protected storage for wines in bulk and cylinders

3 – Specific provision

The experiment system relative to individual complementary volume is regulated by the Decree of October 20, 2005 amended by Decree of 29 November 2007 and the Decree of 23 November 2010.

XII – Basis of presentation and labelling

1 – General Provisions

The wines for which, under this specification, is asserted name of controlled origin 'Petit Chablis' and which are presented under the aforementioned name cannot be declared after harvest, be offered to the public, dispatched, put on sale or sold without, in the harvest declaration, the advertisements, on the leaflets, labels, invoices, containers any, the aforementioned designation of controlled origin be included.

2 – Special Provisions

When the indication of grape variety specified on the label, such indication shall not appear in the same visual field as the mandatory information and is printed in characters whose dimensions do not exceed 2 millimetres.

CHAPTER II
I – Declarative Obligations

1. Statement of claim

Claim statement is addressed, the advocacy organisation and management, fifteen days less before circulation between authorised warehouse, and later in the year to December 10 harvest.

   It shall indicate:
 – The designation claimed;
 – The volume of wine;
 – EVV or the SIRET number;
 – The name and address of the applicant;
 – The place of the wine warehouse.

It is accompanied in particular by a copy of the declaration of harvest and, as appropriate, a copy Production of the statement or extract the records for grapes buyers and musts.

2. Declaration prior to the transaction and retiraisons

Any operator wishing to market bulk wines with the appellation of origin controlled performs, with the inspection body, a transaction report for lot concerned in time set in the control plane, between six and fifteen days before any retiraison.

This statement, possibly accompanied by a copy of the purchase contract specifies in particular:

- Operator's identity;
- EVV or the SIRET number;
- Lot identification;
- The volume of the lot;
- The identification of containers;
- The identity of the buyer.

If retiraisons carried out for volumes less than those specified in the declaration of transaction, the operator informs the inspection body in writing.

3. For consumption Statement

Any operator declares that each batch of wine to be released for consumption within the meaning of Article D.645-18-1 of the Code rural and maritime fishing, has been confirmed with the inspection body.

This statement may also be made for batches already packed. It is made in time set in the control plan, between six and fifteen days before consumption or before shipping the affected lots outside the operator's cellars.

In particular, it states:

- Operator's identity;
- EVV or the SIRET number;
- Lot identification;
- The volume of the lot;
- The lot number for wines already packed;
- The identification of containers for unpackaged wine.

However the provision, by the operator of the register referred to in Article D.645-18 11 of the Rural Code and marine fisheries, approved inspection body, is for consumption declaration as set in the control plan.

4. Declaration on the dispatch outside the national territory of a non-conditioned wine

Any operator wishing to make a shipment outside the territory of a non-conditioned wine benefiting from the AOC makes the declaration, with the organisation of approved inspection within the deadlines set in the control plan, between six and fifteen days prior to shipment.

5. Decommissioning Statement

Any operator performing a downgrade wines profiting from the controlled appellation of origin address to the advocacy organisation and management and the inspection body a statement monthly within deadlines set in the control plan. This statement shall indicate:

– Operator's identity;
– No. EVV or SIRET;
– The volume that has been decommissioning;
– The vintage;
– The date of decommissioning.

6. Redesign plots

Before any development or any work likely to alter the morphology, the basement, the Topsoil (including any exogenous supply of land) or elements to ensure integrity and sustainability of a parcel of land for the production of designation of origin controlled, excluding ripping classic work, the operator sends a statement to the defence and management body, at least four weeks before the date set for the start of works envisaged.

The defence and management body shall, without delay, send a copy of that statement to services National Institute of Origin and Quality.

II – Keeping records

General terms of storage rooms and winemaking
Any operator winemaker maintains and available to the control body approved a plan general places of storage and winemaking, particularly to identify the number, designation and capacity of the containers.

CHAPTER III

I – Key Points to control and evaluation methods

MAIN POINTS TO BE TESTED	VALUATION METHODS
A – STRUCTURAL RULES	
A1 – Location of operators in the area of close	– Documentary check
A2 – Ownership of lots planted to the area delimited	– Documentary control: patchy record CV1 maintenance
A3 – Claimable Production Potential (grape varieties, followed by transitional measures, planting density, plant material)	– Documentary control; – Field control
A4 – processing tool, breeding, packaging and storage	– Documentary control: General plan storage areas;
Capacity winery	– Checking on site
Livestock (temperature control and duration farmed)	– Documentary control: making statement Consumption or register bottling; – Checking on site
Maintenance of state chai and equipment (hygiene)	– On-site inspection
Storage location protected	– On-site inspection

B – RULES RELATING TO THE PRODUCTION CYCLE

B1 – Vineyard management

Size	Field control
Average maximum load plot	Field control
Cultural and health state of the vine (health status foliage and berries, soil maintenance, maintenance of trellising)	Field control
B2 – Harvest, transport and grape maturity	– Documentary control: registration followed by maturity;
Grape maturity	– Field control
B3 – processing, preparation, breeding, packaging, storage	– Documentary control: register enrichment, acidification;
Oenological practices and processes (enrichment, prohibited practices,…)	– Checking on site
Accounting matters, analytical tractability	– Documentary Check: keeping, analysis bulletins
B4 – Declaration and harvest statement claim	
Missing	– Documentary control (held the day list);
	– Field Control
Authorised return	– Documentary control: control statements, tracking permits granted by the INAO, after investigation said services on individual demand operator
VSI, harvest volumes in excess of authorised return	– Documentary check: monitoring of certificates destruction
Volume Complementary Individual (VCI)	– Documentary check: Harvest Declaration VCI register

Declaration of claim	– Documentary and on-site control: compliance with the terms and deadlines, in accordance with the declaration of harvest, production
	Control of products into circulation

C – CONTROL PRODUCTS

Wine not put (the transaction or retiraison)	Analysis and taste test
Packaged wine (before or after preparation for home use)	Analysis and taste test
Unconditioned wines for a shipment outside the national territory	Analysis and taste test of all the lots

D – PRESENTATION OF PRODUCTS

Labelling	On-site inspection

II – References for the control structure

SAS ICON Burgundy
132/134 road Dijon
BP266
21207 BEAUNE CEDEX
Tel: (33) (0) 3 80 25 09 50
Fax: (33) (0) 3 80 24 63 23
E-mail: beaune@icone-sas.com

This regulatory body is accredited in accordance with the 45011 standard.

This monitoring of compliance with this specification is performed by a third party organisation offering guarantees of competence, impartiality and independence on behalf of the INAO on the basis of an approved monitoring plan.

The control plan recalls the self-checks carried out by operators on their own activity and internal controls conducted under the responsibility of the defence organisation and management. It shows the external audits by the third party and the analytical and organoleptic tests.

The set of controls is performed by sampling. Unconditional wines for a shipment outside national territory are subject to an analytical and systematic organoleptic control.

APPENDIX 9

GLOSSARY OF WINE TERMS

A whole new vocabulary has evolved over the years relating to both the production and in particular the tasting of wine.

In the modern world the international wine experts, through their exceptional tasting and quality evaluation skills, dominate the selection process for fine wines and the extent and aura of the related vocabulary can only be described as awesome.

WINE TASTING

The following terms are provided by Robert Parker who is recognised as pre-eminent in the international world of wine tasting and quality evaluation.

Acetic: Wines, no matter how well made, contain quantities of acetic acidity that have a vinegary smell. If there is an excessive amount of acetic acidity, the wine will have a vinegary smell and be a flawed, acetic wine.

Acidic: Wines need natural acidity to taste fresh and lively, but an excess of acidity results in an acidic wine that is tart and sour.

Acidity: The acidity level in a wine is critical to its enjoyment and livelihood. The natural acids that appear in wine are citric, tartaric, malic, and lactic. Wines from hot years tend to be lower in acidity, whereas wines from cool, rainy years tend to be high in acidity. Acidity in a wine can preserve the wine's freshness and keep the wine lively, but too much acidity, which masks the wines flavours and compresses its texture, is a flaw.

Aftertaste: As the term suggests, the taste left in the mouth when one swallows is the aftertaste. This word is a synonym for length or finish. The longer the aftertaste lingers in the mouth (assuming it is a pleasant taste), the finer the quality of the wine.

Aggressive: Aggressive is usually applied to wines that are either high in acidity or have harsh tannins, or both.

Angular: Angular wines are wines that lack roundness, generosity, and depth. Wine from poor vintages or wines that are too acidic are often described as being angular.

Aroma: Aroma is the smell of a young wine before it has had sufficient time to develop nuances of smell that are then called its bouquet. The word aroma is commonly used to mean the smell of a relatively young, unevolved wine.

Astringent. Wines that are astringent are not necessarily bad or good wines. Astringent wines are harsh and coarse to taste, either because they are too young and tannic and just need time to develop, or because they are not well made. The level of tannins (if it is harsh) in a wine contributes to its degree of astringency.

Austere: Wines that are austere are generally not terribly pleasant wines to drink. An austere wine is a hard, rather dry wine that lacks richness and generosity.

Backward: An adjective used to described (1) a young largely unevolved, closed, and undrinkable wine, (2) a wine that is not read to drink, or (3) a wine that simply refuses to release its charms and personality.

Balance: One of the most desired traits in a wine is good balance, where the concentration of fruit, level of tannins, and acidity are in total harmony. Balanced wines are symmetrical and tend to age gracefully.

Barnyard: An unclean, farmyard, fecal aroma that is imparted to a wine because of unclean barrels or unsanitary winemaking facilities.

Berrylike: As this descriptive term implies, most red wines have an intense berry fruit character that can suggest blackberries, raspberries, black cherries, mulberries, or even strawberries and cranberries.

Big: A big wine is a large-framed, full-bodied wine with an intense and concentrated feel on the palate.

Blackcurrant: A pronounced smell of blackcurrant fruit. It can vary in intensity from faint to very deep and rich.

Body: Body is the weight and fullness of a wine that can be sensed as it crosses the palate. Full-bodied wines tend to have a lot of alcohol, concentration, and glycerine.

Botrytis cinerea: The fungus that attacks the grape skins under specific climatic conditions (usually alternating period of moisture and sunny weather). It causes the grape to become super-concentrated because it causes a natural dehydration. Botrytis cinerea is essential for the great sweet white wines of Barsac and Sauternes.

Bouquet: As a wine's aroma becomes more developed from bottle aging, the aroma is transformed into a bouquet that is hopefully more than just the smell of the grape.

Brawny: A hefty, muscular, full-bodied wine with plenty of weight and flavour, although not always the most elegant or refined sort of wine.

Briery: Denotes that the wine is aggressive and rather spicy.

Brilliant: Brilliant relates to the colour of the wine. A brilliant wine is one that is clear, with no haze or cloudiness to the colour.

Browning: As red wines age, their colour changes from ruby/purple to dark ruby, to medium ruby, to ruby with an amber edge, to ruby with a brown edge. When a wine is browning it is usually fully mature and not likely to get better.

Chewy: If a wine has a rather dense, viscous texture from a high glycerine content, it is often referred to as being chewy. High-extract wines from great vintages can often be chewy, largely because they have higher alcohol hence high levels of glycerine, which imparts a fleshy mouthfeel.

Closed: The term closed is used to denote that the wine is not showing its potential, which remains locked in because it is too young. Young wines often close up about 12–18 months after bottling, and depending on the vintage and storage conditions, remain in such a state for several years to more than a decade.

Complex: One of the most subjective descriptive terms used, a complex wine is a wine that the taster never gets bored with and finds interesting to drink. Complex wines tend to have a variety of subtle scents and flavours that hold one's interest in the wine.

Concentrated: Fine wines, whether they are light, medium, or full-bodied, should have concentrated flavours. Concentrated denotes that the wine has a depth and richness of fruit that gives it appeal and interest. Deep is a synonym for concentrated.

Corked: A corked wine is a flawed wine that has taken on the smell of cork as a result of an unclean or faulty cork. It is perceptible in a bouquet that shows no fruit, only the smell of musty cork, which reminds me of wet cardboard.

Decadent: If you are an ice cream and chocolate lover, you know the feeling of eating a huge sundae of rich vanilla ice cream lavished with hot fudge and real whipped cream. If you are a wine enthusiast, a wine loaded with opulent, even unctuous layers of fruit, with a huge bouquet, and a plump, luxurious texture can be said to be decadent.

Deep: Essentially the same as concentrated, expressing the fact that the wine is rich, full of extract, and mouth filling.

Delicate: As this word implies, delicate wines are light, subtle, understated wines that are prized for their shyness rather than for an extroverted, robust character. White wines are usually more delicate than red wines.

Diffuse: Wines that smell and taste unstructured and unfocused are said to be diffuse. When red wines are served at too warm a temperature they often become diffuse.

Double decanting: This is done by first decanting the wine into a decanter and then rinsing the original bottle out with non-chlorinated water and then immediately repouring the wine from the decanter back into the bottle. It varies with the wine as to how long you cork it.

Dumb: A dumb wine is also a closed wine, but the term dumb is used more pejoratively. Closed wines may need only time to reveal their richness and intensity. Dumb wines may never get any better.

Earthy: May be used in both a negative and a positive sense; however, I prefer to use earthy to denote a positive aroma of fresh, rich, clean soil. Earthy is a more intense smell than woody or truffle scents.

Elegant: Although more white wines than red are described as being elegant, lighter-styled, graceful, balanced red wines can be elegant.

Extract: This is everything in a wine besides water, sugar, alcohol, and acidity.

Exuberant: Like extroverted, somewhat hyper people, wines too can be gushing with fruit and seem nervous and intensely vigorous.

Fat: In an exceptionally hot year the crop and the wines attain a super sort of maturity, they are often quite rich and concentrated, with low to average acidity. Often such wines are said to be fat, which is a prized commodity. If they become too fat, that is a flaw and they are then called flabby.

Flabby: A wine that is too fat or obese is a flabby wine. Flabby wines lack structure and are heavy to taste.

Fleshy: Fleshy is a synonym for chewy, meaty, or beefy. It denotes that the wine has a lot of body, alcohol, and extract, and usually a high glycerine content.

Focused: Both a fine wine's bouquet and flavour should be focused. Focused simply means that the scents, aromas, and flavours are precise and clearly delineated. If they are not, the wine is like an out-of-focus picture-diffuse, hazy, and possibly problematic.

Forward: An adjective used to described wines that are (1) delicious, evolved, and close to maturity, (2) wines that border on being flamboyant or ostentatious, or (3) unusually evolved and/or quickly maturing wines.

Fresh: Freshness in both young and old wines is a welcome and pleasing component. A wine is said to be fresh when it is lively and cleanly made. The opposite of fresh is stale.

Fruity: A very good wine should have enough concentration of fruit so that it can be said to be fruity. Fortunately, the best wines will have more than just a fruity personality.

Full-bodied: Wines rich in extract, alcohol, and glycerine are full-bodied wines.

Green: Green wines are wines made from underripe grapes; they lack richness and generosity as well as having a vegetal character.

Hard: Wines with abrasive, astringent tannins or high acidity are said to be hard.

Harsh: If a wine is too hard it is said to be harsh. Harshness in a wine, young or old, is a flaw.

Hedonistic: Certain styles of wine are meant to be inspected; they are introspective and intellectual wines. Others are designed to provide sheer delight, joy, and euphoria. Hedonistic wines can be criticized because in one sense they provide so much ecstasy that they can be called obvious, but in essence, they are totally gratifying wines meant to fascinate and enthral pleasure at its best.

Herbaceous: Many wines have a distinctive herbal smell that is generally said to be herbaceous. Specific herbal smells can be of thyme, lavender, rosemary, oregano, fennel, or basil.

Hollow: Also known as shallow, hollow wines are diluted and lack depth and concentration.

Hot: Rather than meaning that the temperature of the wine is too warm to drink, hot denotes that the wine is too high in alcohol and therefore leaves a burning sensation in the back of the throat when swallowed. Wines with alcohol levels in excess of 14.5% often taste hot if the requisite depth of fruit is not present.

Intensity: Intensity is one of the most desirable traits of a high-quality wine. Wines of great intensity must also have balance. They should never be heavy or cloying. Intensely concentrated great wines are alive, vibrant, aromatic, layered, and texturally compelling. Their intensity adds to their character, rather than detracting from it.

Jammy: When wines have a great intensity of fruit from excellent ripeness they can be jammy, which is a very concentrated, flavourful wine with superb extract.

Leafy: A leafy character in a wine is similar to a herbaceous character only in that it refers to the smell of leaves rather than herbs. A wine that is too leafy is a vegetal or green wine.

Lean: Lean wines are slim, rather streamlined wines that lack generosity and fatness but can still be enjoyable and pleasant.

Lively: A synonym for fresh or exuberant, lively wine is usually young wine with good acidity and a thirst-quenching personality.

Long: A very desirable trait in any fine wine is that it be long in the mouth. Long (or length) relates to a wine's finish, meaning that after you swallow the wine, you sense its presence for a long time. (Thirty seconds to several minutes is great length.) In a young wine, the difference between something good and something great is a length of the wine.

Lush: Lush wines are velvety, soft, richly fruity wines that are both concentrated and fat. A lush wine can never be an astringent or hard wine.

Massive: In great vintages where there is a high degree of ripeness and superb concentration, some wines can turn out to be so big, full-bodied, and rich that they are called massive.

Meaty: A chewy, fleshy wine is also said to be meaty.

Monocepage: This term describes a wine made totally of one specific varietal.

Mouth-filling: Big, rich, concentrated wines that are filled with fruit extract and are high in alcohol and glycerine are wines that tend to texturally fill the mouth. A mouth-filling wine is also a chewy, fleshy, fat wine.

Musty: Wines aged in dirty barrels or unkept cellars or exposed to a bad cork take on a damp, musty character that is a flaw.

Nose: The general smell and aroma of a wine as sensed through one's nose and olfactory senses is often called the wine's nose.

Oaky. At some properties, a percentage of the oak barrels may be new, and these barrels impart a toasty, vanillin flavour and smell to the wine. If the wine is not rich and concentrated, the barrels can overwhelm the wine, making it taste overly oaky. Where the wine is rich and concentrated and the winemaker has made a judicious use of barrels, however, the results are a wonderful marriage of fruit and oak.

Off: If a wine is not showing its true character, or is flawed or spoiled in some way, it is said to be 'off'.

Oxidized: If a wine has been excessively exposed to air during either its making or aging, the wine loses freshness and takes on a stale, old smell and taste. Such a wine is said to be oxidized.

Peppery: A peppery quality to a wine that has an aroma of black or white pepper and a pungent flavour.

Perfumed: This term usually is more applicable to fragrant, aromatic white wines than to red wines. However, some of the dry white wines and sweet white wines can have a strong perfumed smell.

Plummy: Rich, concentrated wines can often have the smell and taste of ripe plums. When they do, the term plummy is applicable.

Ponderous: Ponderous is often used as a synonym for massive, but in my usage a massive wine is simply a big, rich, very concentrated wine with balance, whereas a ponderous wine is a wine that has become heavy and tiring to drink.

Precocious: Wines that mature quickly are precocious. However the term also applies to wines that may last and evolve gracefully over a long period of time, but taste as if they are aging quickly because of their tastiness and soft, early charms.

Pruney: Wines produced from grapes that are overripe take on the character of prunes. Pruney wines are flawed wines.

Rich: Wines that are high in extract, flavour, and intensity of fruit.

Ripe: A wine is ripe when its grapes have reached the optimum level of maturity. Less than fully mature grapes produce wines that are underripe, and overly mature grapes produced wines that are overripe.

Round: A very desirable character of wines, roundness occurs in fully mature wines that have lost their youthful, astringent tannins, and also in young wines that have soft tannins and low acidity.

Savory: A general descriptive term that denotes that the wine is round, flavourful, and interesting to drink.

Shallow: A weak, feeble, watery or diluted wine lacking concentration is said to be shallow.

Sharp: An undesirable trait, sharp wines are bitter and unpleasant with hard, pointed edges.

Silky: A synonym for velvety or lush, silky wines are soft, sometimes fat, but never hard or angular.

Smoky: Some wines, either because of the soil or because of the barrels used to age the wine, have a distinctive smoky character.

Soft: A soft wine is one that is round and fruity, low in acidity, and has an absence of aggressive, hard tannins.

Spicy: Wines often smell quite spicy with aromas of pepper, cinnamon, and other well-known species. These pungent aromas are usually lumped together and called spicy.

Stale: Dull, heavy wines that are oxidized or lack balancing acidity for freshness are called stale.

Stalky: A synonym for vegetal, but used more frequently to denote that the wine has probably had too much contact with the stems, resulting in a green, vegetal, or stalky character to the wine.

Supple: A supple wine is one that is soft, lush, velvety, and very attractively round and tasty. It is a highly desirable characteristic because it suggests that the wine is harmonious.

Tannic: The tannins of a wine, which are extracted from the grape skins and stems, are, along with a wine's acidity and alcohol, its lifeline. Tannins give a wine firmness and some roughness when young, but gradually fall away and dissipate. A tannic wine is one that is young and unready to drink.

Tart: Sharp, acidic, lean, unripe wines are called tart. In general, a wine that is tart is not pleasurable.

Thick: Rich, ripe, concentrated wines that are low in acidity are often said to be thick.

Thin: A synonym for shallow, it is an undesirable characteristic for a wine to be thin, meaning that it is watery, lacking in body, and just diluted.

Tightly knit: Young wines that have good acidity levels, good tannin levels, and are well made are called tightly knit, meaning they have yet to open up and develop.

Toasty: A smell of grilled toast can often be found in wines because the barrels the wines are aged in are charred or toasted on the inside.

Tobacco: Some red wines have the scent of fresh tobacco. It is a distinctive and wonderful smell in wine.

Troncais oak: This type of oak comes from the forest of Troncais in central France.

Unctuous: Rich, lush, intense wines with layers of concentrated, soft, velvety fruit are said to be unctuous.

Vegetal: An undesirable characteristic, wines that smell and taste vegetal are usually made from unripe grapes. In some wines, a subtle vegetable garden smell is pleasant and adds complexity, but if it is the predominant character, is a major flaw.

Velvety: A textural description and synonym for lush or silky, a velvety wine is a rich, soft, smooth wine to taste. It is a very desirable characteristic.

Viscous: Viscous wines tend to be relatively concentrated, fat, almost thick wines with a great density of fruit extract, plenty of glycerine, and high alcohol content. If they have balancing acidity, they can be tremendously flavourful and exciting wines. If they lack acidity they are often flabby and heavy.

Volatile: A volatile wine is one that smells of vinegar as a result of an excessive amount of acetic bacteria present. It is a seriously flawed wine.

Woody: When a wine is overly oaky it is often said to be woody. Oakiness in a wine's bouquet and taste is good up to a point. Once past that point, the wine is woody and its fruity qualities are masked by excessive oak aging.

WINE PRODUCTION

Assemblage: The process of amalgamating the contents of various vats or casks to unify the wine and make a single cuvée for bottling, which is then known as the '*ensemble*'.

Base elements: Nitrogen, potassium and phosphorus. These are the essential active soil ingredients to support plant life.

Batonnage: The practice of stirring the lees to increase contact with the wine.

Botrytis: A fungus which attacks grapes and rots them.

Cap: The solids which rise to the top of a fermentation vat to form a cap over the fermenting red wine.

Carbonic maceration: A system of fermentation in which bunches of grapes are deposited in a vat. The weight on the lower grapes causes them to crush and ferment. The heat released causes the upper grapes to ferment in their skins. This method is used for the production of Beaujolais wine.

Cépage: Grape variety.

Chapeau immerge: The practice of keeping the cap of skins and pips moist, in a vat of red *must,* by submerging it permanently underneath a ceiling of wooden planks.

Chapalisation: The addition of sugar to fermenting *must* to correct a natural deficiency and thus bring the final alcohol level up to the legal minimum. Introduced by Chaptal in 1801.

Coupage: The practice of cutting (blending) one, usually more expensive, wine with something inferior.

Court-noué: A virus disease, endemic in Burgundy, especially in white wines. Known as the 'fan-leaf', this malady attacks the vine's leaves, reducing their photosynthetic ability.

Cuvaison: The *maceration* time.

Cuve: The vessel in which fermentation takes place. This can be made of wood, stainless-steel, glass-lined epoxy etc.

Débourbage: The process of allowing the heavier, *lees* desirable lees to precipitate out.

Écoulage: Running off juice from a vat or press.

Égalisage: The process of unifying several casks of wine from the same vineyard or appellation, to eliminate any differences in taste between them. This usually takes place at *racking* just before bottling.

Égrappage: The de-stemming of the harvested grapes either fully or partially prior to fermentation.

Élevage: The process between vinification and bottling. *Racking, fining, filtration* etc. are all part of a wine's *élevage*.

Fermentation: The process where the sugar of the crushed grape is converted to alcohol and carbon dioxide.

Foudre: A large, wooden, fermenting vat.

Lees: The solid particles which settle out at the bottom of the barrel.

Macération: The absorption by the juice of elements contained in the *pomace* and what is extracted is known as '*mattiere*'.

Malolactic: A bacterial fermentation which turns harsh malic acid, naturally present in wine, into softer tasting lactic acid. It follows alcoholic fermentation.

Mattiere: What is absorbed by the juice from the *pomace*.

Monopole: A vineyard in single ownership.

Must: The mixture of the solid parts *(pomace)* of the crushed grape and the juice.

Noble rot (Pourriture noble): Whilst an important condition in grapes for the production of sweet white wine, a small amount can also improve a dry white wine.

Pomace: The solid parts (skins, stems, and seeds) of the crushed grape.

Phylloxera: An aphid, which feeds on vine-roots, eventually killing the vine. It is permanently present in the soils of most European vineyards, which it devastated at the end of the 19th century. It is prevented by grafting onto resistant rootstock.

Pièce: The standard Burgundy barrel, containing 228 litres. The standard Bordeaux 'barrique' contains 225 litres.

Pigéage: The practice of breaking up the cap of solids which forms on top of a vat of fermenting red grapes to increase contact with the fermenting wine.

Racking: The transfer of the clear wine from the barrel containing the lees to a clean barrel.

Régisseur: The manager or cellar-master of an estate.

PLC (*Plafond Limite de Classement*): This is the ceiling yield for any given appellation, expressed in hl/ha, and represents a percentage increase – normally 20% – on the *rendement de base.*

Rendement de base: The base yield. This is the maximum yield set for each appellation, for a normal vintage. It is expressed as hl/ha. In exceptional vintages, it may be augmented by the *PLC.*

Remontage: Pumping-over juice from the bottom to the top of a vat during red wine fermentation to mix the juice or fermenting wine with the solids in the cap.

SO: Sulphur dioxide. This is widely used in wine-making as an all-purpose disinfectant, since it kills microbes and prevents oxidation.

Trace elements: Inorganic compounds found in usually minute quantities in soil for example: beryllium, iron, cobalt, manganese, magnesium, chromium. They contribute in different ways to grape-maturity, fertilisation, photosynthesis and sugar.

Vendange verte: Literally 'green harvest' – cutting and disposing of a proportion of bunches before the proper harvest referred to as the '*vendange*' to reduce the load on each vine. The official opening day of the harvest declared by the INAO is the '*Bon de Vendange*'.

Ver de la grappe: Grape-worm. Insect which punctures the skin of the grape leaving a wound which rapidly turns the grape rotten.

Vin de garde*:* Wine for keeping, as opposed wine designed for early drinking.

Vin de goutte: Free-run wine.

Vin de presse: Wine resulting from the pressing process.

INDEX

References to photographs and maps are shown in **bold**

W

Warner Allen, H. 71
wine bottles 236–9
wine production, countries 239–40
wine tasting 209–15
  Judgement of Paris 241–4
winemaking xi–xii, 18, 189, 219–
  26

Y

yield 228–30
Yquem 116–17, **118**, 136, 183, 189